THE BEST OF
IRISH WIT AND WISDOM

Also by John McCarthy

THE HOME BOOK OF

IRISH HUMOR

THE BEST OF IRISH WIT AND WISDOM

SELECTED AND EDITED
by John McCarthy

CONTINUUM / NEW YORK

1990

The Continuum Publishing Company
370 Lexington Avenue
New York, NY 10017

Printed in the United States of America

Library of Congress Cataloging-in-Publication Data

The Best of Irish wit and wisdom / selected and edited by John
  McCarthy.
      p.   cm.
  Reprint. Originally published: New York : Dodd, Mead, c1987.
  ISBN 0-8264-0511-8
  1. English literature—Irish authors.   2. Ireland—Literary
collections.   3. Irish wit and humor.   I. McCarthy, John, 1898–
PR8835.B47   1990
820.8'09415—dc20   89-38920
                                                            CIP

Acknowledgments will be found on page vi, which
constitutes an extension of this page.

*To my wife, Evelyn Boyle McCarthy,
and our children, Molly Brueger, John Junior,
Nora Archibald and Michael*

Acknowledgments

Thanks are due the following for permission to reprint the material indicated: Joan Daves for "The Party" by Frank O'Connor. Copyright © 1969 by Frank O'Connor. Curtis Brown, Ltd. for "The Gold in the Sea" by Brian Friel. Copyright © 1965 by Brian Friel. A D Peters & Co Ltd for "The Scoop" by James Plunkett. Viking Penguin Inc., the Estate of Flann O'Brien and Grafton Books for "The Martyr's Crown" from *Stories and Plays* by Flann O'Brien. Copyright 1941, 1943, 1950, 1951 by Brian O'Nolan. Copyright © 1973 by Evelyn O'Nolan. John Farquharson, Ltd for "Poisson d'Avril" by Sommerville & Ross. Deborah Rogers, Ltd for "Her Trademark" by Julia O'Faolain. Copyright © by Julia O'Faolain from the collection *We Might See Sights!*, 1968, published by Faber & Faber. Poolbeg Press for "The Priest's Housekeeper" by Michael McLaverty from *Collected Short Stories of Michael McLaverty* published by Poolbeg Press, Dublin. Copyright © by Michael McLaverty. Colin Smythe Limited on behalf of the heirs of John Christopher Medley for "A Letter to Rome" by George Moore. E.P. Dutton, a division of New American Library, for "Exile's Return" from *The Red Petticoat and Other Stories* by Bryan MacMahon. Copyright © 1955 by Bryan MacMahon, renewed 1983 by Bryan MacMahon. The Mercier Press for "The Can With the Diamond Notch" from *Irish Short Stories* by Seamus O'Kelly published by The Mercier Press, 4 Bridge Street, Cork, Ireland. André Deutsch Ltd for "The Anticlerical Pup" from *Home Before Night*, 1980, by Hugh Leonard. Viking Penguin Inc. and the Executors of the James Joyce Estate for "The Boarding House" from *Dubliners* by James Joyce. Copyright 1916 by B.W. Huebsch. Definitive text Copyright © 1967 by the Estate of James Joyce. Mary Lavin for "A Voice from the Dead (A Monologue)." Curtis Brown, Ltd. for "A Rest and a Change" by Honor Tracy. Copyright © 1966 by Honor Tracy. Viking Penguin Inc. and AD Peters & Co Ltd for "Death in Jerusalem" from *Lovers of Their Time* by William Trevor. Copyright © 1978 by William Trevor. Originally published in *The New Yorker*. David R. Godine, Publisher, Boston, for "A Journey to the Seven Streams" from *The State of Ireland* by Benedict Kiely. Copyright © 1963, 1978, 1979, 1980 by Benedict Kiely. The Educational Company of Ireland for "They Also Serve..." by Mervyn Wall, published by Talbot Press, Ltd. Jonathan Cape Ltd for "The Stolen Ass" by Liam O'Flaherty from *The Short Stories of Liam O'Flaherty*. Devin-Adair Publishers for "The Fur Coat" by Sean O'Faolain. Copyright © 1948 by the Devin-Adair Company, renewed in 1976. The O'Brien Press for "The Last of Mrs. Murphy" from *After the Wake* by Brendan Behan. *Our Sunday Visitor* for "Irish Bulls" by John McCarthy. *The New Yorker* for "A Man Like Grady, You Got to Know Him First" from *The World of John McNulty* (Doubleday). Copyright © 1942, 1970 by John McNulty. This appeared originally in *The New Yorker*. *The Irish Press* for "Help for the Hay" by Cormac MacConnell. Irish Distillers Group Plc. for "Irish Toasts." Copyright © 1980, Irish Distillers Group Plc. Jim McGarry for "Old Irish Songs Still Popular Today." A P Watt Ltd on behalf of Michael Holroyd for "Oscar Wilde's Wit" by Hesketh Pearson from *Oscar Wilde, His Life and Wit*. *The New York Times* for "The Man Who Knew It All" by Hugh Kenner. Copyright © 1985 by The New York Times Company. Hugh A. Mulligan for "Language That the Strangers Never Knew" by Hugh A. Mulligan. *The New York Times* for "The Only Way to Go in Ireland" by Eugene J. McCarthy © 1981 by The New York Times Company. *Our Sunday Visitor* for "A Visit to Paddy Joe's Pub" by John McCarthy. *The New York Times* for "To Ireland for Talk" by David Dempsey. Copyright © 1968 by The New York Times Company. McIntosh and Otis, Inc. for "The Willing Heart" by Leonard Wibberly. Copyright © 1960 by Leonard Wibberly.

Contents

INTERESTING CHARACTERS

TOASTS & SONGS

WILDE AND SHAW: TWO OF THE GREATS

STRANGERS IN IRELAND

Introduction

"The Irish are a very fair people," said Dr. Samuel Johnson in the 1730's. "They rarely speak well of one another."

That observation is as true today as it was a couple of centuries ago. This Celtic racial trait frequently results in apt, amusing descriptions of an Irishman's friends and foes. Interestingly, most Irishmen do not mind in the least how their peers describe them. Even if it is not entirely complimentary, but witty, the Irish affected will accept and enjoy it. Besides, they will smilingly repeat it to others.

Take Oscar Wilde's famous witticism about Bernard Shaw— "Shaw has not an enemy in the world; and none of his friends like him."

Actually, through his long lifetime habit of jocular plain speaking with its plummy intellectual blarney, Shaw had a host of enemies, albeit he had a sizable segment of friends and admirers who relished his good tempered tall talks and suave criticisms, plays, and writings.

Certainly, Shaw was delighted with his friend Wilde's comment and oft mentioned it to others. Once a biographer of Shaw, Archibald Henderson, devised to change Wilde's witticism into a weak, pointless statement: "Shaw has many enemies and none of his friends like him." Pronto, Shaw protested vigorously and wrote him:

"I tell you with brutal violence that not only is the version I gave you the correct one, but that it is well known and has been quoted again and again in its original form. Oscar must have turned in his grave when you not only spoilt it, but turned it into an ill-natured platitude. When you added that Shaw gave it brilliance by turning it into a really witty saying, all Pere La Chaise must have rocked."

Hugh Kenner, in his contribution to this book, "The Man Who Knew It All," truly describes Bernard Shaw. Oscar Wilde is recorded in a piece titled "Wilde as a Wit" by Hesketh Pearson.

Among the Irish, it is not just their heralded like Shaw, Wilde, and other prominent writers who can deliver apt, crypt descriptions of personalities and places. It's been my personal observation from traveling and living in Ireland that the vast majority of its citizens are mirthful, with talented tongues producing regularly "cute cracks," the Irish equivalent of the American wisecrack. Naturally, there are serious Irishers devoid of humor, but their comparative quota is probably smaller than in most nations.

For some years, we summered in a friendly, lovely seaside village in County Donegal located in the remote northwest section of the Republic of Ireland. Once at a band concert there, I overheard a visitor ask who I was? The inquirer got an immediate reply from one of the locals who said, "He is the Yank who comes with the cuckoo." Since we always arrived in Donegal in May as does the cuckoo, the local's response was gospel correct. Whether or not the local also thought this Yank was in the same category as the cuckoo, I never had the courage to ask him, fearing his likely frank affirmative reply.

Another time while leaving the village pub after an enjoyable evening with a group of locals, I heard one of them saying, "Although he's a Yank, McCarthy is not a bad chap." That's a typical Irish compliment with the usual putdown.

Another inherited Irish trait is that of being contrary, as are the politicians both in the Irish Republic in the South and in Northern Ireland, known also as Ulster, which is still part of Britain. In the North, the politicians are known as Unionists because they desire to remain British and not unite with the Southern Republic. Their motto; "We will never surrender!,"

meaning they will never consent to joining their sector with the
Irish Republic.

To publicize their protests, the Northern Unionist politicians
have in recent years walked out of the local Ulster councils en
masse and resigned from the British Parliament in London.
However, when the next elections come around, the same
Unionist political candidates participate, get re-elected and then
march en masse right back to their former places in the local
councils and in the London Parliament.

In the southern Republic of Ireland, the politicians there can
be just as contrary. For instance, few heads of governments will
boast about their national debt. Yet Liam Cosgrave, who headed
the Fine Gael party in the 1970's and served as the Republic's
Taoiseach, as the Irish Prime Minister is known, reportedly
publicly stated, "So what about our big debt? It shows the world
that Ireland is good for it!"

Cosgrave's contemporary opponent was Jack Lynch, leader of
the Fianna Fail party. To win a national election, Lynch and his
party offered the Irish voters a unique program that included
the elimination of the taxes on family private dwellings and also
a grant of £1,000 to newlyweds toward either building or buying
a house. Lynch and his Fianna Fail party won a resounding
national victory, capturing a historic majority of parliamentary
seats.

Despite the tremendous triumph of Lynch's contrary political
policy, it is rather doubtful if it would be accepted or adopted by
any other democracies elsewhere in the Western world. Few
governments would risk losing the perennially accepted and
stabilizing taxes on dwellings or encourage newlyweds with
£1,000 grants to buy or to build homes. Few governments could
afford such generous gestures.

Before long, the Lynch-Fianna Fail government discovered
that finding income in lieu of the traditional taxes on home
dwellings was difficult; this proved to be a potent factor in the
Fianna Fail losing the next national election to a coalition of
opposing Fine Gael and Labour parties.

Besides the appealing contrariness, quick retort and ready
wit, the Irish, too, have their ingratiating faults. Nevertheless,
overall, the lives of the Irish in Ireland, or wherever they have

settled, are usually worthwhile. Certainly, the Irish have well earned and deserve their worldwide reputation for well-being, good humor, and good fellowship.

This collection of stories and articles by leading Irish and American-Irish writers, past and present, has been selected and designed to catch at firsthand the many colorful facets of the Irish and their lifestyle at home and abroad.

Stories from the Great Irish Writers

The Party

By Frank O'Connor

Old Johnny, one of the Gas Company's watchmen, was a man with a real appreciation of his job. Most of the time, of course, it was a cold, comfortless job, with no one to talk to, and he envied his younger friend Tim Coakley, the postman. Postmen had a cushy time of it—always watched and waited for, bringing good news or bad news, often called in to advise, and (according to Tim, at least) occasionally called in for more intimate purposes. Tim, of course, was an excitable man, and he could be imagining a lot of that, though Johnny gave him the benefit of the doubt. At the same time, queer things happened to Johnny now and again that were stranger than anything Tim could tell. As it seemed to Johnny, people got it worse at night; the wild ones grew wilder, the gloomy ones gloomier. Whatever it was in them that had light in it burned more clearly, the way the stars and moon did when the sun went down. It was the darkness that did it. Johnny would be sitting in his hut for hours in the daylight and no one even gave him a second glance, but once darkness fell, people would cross the street to look at his brazier, and even stop to speak to him.

One night, for instance, in the week before Christmas, he was watching in a big Dublin square, with a railed-off park in the middle of it and doctors' and lawyers' houses on all the streets about it. That suited Johnny fine, particularly at that time of year, when there was lots of visiting and entertaining. He liked to be at the center of things, and he always appreciated the touch of elegance; the stone steps leading up to the tall door, with the figures entering and leaving looking small in the lighted doorway, and the slight voices echoing on the great brick sounding board of the square.

3

One house in particular attracted him. It was all lit up as if for a party, and the curtains were pulled back to reveal the tall handsome rooms with decorated plaster ceilings. A boy with a basket came and rang, and a young man in evening dress leaned out of the window and told the boy to leave the stuff in the basement. As he did so, a girl came and rested her hand on his shoulder, and she was in evening dress, too. Johnny liked that. He liked people with a bit of style. If he had had the good fortune to grow up in a house like that, he would have done the right thing, too. And even though he hadn't, it pleased him to watch the show. Johnny, who came of a generation before trade unions, knew that in many ways it is pleasanter to observe than to participate. He only hoped there would be singing; he was very partial to a bit of music.

But this night a thing happened the like of which had never happened to Johnny before. The door of the house opened and closed, and a man in a big cloth coat like fur came across the road to him. When he came closer, Johnny saw that he was a tall, thin man with graying hair and a pale discontented face.

"Like to go home to bed for a couple of hours?" the man asked in a low voice.

"What's that?" said Johnny, in astonishment.

"I'll stay here and mind your box."

"Oh, you would, would you?" Johnny said, under the impression that the man must have drink taken.

"I'm not joking," said the man shortly.

The grin faded on Johnny's face, and he hoped God would direct him to say the right thing. This could be dangerous. It suggested only one thing—a checkup—though in this season of good will you'd think people would be a bit more charitable, even if a man had slipped away for a few minutes for a drink. But that was the way of bosses everywhere. Even Christmas wasn't sacred to them. Johnny put on an appearance of great sternness. "Oho," he said, "I can't afford to do things like that. There's valuable property here belonging to the Gas Company. I could lose my job over a thing like that."

"You won't lose your job," the man said. "I won't leave here till you come back. If there's any trouble about it, I'll get you another job. I suppose it's money you want."

"I never asked you for anything," Johnny replied indignantly.

"And I can't go home at this hour, with no bus to bring me back."

"I suppose there's other places you can go," the man replied. "There's a quid, and I won't expect you till two."

The sight of the money changed Johnny's view of the matter. If a rich man wanted to amuse himself doing Johnny's job for a while—a little weakness of rich men that Johnny had heard of in other connections—and was willing to pay for it, that was all right. Rich men had to have their little jokes. Or, of course, it could be a bet.

"Oh, well," he said, rising and giving himself a shake, "so long as there's no harm in it!" He hadn't seen the man go into the house where they were having the party, so he must live there. "I suppose it's a joke?" he added, looking at the man out of the corner of his eye.

"It's no joke to me," the man said gloomily.

"Oh, I wasn't being inquisitive, of course," Johnny said hastily. "But I see there was to be a party in the house. I thought it might be something to do with that."

"There's your quid," said the man. "You needn't be back till three unless you want to. I won't get much sleep anyway."

Johnny thanked him profusely and left in high good humor. He foresaw that the man would probably be of great use to him sometime. A man who could offer to get you a job just like that was not to be slighted. And besides he had an idea of how he was going to spend the next hour or so, at least, and a very pleasant way it was. He took a bus to Ringsend to the house of Tim Coakley, the postman. Tim, though a good deal younger, was very friendly with him, and he was an expansive man who loved any excuse for a party.

As Johnny expected, Tim, already on his way to bed, welcomed him with his two arms out and a great shout of laughter. He was bald and fat, with a high-pitched voice. Johnny showed Tim and his wife the money and announced that he was treating them to a dozen of stout. Like the decent man he was, Tim didn't want to take the money for the stout from Johnny, but Johnny insisted. "Wait till I tell you, man!" he said triumphantly. "The like of it never happened before in the whole history of the Gas Company."

As Johnny told the story, it took close to half an hour, though this included Mrs. Coakley's departure and return with the dozen of stout. And then the real pleasure began, because the three of them had to discuss what it all meant. Why was the gentleman in the big coach sitting in the cold of the square looking at the lights and listening to the noise of the party in his own home? It was a real joy to Johnny to hear his friend analyze it, for Tim had a powerful intellect, full of novel ideas, and in no time what had begun as a curious incident in a watchman's life was beginning to expand into a romance, a newspaper case. Tim at once ruled out the idea of a joke. What would be the point in a joke like that? A bet was the more likely possibility. It could be that the man had bet someone he could take the watchman's place for the best part of the night without being detected, but in Tim's view there was one fatal flaw in this explanation. Why would the man wear a coat as conspicuous as the one that Johnny had described? There would be big money on a wager like that, and the man would be bound to try and disguise himself better. No, there must be another explanation, and as Tim drank more stout, his imagination played over the theme with greater audacity and logic, till Johnny himself began to feel uncomfortable. He began to perceive that it might be a more serious matter than he had thought.

"We've agreed that it isn't a joke," said Tim, holding up one finger. "We've agreed that it isn't a bet," he added, holding up another finger. "There is only one explanation that covers the whole facts," he said, holding up his open hand. "The man is watching the house."

"Watching his own house?" Johnny asked incredulously.

"Exactly. Why else would he pay you good money to sit in your box? A man like that, that could go to his club and be drinking champagne and playing cards all night in the best of company? Isn't it plain that he's doing it only to have cover?"

"So 'twould seem," said Johnny meekly, like any interlocutor of Socrates.

"Now, the next question is: Who is he watching?" said Tim.

"Just so," said Johnny with a mystified air.

"So we ask ourselves: Who would a man like that be watching?" Tim went on triumphantly.

"Burglars," said Mrs. Coakley.

"Burglars?" her husband asked with quiet scorn. "I suppose they'd walk in the front door?"

"He might be watching the cars, though," Johnny said. "There's a lot of them young hooligans around, breaking into cars. I seen them."

"Ah, Johnny, will you have sense?" Tim asked wearily. "Look, if that was all the man wanted, couldn't he give you a couple of bob to keep an eye on the cars? For the matter of that, couldn't he have a couple of plain-clothesmen round the square? Not at all, man! He's watching somebody, and what I say is, the one he's watching is his own wife."

"His wife?" Johnny exclaimed, aghast. "What would he want to watch his wife for?"

"Because he thinks someone is going to that house tonight that should not be there. Someone that wouldn't come at all unless he knew the husband was out. So what does the husband do? He pretends to go out, but instead of that he hides in a watchman's box across the road and waits for him. What other explanation is there?"

"Now, couldn't it be someone after his daughter?" said Johnny.

"What daughter?" Tim asked, hurt at Johnny's lack of logic. "What would a well-to-do man like that do if his daughter was going with a fellow he considered unsuitable? First, he would give the daughter a clock in the jaw, and then he would say to the maid or butler or whoever he have, 'If a Mr. Murphy comes to this house again looking for Miss Alice, kindly tell him she is not at home.' That's all he'd do, and that would be the end of your man. No, Johnny, the one he's watching is the wife, and I can only hope it won't get you into any trouble."

"You don't think I should tell the bobbies about it?" Johnny asked in alarm.

"What *could* you tell the bobbies, though?" Tim asked. "That there was a man in your box that paid you a quid to let him use it? What proof have you that a crime is going to be committed? None! All this is only suspicion. There's nothing you can do now, only let things take their course till two o'clock, and then I'll go round with you and see what really happened."

"But what could happen?" Johnny asked irritably.

"He sounds to me like a desperate man," Tim said gravely.

"Oh, desperate entirely," agreed his wife, who was swallowing it all like a box of creams.

"You don't mean you think he might do him in?" asked Johnny.

"Him, or the wife, Johnny," said Tim. "Or both. Of course, it's nothing to do with you what he does," he added comfortingly. "Whatever it is, you had neither hand, act, nor part in it. It is only the annoyance of seeing your name in the papers."

"A man should never take advice from anybody," Johnny commented bitterly, opening another bottle of stout. Johnny was not a drinking man, but he was worried. He valued his own blameless character, and he knew there were people bad enough to pretend he ought not to have left his post for a couple of hours, even at Christmastime, when everybody was visiting friends. He was not a scholar like Tim, and nobody had warned him of the desperate steps that rich men took when their wives acted flighty.

"Come on," Tim said, putting on his coat. "I'm coming with you."

"Now, I don't want your name dragged into this," Johnny protested. "You have a family to think of, too."

"I'm coming with you, Johnny," Tim said in a deep voice, laying his hand on Johnny's arm. "We're old friends, and friends stick together. Besides, as a postman, I'm more accustomed to this sort of thing than you are. You're a simple man. You might say the wrong thing. Leave it to me to answer the questions."

Johnny was grateful and said so. He was a simple man, as Tim said, and, walking back through the sleeping town, expecting to see police cordons and dead bodies all over the place, he was relieved to have a levelheaded fellow like Tim along with him. As they approached the square and their steps perceptibly slowed, Tim suggested in a low voice that Johnny should stand at the corner of the square while he himself scouted round to see if everything was all right. Johnny agreed, and stopped at the corner. Everything seemed quiet enough. There were only two cars outside the house. There were lights still burning in it, but though the windows were open, as though to clear the air, there was no sound from within. His brazier still burned bright and even in the darkness under the trees of the park. Johnny wished he had never left it.

He saw Tim cross to the other side of the road and go slowly by the brazier. Then Tim stopped and said something, but Johnny could not catch the words. After a few moments, Tim went on, turned the corner, and came back round the square. It took him close on ten minutes, and when he reached Johnny it was clear that something was wrong.

"What is it?" Johnny asked in agony.

"Nothing, Johnny," Tim said sadly. "But do you know who that man is?"

"Sure I told you I never saw him before," said Johnny.

"I know him," said Tim. "That's Hardy that owns the big stores in George's Street. It's his house. The man must be worth hundreds of thousands."

"But what about his wife, man?" asked Johnny.

"Ah, his wife died ten years ago. He's a most respectable man. I don't know what he's doing here, but it's nothing for you to fret about. I'm glad for everyone's sake. Good night, Johnny."

"Good night, Tim, and thanks, thanks!" cried Johnny, his heart already lighter.

The Gas Company's property and his reputation were both secure. The strange man had not killed his wife or his wife's admirer, because the poor soul, having been dead for ten years, couldn't have an admirer for her husband or anyone else to kill. And now he could sit in peace by his brazier and watch the dawn come up over the decent city of Dublin. The relief was so sharp that he felt himself superior to Tim. It was all very well for postmen to talk about the interesting life they led, but they hadn't the same experiences as watchmen. Watchmen might seem simple to postmen, but they had a wisdom of their own, a wisdom that came of the silence and darkness when a man is left alone with his thoughts, like a sailor aboard ship. Thinking of the poor man sitting like that in the cold under the stars watching a party at his own house, Johnny wondered that he could ever have paid attention to Tim. He approached his brazier smiling.

"Everything nice and quiet for you?" he asked.

"Except for some gasbag that stopped for a chat five minutes ago," the other replied with rancor. Johnny felt rather pleased to hear Tim described as a gasbag.

"I know the very man you mean," he said with a nod. "He's a nice poor fellow but he talks too much. Party all over?"

"Except for one couple," the other man said, rising from his box. "It's no use waiting for them. They'll probably be at it till morning."

"I daresay," said Johnny. "Why wouldn't you go in and have a chat with them yourself? You could do with a drink by this time, I suppose."

"A pot they care whether I could or not," the man said bitterly. "All that would happen is that they'd say 'Delighted to see you, Mr. Hardy' and then wait for me to go to bed."

"Ah, now, I wouldn't say that," said Johnny.

"I'm not asking whether you'd say it or not," said the other savagely. "I know it. Here I am, that paid for the party, sitting out here all night, getting my death of cold, and did my daughter or my son as much as come to the door to look for me? Did they even notice I wasn't there?"

"Oh, no, no," Johnny said politely, talking to him as if he were a ten-year-old in a tantrum—which, in a sense, Johnny felt he was. The man might have hundreds of thousands, as Tim said, but there was no difference in the world between him and a little boy sitting out in the back on a frosty night, deliberately trying to give himself pneumonia because his younger brother had got a penny and he hadn't. It was no use being hard on a man like that. "Children are very selfish, of course, but what you must remember is that fathers are selfish, too."

"Selfish?" the other exclaimed angrily. "Do you know what those two cost me between private schools and colleges? Do you know what that one party tonight cost me? As much as you'd earn in a year!"

"Oh, I know, I know!" said Johnny, holding his hands up in distress. "I used to feel the same myself, after the wife died. I'd look at the son putting grease on his hair in front of the mirror, and I'd say to myself, 'That's my grease and that's my mirror, and he's going out to amuse himself with some little piece from the lanes, not caring whether I'm alive or dead!' And daughters are worse. You'd expect more from a daughter somehow."

"You'd expect what you wouldn't get," the other said gloomily. "There's that girl inside that I gave everything to, and she'd think more of some spotty college boy that never earned a pound in his life. And if I open my mouth, my children look at me as if they didn't know was I a fool or a lunatic."

"They think you're old-fashioned, of course," said Johnny. "I know. But all the same you're not being fair to them. Children can be fond enough of you, only you'd never see it till you didn't care whether they were or not. That was the mistake I made. If I might have got an old woman for myself after the Missis died, I'd have enjoyed myself more and seen it sooner. That's what you should do. You're a well-to-do man. You could knock down a very good time for yourself. Get some lively little piece to spend your money on who'll make a fuss over you, and then you won't begrudge it to them so much."

"Yes," said the other, "to have more of them wishing I was dead so they could get at the rest of it."

He strode across the street without even a good night, and Johnny saw the flood of light on the high steps and heard the dull thud of the big door behind him.

Sitting by his brazier, waiting for the dawn over the city square, Johnny felt very fortunate, wise, and good. If ever the man listened to what he had said, he might be very good to Johnny: he might get him a proper job as an indoor watchman; he might even give him a little pension to show his appreciation. If only he took the advice—and it might sink in after a time—it would be worth every penny of it to him. Anyway, if only the job continued for another couple of days, the man would be bound to give him a Christmas box. Five bob. Ten bob. Even a quid. It would be nothing to a man like that.

Though a realist by conviction, Johnny, too, had his dreams.

The Gold in the Sea

BY BRIAN FRIEL

The *Regina Coeli* was the last boat to pull away from the harbour that evening. She was a twenty-footer of graceless proportions, without sails, and with two set of oars. I would have preferred to go in one of the bigger boats, with engines and a full-time crew, but the hotel barman told me they did not welcome passengers.

"Con's your man," he said. "What he catches won't glut the market. But he has travelled a bit, and himself and Philly and Lispy are a comical trio. Aye," he added, smiling at some memory, "even if you don't catch much, it's an education being out with Con."

We were to have set out at eight, at the turn of the tide, but between one thing and another—each of the four of us stood a round of drinks, and then I called a fifth, because they had been so agreeable about taking me salmon fishing with them—it was almost nine before we climbed aboard. The July sun had withered and the Donegal hills were a sullen purple, but the whiskey drew us together, making us feel intimate and purposeful.

"By God, sirs, you'll get more fish tonight than you ever dreamed of!" said Con. "Nothing like a choppy sea to make them jump." He reclined in the stern, an elbow on the tiller, bald and garrulous as Odysseus. He was quick with energy, for all his seventy-two years. I sat in the bow, facing him. Between us were Philly and Lispy, each taut on an oar. They were young men in their thirties.

We had become acquainted in the bar of the hotel where I was spending my two weeks' holiday. There had been no diffidence between myself and the locals, because the appearance of the salmon in the bay two days previously created a happy urgency

that made everyone in Ballybeg partners. After breakfast that
morning, I had watched the boats return from their first night
out, gunwales low in the water, the fishermen ponderous and
slow-moving, as if they had risen, sated, from a huge meal. The
tiny pier was crammed with vehicles—trucks, tractors, battered
vans—and as soon as a catch was weighed and loaded on to a
lorry the driver planted his elbow on the horn, stuck his head
out of the window, and cleared a lane for himself with his oaths.
The distraught official who supervised the noisy weighing had
a moonface that was on the point of tears. "Gentlemen, please!"
he kept whimpering. Young boys on their way to school peered
down into the halfdeckers and saw five, ten and twenty-pound
salmon that would be ten, twenty and forty-pound Salmon
when their friends from the far side of the mountain heard
about them. The vehicles scraped one another. Tyres skidded
on the wet, cobbled pier. Only the conquering fishermen were
calm and aloof. In twos and threes, they came up the steep road
to the village with the walk of kings.

Philly was Con's nephew. They lived in different cottages on
a jointly owned five-acre farm. Con was a bachelor ("But if I had
a penny for every woman I handled, by God, sirs, I'd be a
millionaire!"), and his nephew, he told the bar with unnecessary
gusto, was the father of seven daughters. "But he'll sire a son
yet, never worry!" Lispy, I learned, lived with two maiden aunts
who doted on him, but not to the extent of allowing him to
bring a bride into the house. He was a shy man, whose quietness
suggested depth and whose speech gave no explanation for his
nickname. Perhaps he inherited it. When Lispy had gone to the
toilet, Con told me that Lispy got mad drunk once a year, on
Saint Patrick's Day, when he chased the two screaming aunts
out of the house and over the stunted fields. "Just to assert his
rights," Con concluded. "A saint when sober, but inclined to be
sporty on that one occasion." All three men were full-time
farmers and part-time fishermen, and by any standards they
were very poor.

Two miles out from the harbour, free from the shelter of the
headland, we were struck by a brisk Atlantic wind. We were now
part of an impenetrable blackness.

"At this very moment, friend," Con proclaimed, "you're

sitting on top of more gold than there is in the vaults of Fort Knox."

"We'll get our share," I said, thinking he was referring to the salmon, which he had described earlier as being so plentiful that you could dance a reel on their backs and not wet a toe.

"Real gold!" he said. "At this very spot, on an August morning in 1917, the *Bonipart* was sunk by a German submarine on her way from England to the U.S.A. Fifty fathoms straight below us. A cargo of bullion."

"*Boniface,*" corrected Philly.

"There's no smoke without fire," said Lispy. He had a weakness, I discovered, for proverbs that apparently had relevance only to private thoughts of his own.

"She was slipping down along the coast," Con went on, "when the Huns caught up with her here. By God, sirs, you've got to hand it to them Germans!"

"Was it never recovered?" I asked.

"*Boniface,*" repeated Philly doggedly. "He always get the name wrong."

"Two shells done it," said Con. "One in the bows that made her rise up like a stallion, and then one midships. She went down like a knife."

'And you don't know for sure what she was carrying. No one knows that," said Philly.

"Just two shells," said Con. "And—bang!—requiescat the *Bonipart.*"

"*Boniface,*" said Philly, but without heart.

"Enough gold to develop all the underdeveloped countries of the world—including Alaska."

"The last straw broke the camel's back," said Lispy mildly.

"Right below our feet. By God, sirs, it's a wonderful thought, too, isn't it? It's there and it's safe and no one has laid a finger on it. Happy as an old lark."

While the whiskey was still active in me, I made a few confident calculations. Assuming we caught a hundred fish (this was modest; that morning the *St. Brendan* had waddled into port with three hundred), averaging ten pounds per fish, our night's work, at the current wholesale price of eight shillings and sixpence per pound, would earn us four hundred and twenty-five pounds. I did the calculation again, because this seemed a lot of money, but I got the same result. Then, as one does when easy wealth presents itself, I built myself a chalet above Ballybeg, bought a boat, hired a crew, set up a canning factory and an export business, and was getting down to the details of an advertising campaign when the ghostly hulk of a long powerboat suddenly rose out of the water beside me, towered over me for a second, and vanished, thrumming in the blackness. I was instantly cold and sober.

"By the look of them, that was the McGurk brothers," said Con casually. "Damned near rammed us, didn't they?"

"Why haven't they a light?" I almost shouted.

"A light!" said Philly, with contempt. "And have the patrol boat down on them for fishing without a license? Are you mad?"

"Why don't they take out a license?" I demanded.

"Costs money," said Philly flatly.

"A stitch in time saves nine," said Lispy.

"You mean to say," I went on, "that for all we know there may be dozens of boats all around us, not one with a light? And all of them poaching?"

"Not dozens," said Philly. "Maybe three or four."

"And what happens if they get caught?—If they don't drown us and themselves first."

"Boat's confiscated. Gear's confiscated. Up to six months in jail."

"Too good for them!" I shouted. "It's a disgrace having—"

"By my reckoning, sirs," Con broke in, "we're near the Stags, and it's about time we shot the net. You can argue to your heart's content when we're drifing. Ship the oars, sirs, and let's get the net out."

I heard him fasten the tiller with a rope and the handles of the oars spear towards me. I reached out to catch them, and then it dawned on me for the first time that we had no light, either.

I had examined the net earlier in the day. It was three miles long, four feet deep, made of nylon, and manufactured in Japan. It was designed to float about twelve inches below the surface. Con had explained that these Japanese nets were new to the Irish market, and that they were so transparent the fish couldn't see them even in the daytime. I asked him if this meant that salmon fishing could now be done in the daytime, at which he laughed scornfully and replied that sure God and the world knew that you fished salmon only at night. I left it at that.

Now, while the boat drifted, the net was fed out from the stern. The job took the best part of an hour. The blackness was so dense that the three fishermen had identity only by their voices. Con, I gauged, was on the middle bench, issuing instructions, and Philly and Lispy were throwing out the net. They talked incessantly.

"Hurry up, sirs! It'll be dawn before you know."

"Shut up!"

"The best salmon in the world are got in Peru."

"How would you know?"

"I seen me in my day grilling a seventeen-pounder over an open fire near the town of Pisco, if you ever heard of it."

"It's an ill wind that blows nobody good."

"Come on, sirs! The seven daughters and the two aunts will think you've emigrated."

"For a man with such a big mouth, how is it you never got a thump across it during your famous travels?"

"We'll fill the boat tonight, sirs. I'll settle for nothing short of a boatload."

"Look before you leap."

"Gold, sirs. Cast out the net and bring in the gold."

"Fit you better to talk less and work more."

"This will be a lovely catch. And I've seen apples in Oregon that were as big as a bishop's head. And I seen oranges in San Paulo that two men, eating steady, couldn't get through in a week."

"You and your stories. There's nothing as hateful as an old man that never stops talking."

"Faraway hills look green."

"This is the work'll put muscles on your backs, sirs. A season of this, Philly boy, and you'll father half-a-dozen sons."

"A blathering old woman! Hateful!"

"There's no smoke without fire. Oh, God, no—no smoke at all."

When the net was all out, its end was secured to the stern. Then the three men moved back to their first positions, and the long, long wait began. For the next hour, no one spoke, not even Con. Despite the sound of wind and sea and the rheumaticky groans of the *Regina Coeli*, we seemed to be encased in silence. The elements made their blustering noises above and beyond, but in and around our floating arena there was a curious stillness. In the drifting blackness of the night I could hear Philly's deep, regular breathing and the coins rattle in Con's trousers every time he searched for matches to light his pipe. It was a strange sensation, floating in blackness across an unknown sea, with men one couldn't see but whose intimate movements one could hear distinctly. And as time crept by, my senses sharpened and became responsive to a shift in the direction of the boat, to the slightest movement of a body, almost to the very presence of the fish beneath us. It was a strange, thrilling perceptivity like playing blindman's bluff for the first time as a child. I wondered if the others experienced it, and as soon as this thought occurred to me I found myself going absolutely still, opening my mouth so that even my breathing would not be audible, speculating with absurd cunning that my thinking might be somehow perceptible.

Con's booming voice smashed the secrecy, and the noise of the wind and the seas crashed in.

"It was in the winter of 1918," he said, "and I was assing about in the region of a town called Fort Good Hope on the Mackenzie River, if you ever heard of it."

"I did not," said Philly curtly.

"And there was no work, and the whole damned place was under sixteen foot of snow, and there was a famine in my belly and not a cent in my pocket."

"Oh-ho, oh-ho," said Lispy mildly.

"So bloody bad was that winter, sirs, that the wolves came down from the hills, down into the very streets of Fort Good Hope, and ate all before them."

"Pity they missed you—if you were there at all."

"Anyhow, to cut a long story short the townsfolk held a meeting, and it was agreed that they would pay a dollar out of the public funds for every wolf's head that was brought into

McFeterson's trading station. And a dollar in them days was something, sirs. You wouldn't light your pipe with a dollar in them days." He waited for a comment. None came.

"So, off I went into the hills with a Winchester—"

"Through sixteen foot of snow!" said Philly.

"—shot two dozen wolves, cut the heads off them, and carried them back to Good Hope."

"Will you listen to the man!"

"Still waters run deep."

"Presented my load to old Robbie McFeterson and said, 'Twenty-four dollars, Robbie, please.' Robbie counted the heads and gave me my money. And then says he, 'Here, sonny boy, take them heads out to the back and bury them.' And that's what I done. Buried them in the snow behind the trading station, and then went back in and bought food and whiskey and had a hell of a week to myself. But when the week was up, I was broke again and hungry again, and my tongue was out a mile for a drink. So what did I do, friend?"

"You loaded the Winchester, Con," I said.

"I went down that Sunday night to the plot behind the trading station and dug up them heads and the next morning presented them to Robbie! That's what I done! And he paid me—twenty-four dollars! And I done the same thing the following Monday and the following Monday and the following—"

"Damned things would have been rotten after four days!" Philly said.

"In twenty foot of snow, man? Fresh as a daisy! And old Robbie never suspected a thing. As straight a man as ever drew breath."

"A man who never told a lie," Philly said bitterly.

"By God, sirs, you've got to hand it to them Canadians!"

About two in the morning, we had cold tea and huge hunks of homemade bread. The tea tasted of disinfectant, and I furtively emptied mine over the side. I chewed mouthfuls of the bread until it became a thick, dry paste in my mouth, and then I tried to swallow it in a piece, without tasting it, the way one swallows medicine. When I had got through my ration, Lispy insisted I share his—"The old aunts aren't too bad at the soda bread"— and I took two more slices. One I ate with effort. The other I dropped into the sea, and then wondered if it might not get caught in the net and be hauled back into the boat later.

After we had eaten, Con resumed his tales of his travels; Philly must have dozed, because his uncle held forth without interruption. Lispy threw in an occasional proverb, perhaps to show that he was awake and listening. I was cold and tired and eager for the night to end. My dreams of a salmon industry had lost some of their sparkle.

It was still pitch black when they began to haul the net. It was then about 4 A.M., and the darkness was as dense as ever, but one felt that it had lost its terrible permanence; a change was imminent. The blackness would soon be fragmented. When they began to haul the net—Philly and Lispy again doing the donkey work, Con instructing and encouraging, and me mumbling an occasional commendation just to establish my participation—we rediscovered the purpose and intimacy that had animated us when we had set out. We knew again that out of the black, invisible waters we were about to draw in a small fortune in fish. It was a lovely feeling.

"She's a grand boat, this," Lispy said to me with sudden friendliness. "And her name is *Regina Coeli*. That's Latin, and it means "Star of the Sea.""

They were still hauling when the sky and sea became distinct. The sky was a fuzz of mist that ringed our craft at a discreet distance. The last fifty yards of net had still to be pulled in when the sky suddenly broke into black and orange and grey streaks. I could see Con's bald head glistening with salt water, and Philly's and Lispy's yellow waterproofs billowing like sails in the morning breeze. Now all the net was lifted. The young men straightened up and waited to get their breath back, and Con released the fish from the mesh. His broad shoulders concealed his movements. I could not see how many we had landed.

"Well?" said Philly.

"Salmon caught in the net, friend, is never as good to eat as salmon caught with a fishing line," said Con. "And I'll tell you why. When they get caught in the net, they can't breathe, and their lungs burst, and unless you gut them and pack them right off, they go bad very quick."

"How many's in it?" said Philly impatiently.

"But if you catch a fish with a rod and line," Con went on "you kill him before his lungs burst, and he's a better fish to eat—far better."

"I asked you—how many are there?"

Con straightened and grimaced at the sky. "Six," he said flatly. "There's six in it. Six wee ones."

"Oh-ho, oh-ho," said Lispy.

Philly spat out a curse. There was a long silence.

"Right, sirs!" Con announced suddenly in a new, vigorous voice. "Back to the oars, and home to the daughters and the aunts. There'll be another day. Oh, by God, there'll be another day!"

He moved back to the stern, and Philly and Lispy each took an oar, and we headed for home, taking our direction from a cold, grey sky. Six small fish, I calculated, would fetch about fifteen pounds—five pounds for each of the three men. Then, I remembered Con telling me that the Japanese net cost eighty pounds, more than half of which had still to be paid. He said it could be lost in a storm or destroyed by seals before it had been paid off. To balance my rising sympathy, I told myself that they were not, after all, real fishermen, but poachers; that they had no right to fish and so could not be disappointed with their catch. But it was no time for assessments. The sky had grown brilliant and the headland was strong and permanent ahead of us. The night was a failure. I was wet and hungry and miserable.

"At this very moment, friend," Con proclaimed suddenly, "you're sitting on top of more gold than there is in the vaults of Fort Knox."

"You were telling me about that," I said coldly.

"A cargo of bullion. Heading for the States."

"Tell him about the salvage ships," said Philly.

"None of us knows what it got—if it got anything," replied Con sharply.

"Tell him all the same."

"The proof of the pudding is in the eating," said Lispy.

"What's this about a salvage ship?" I asked.

"Five years ago," said Con, addressing me but watching Philly and Lispy with his sailor's eyes, "on a clear spring morning a Dutch salvage vessel dropped anchor at this very spot and didn't move away for twenty-seven days. She had divers and equipment and all the rest of it. But none of us knows did she get anything."

"They weren't here for the good of their health," said Philly. He turned to me. "What do you think?"

"Take my word for it," Con broke in. "They got nothing. Didn't I watch them through the glasses day and night? And didn't I tell you dozens of times they pulled up nothing but seaweed?"

"You couldn't swear to it."

"For God's sake, I'm not a swearing man. I'm telling you—the gold's still down there in the *Bonipart*."

"*Boniface*."

"Call it what you like. It's all there, happy as an old lark."

"Maybe you're right," said Philly, with surprising amiability. "I'm not saying you're wrong. All I'm saying is that we don't know for sure."

"Take my word for it," said Con with finality. "We're sitting on a gold mine." He spoke with such authority that somehow we all felt that he must be right.

We were the first to tie up at the harbour. The place was deserted, silent in the clean morning light. There was only the sharp smell of old fish and the light, echoey sound of the water under the dock. Now that we were on land again, our bodies were slow and unsure with fatigue. I thanked them for taking me with them, and we shook hands formally. Con held me by the elbow until the young men were out of earshot.

"It wasn't much good, was it?" he asked.

"I enjoyed it, Con." I said.

In the daylight, he looked every one of his seventy-two years—an old man with tired eyes. "The point is," he said, "the fish are there, a bloody harvest of them. You saw for yourself the catches them big boats landed. What we need is an out-board. That's what we need, I keep telling the boys that. 'The fish is there,' I say to them when they lose heart."

He stood looking back at the sea, still holding my arm. Then he spoke in a rush. "I told you a lie about the *Bonipart.*"

"Yes?" I said cautiously. I thought he was going to ask me for money.

"The Dutchmen cleaned her out from head to foot. I seen it all through the glasses from the point of the headland. They took cartloads of stuff off her. Didn't leave a bolt on her."

"And was she really carrying bullion?"

He didn't hear me, but went on as if I hadn't spoken.

"I don't want Philly or Lispy to know this. It's better for them to think it's still there. They're young men.... You see, friend, they never got much out of life. Not like me."

His voice trailed off, and I suddenly understood that he was asking me for something more important than money.

"You saw the world, Con," I said. "You've been everywhere."

"Damned right I have!" he said. "Canada, the United States, South America—right round the world before I was twenty!"

He turned, and we walked off the dock and started up the hill together.

"By God, sirs," he said, "you've got to hand it to them Dutchmen!"

The Scoop

BY JAMES PLUNKETT

A discreet glance to right and left assured Murphy that no undesirable interest was being taken in his movements. He tilted his umbrella, turned expertly into the alleyway and entered the Poolebeg by the side door. He shook the January snow from his clothes before mounting the narrow stairs, and once inside the lounge called for the hot whiskey he had been promising himself all morning. He then looked around to see who was present.

There was the usual lunch break crowd; some actors from the nearby theatre, a producer, a sprinkling of civil servants who, like himself, worked in the nearby Ministry for Exports. His friend Casey was in deep conversation with a group which included three of the actors. There was a stranger among them, who seemed to be the focus of their attention.

Murphy's head was not in the best of health. He found the friendly buzz and the artificial brightness a relief after the drabness of the streets. He curled his fingers about his glass and sighed deeply. It was comfortably warm to the touch. As he lowered it from his lips his eye met Casey's and he nodded. Casey in return winked broadly. At first Murphy interpreted the wink as a wry reference to their mutual drinking bout of the previous evening, an acknowledgement of suffering shared. But Casey followed the wink by indicating the stranger with his thumb.

So that was it. The stranger had fallen into the clutches of the actors and there was some joke going on at his expense. Strangers who entered the Poolebeg had to run that risk. The actors were adept practical jokers who had given the other regulars many a memorable laugh at some casual's expense. They were good fellows, whose companionship Casey and

Murphy relished. Murphy, eyeing the group with added interest, smiled with fellow feeling. In matters of this kind, he was one of the initiates.

He had called for his second whiskey and was wondering who the stranger could be, when Casey stood up and came across to him.

"What goes on?" Murphy asked.

"It's priceless," Casey said in an undertone. "Come on over and join us."

"Who's his nibs?"

"An English journalist. Name of Smith."

Murphy, preparing to relish the fun, asked, "What's extraordinary about a journalist?"

"Do you know what he wants?" Casey said. "A photograph of the I.R.A. drilling and an interview with one of the leaders."

"He doesn't want much," Murphy said, his eyes widening.

"Someone told him the Poolebeg was an I.R.A. hangout. The actors are playing up to him. Come on over for God's sake. It's gas."

"Wait a minute," Murphy said. "I'll call another drink first."

He did so. This was one of the things that distinguished the Poolebeg from other houses. There was colour and life in it, the regulars were a cut above the ordinary. One could discuss philosophy and religion with them. They knew what they were talking about. Or poetry. Or, if the mood prevailed, horse racing and dogs. And there was always the chance of some well-manoeuvered joke, the telling of which would enliven the dull hours in the office of the Ministry for Exports.

Murphy got his drink and followed Casey. He was introduced as Sean O'Murchu. The use of the Irish form of his name puzzled him but after a while he concluded that it must be part of the joke. The journalist took an immediate interest in him. He spoke of several recent raids on Northern Ireland by the illegal army and of the interest which his paper took in them. The editor wanted photographs and an interview. Since his arrival in Dublin he had been trying to make contact. Murphy hid his amusement behind an unsmiling mask. Then the journalist said:

"When I got the tip-off about this place I wasn't inclined to believe it, Mr. O'Murchew. I don't easily despair, but I'd got several false leads already. But the moment I heard the Erse I knew you boys were straight."

One of the actors affected a guilty start.

"We were speaking Irish and he overheard us," he explained.

He said it directly to Murphy, in a tone of embarrassed apology, as though to forestall a possible reprimand.

"That's right," another added, "Mr. Smith here took us completely by surprise."

The first, fawning on Murphy, said:

"Oh—completely, sir."

The word "Sir" alarmed Murphy. He began to see what they were up to.

"What the hell do you mean by 'Sir'," he demanded.

"Sorry—it slipped out," the actor said. To Murphy's horrified eyes the actor appeared to blush.

He decided to take control of the situation at once. It was one thing to enjoy their leg-pull of an English journalist who was fool enough to think he could collect photographs of an illegal organisation such as the Irish Republican Army by walking into a public house and making a simple request. It was another thing if Murphy himself was to be pushed forward as an officer of that organisation and find God knows what dangerous reference to himself appearing in the English papers. Apart from the law, he was a civil servant and supposed to keep a mile clear of such things. It wouldn't do at all.

"Look here," Murphy said, with a show of tolerance, "I don't know what yarns these fellows have been spinning for you, Mr. Smith, but I know nothing whatever about the I.R.A."

"I appreciate your reticence, Mr. O'Murchew," the journalist assured him. "Don't think I'd betray anything. Or that our paper is going to be unsympathetic. We know the wrongs of the Irish. We've carried articles on the Irish question that have rattled the Tories. That's why we want these pictures."

"After all, think of the publicity," one of the actors suggested.

"That's right. The organisation needs it," said the other.

"A sympathetic review of *Aims*," the first urged.

It took Murphy some time to collect his thoughts. The combined attack petrified him. The journalist, interpreting his silence for indecision, looked on hopefully.

"Look here," Murphy said loudly, "I know nothing about the bloody I.R.A. I'm a peaceable man with twenty years' service in the Ministry for Exports. I came here to have a quiet, contemplative drink…"

Casey suddenly gripped his sleeve.

"Keep your voice down, For God's sake."

This Judas touch from his closest friend made Murphy almost shoot out of his chair.

"Are you going to side with them too. Holy God…"

"No, no, no," Casey interrupted. "Look who's just come in."

Murphy looked up and immediately subsided.

A newcomer had taken his place at the counter and was ordering a drink with a grim inclination. He was tall, spare and hatchet-faced. He acknowledged those nearest him with a curt nod of the head and immediately excluded them again by studying his newspaper. Hempenstall was Murphy's immediate superior in the office. He seldom appeared in the Poolebeg. If he drank it was for a strict medicinal purpose. A sneeze in the course of the morning had caused him a moment of apprehension. Or a spasm of stomach cramp. Or a touch of flu. His world was essentially humourless and, since his wife's tragic death, a deliberately joyless one. His only release was the study of Regulations—all kinds of Regulations, which he applied rigorously. They were his only scruples. He spoke little, and that little only in the way of business.

"Do you think he heard?" Murphy asked in an undertone.

"If he didn't it wasn't *your* fault," Casey answered sourly.

Hempenstall was Casey's superior too. The journalist leaned forward avidly. "Who is he?"

"My superior," Murphy whispered, using only the side of his mouth.

One of the actors said, "The Wig."

"I beg your pardon?"

"No one must know his real name," the actor explained, "so we call him The Wig."

"Ah!" the journalist said, with complete understanding.

This was too much for Murphy. He tried to speak quietly, but emotion amplified what he had to say.

"Lookit here. This has got to stop. When I said it was my superior I meant my superior. I'm not going to sit here..."

Hempenstall was seen to lower his paper.

"Keep your goddam voice quiet," Casey appealed. "He's looking straight over."

The journalist, who had formed his own conclusions, said:

"I suppose there's no use me making a direct approach to the...eh...Wig?"

The sudden change in Murphy's face gave him his answer. He added almost immediately: "Sorry, Mr. O'Murchew. I know how these things are. Forget it."

He lowered his voice further and asked for what he termed a tip-off. A photograph of a contingent drilling would complete his assignment. It would be used in a manner which would reflect nothing but credit on a brave and resourceful organisation.

"You might as well tell him," said one of the actors.

"He's a sympathiser. I've read his articles before."

But the journalist was meticulous. It was the effect of four hot whiskies.

"Not a sympathiser—quite," he corrected. "My rule is— Understand one another first. Then judge. Present the case. I mean—fair hunt. What my colleagues and I are proud to call British Impartiality."

"British Impartiality," the actor approved, with the hearty air of being man enough to give the enemy his due.

Impulsively his colleague said, "Shake."

The journalist looked at the outstretched hand in surprise, then gripped it with genuine emotion.

"Now tell him," the first actor said to Murphy.

Two matters troubled Murphy simultaneously. The first was the continuing presence of Hempenstall, who was uncomfortably within earshot. The second concerned the journalist and the actors. He found it impossible to decide which of them he would annihilate first—given the ability and the opportunity. He thought the journalist. He glanced around at the windows on his left and saw the snow dissolving in endless blobs against them. It tempted him with an idea for revenge. There was a mountain valley about seventeen miles distant, a lost, isolated spot which boasted a crossroads, a good fishing river and a public house. In summer Casey and he sometimes journeyed there by bus, for a little air and plenty of drink. In winter it was a godforsaken wilderness, frequently cut off from the outside world by deep drifts.

"Keep it very quiet," Murphy whispered. They all leaned forward.

"There's a valley about seventeen miles out to the south, Slievefada," he continued. "Go there tomorrow and visit John Joe Flynn's public house."

"How do I get there?" the journalist asked.

"Any of the car-hire firms will fix you up. Just tell them you want to go to Slievefada."

"And what do I say to Flynn?"

One of the actors took over.

"When you walk in just say Dia Dhuit."

"I get it—a password."

This was better than the actor intended.

"Exactly. If Flynn answers Dia's Muire Dhuit, everything's O.K."

"Do I mention Mr. Murchew sent me?"

"No. If he asks you that, just say—The Mask."

"The Mask."

"Now you've got it."

They spent some time teaching the journalist how to pronounce the simple Irish greeting which he had concluded to be a password and they wrote down the customary response phonetically so that he could study and recognize it. While they were talking Hempenstall left. Then the journalist found it was time to go too. His leave-taking was the occasion of a series of warm handshakes. As his bulk disappeared through the door, Casey felt the need of emotional release.

"Well...I declare to God," he began. But having got that far, words failed him. He looked at the rest and they began to laugh, the actors helplessly, Murphy uneasily. He was already apprehensive and inclined to regret his surrender to temptation.

His regret grew as the afternoon wore on. The office of the Ministry for Exports was an oppressive warren of corridors and offices, lit by hanging bulbs under ancient cowls. The whiskey had left an unpleasant aftertaste. He felt depressed. Life, from no tangible cause, bristled with vague but threatening uncertainties. On afternoons such as this the thought often suggested itself to Murphy that he was growing too old for the joking and the drinking, a thought he now and then discussed with Casey. They referred to the feeling mutually as a touch of Anno Domini. Sometimes they wondered if it would have been better to marry, even on the salary their modest abilities commanded. There was troublesome correspondence on his desk too. A Lady Blunton-Gough had started a campaign against the export of live horses to France for use as food. She had founded a "Save-the-Horses" Committee.The trades unions had also made representation to the Minister because the horses were being exported. Lady Blunton-Gough had publicly praised the humanity of the working class. As it happened, prematurely. The trades unions had soon made it clear that they had no objection to the French getting their horse meat. They simply wanted to export the meat in cans, in order to provide employment for the butchering trade and the factory hands. As a result Lady Blunton-Gough and the trades unions were now at daggers drawn. It was part of Murphy's job to make a first draft of a letter to Lady Blunton-Gough advising her that her representations were being closely considered, and one to the Trade Union Congress to the effect that in view of the heavy unemployment figures their suggestion was receiving the sympathetic attention of the Minister. Both organisations would publicise the respective replies. He was struggling for the fifth successive afternoon with this unwelcome problem when the buzzer indicated that he was wanted in Hempenstall's office.

He found his superior sitting in an aroma of disinfectant, sucking throat lozenges from a box on his desk.

"What I have to say is not official," Hempenstall opened, waving him to a chair.

Murphy made signs which conveyed that anything Mr. Hempenstall cared to address to him would be avidly received.

"I speak in your own interest and that of the Department."

"I understand, sir."

"At lunch break today I visited the Poolebeg. I had a premonition of flu and felt the need of a preventative. You may have seen me?"

"Now that you mention it, I believe I did."

"I happened to overhear a remark of yours, a reference to an illegal organisation. I have no doubt that it arose in the course of conversation..."

"I assure you it did."

"Still, I think it my duty to remind you that even during his free time a civil servant remains a civil servant. Prudence requires him to avoid discussions of a political nature. Especially conversations involving the activities of an illegal army which operates in defiance of the Government he serves. I don't think I need labour the point. In mentioning it I have your career in mind. You are a long time with us."

"Twenty years."

"I thought even longer."

"I'd like to explain that the subject of the I.R.A..."

"Quite. I trust it won't be necessary to refer to it again."

"It arose, Mr. Hempenstall..."

"Excellent. I won't keep you any longer from your desk."

Frustrated and upset, Murphy returned to his desk. He found it more difficult than ever to concentrate on the question of horse meat. The evening dragged on; against the darkened windows he could sense the silent melting of snowflakes. After some neverous reflection he phoned Casey, who seemed to be in remarkably good form, and said to him:

"That was desperate carry on."

"What was?"

"What-you-know."

"Lord, yes. Priceless."

"He seemed a bit of an ass."

"Who?"

"Who-you-know."

"It was good fun."

"Do you think he'll really go?"

"Where?"

"Where-you-know."

"It wouldn't surprise me."

"Look. Meet me after the office."

"The usual?"

"No. I think the other place."

"Dammit. I can't. I've got an appointment."

"That's a pity. Oh well. See you tomorrow. Lunchtime."

"In the other place?"

"No. Better make it the usual."

"Righto. By the way, I thought it very funny."

"What?"

"Calling you The Mask."

Murphy shuddered and replaced the phone.

Two days later nothing had happened and Murphy was beginning to see the bright side of the incident. The story of his
sending the journalist on a wild goose chase to Slievefada had
gone the rounds of the bars. In three different haunts he found
himself invited to give the story to the *habitués*. It was received
with tremendous hilarity. Here, their inner phantasies had been
translated into reality. A man with a camera, armed with a
harmless Irish greeting as a password, had gone off into the
snow-bound wilderness for a glimpse of the I.R.A. It was as
though Murphy had sent him hunting a Unicorn. Someone said
it was typical of the English and showed that they lacked
imagination. Another said it didn't. On the contrary, it showed
they had too much imagination. Somebody else said imagination had nothing to do with it. It showed that the English had
what the Irish always lacked, faith in themselves. Another said
not at all; if it demonstrated anything it was that the English had
faith in the Irish. Murphy, when asked for his opinion, modestly
owned himself at a loss. It was dangerous to generalise. It was a
matter of judging the individual character he said, weighing
him up carefully and deciding how best to exploit his weak
points. Of course, it was all easier said than done.

"And you were the man to do it," someone enthused. "I take
off my hat to you."

Then they all took off their hats to him, even those who were
not wearing them. Murphy found the experience pleas-

ant. To be well thought of in such company was the only taint of ambition in his make-up.

Life had taught Murphy to believe in Fate. It had also taught him not to trust it, a fact of which he was reminded the following day when Hempenstall again called him to his office.

"You will remember our recent interview?" Hempenstall began.

"Of course, sir."

"Have you seen the *Daily Echo*?"

"No, sir, I don't get the English dailies."

"I have this morning's issue here. There is a photograph in it."

Hempenstall unfolded a paper and laid it before Murphy who bent down to examine it. His heart missed a beat. The photograph showed about twelve men, spread out in wide formation, advancing up a snowy clearing which was flanked by pine trees. The men were armed with rifles. The top caption read, *I.R.A. Manoeuvres,* and underneath, *Our Special Reporter scooped this candid shot of warlike preparations in the Irish mountains* (see below).

The accompanying article began:

Within twelve hours of his arrival in Dublin, enquiries sent our special reporter battling through snow and ice to a little known village less than seventeen miles from the heart of the Capital. The village— Slievefada, the mission . . .

"Slievefada," Murphy echoed involuntarily.

"You know the place?" Hempenstall said.

"Vaguely," Murphy confessed.

"You are hardly being frank, Mr. Murphy," Hempenstall accused. "You spent your vacation there two years in succession. We have it on your file. You will remember that during the recent war the regulations required everyone of this staff to furnish information as to his whereabouts when going on leave."

"Now I remember," Murphy said. "I was there for the fishing. Funny I should forget."

Hempenstall looked at him closely. He had the lowest possible opinion of Murphy's intelligence, yet this new sample of its level surprised him.

"I show you the photograph because you may feel I was over-severe the other day. I realize, of course, that your choice of Slievefada as a holiday resort and the present picture have no connection. But I trust it will help to drive home my point about careless talk in public places."

"Very forcibly, sir."

"These English reporters are everywhere. Think of your situation as a civil servant if one of them were to overhear you and approach you."

"You make it very clear, sir."

"Good. I want no action of any officer under my control to reflect discredit on my Section. You may go back to your desk."

"Thank you, Mr. Hempenstall."

Murphy's appointment with Casey that evening was in none of their usual haunts. He was thankful for the darkness of the snowbound streets, thankful for the swarming tea-time crowds. He felt he might already be a hunted man. Now and again the picture flashed into his mind of a middle-aged body spreadeagled and lifeless among the shadows of some court-yard, the word "Informer" pinned to its shabby coat. The body was his. Casey was already waiting for him in the restaurant. It was a cheap and noisy basement with a multi-coloured juke box around which a group of teenagers wagged assorted bottoms. They drank two bowls of indescribable soup while Murphy urged the wisdom of going at once to Slievefada to question John Joe Flynn. Casey was disinclined.

"I don't see any sense in it," he objected.

"Maybe you don't. But I do. It's the talk of every bar that I sent the reporter out there. If the I.R.A. get to hear it God knows what will happen. They might even shoot me."

"That's what I mean," Casey said, making his point clearly. "If we go to Slievefada they might shoot both of us."

"John Joe's a friend of ours," Murphy pleaded, "he'll advise us for the best and let us know how we stand."

"The roads are too bad," Casey resisted, changing ground.

"There's no harm trying."

"And look at the expense. Even if we persuade some driver to chance it, he's bound to charge us through the nose."

"Not if we hire a self-drive."

"And who'll drive it?"

"I will."

"You," Casey protested. "Not bloody likely. I'd rather give myself up to the I.R.A. and be done with it."

"All right," Murphy said at last, with a look of pitiable resignation. "I'll go by myself."

Two hours later Casey bitterly regretted the sense of loyalty which had made him yield to the unspoken challenge. He looked sideways at Murphy and wondered what strange love it was that induced him to stand by this thin, miserable, unprepossessing piece of humanity. He had a half bottle of whiskey in his lap which they had brought with them in case of emergency, but the potential comfort it contained failed to cheer him. The hired car slithered from ditch to ditch when they went downhill and slipped alarmingly when they climbed. Murphy crouched inexpertly over the wheel, his chin out, the rest of his face pinched and small with concentration and the cold.

"If I ever get back home alive," Casey said finally, "I'm going straight in to have myself certified."

The car swung wildly but righted itself. Murphy's nerves were in a bad way. He snapped at him.

"There you go—distracting my attention."

He crouched over the wheel once more. For some miles the headlights lit up a snowy wilderness. Soon it narrowed to a few yards. Slanting streamers of white surrounded and enclosed them. It was snowing again. The pine trees which marched up steep slopes on either side of the road disappeared. Once the near wheel slithered into the ditch and Casey got his shoes full of snow as he pushed and strained to lift it out. After less than a mile his feet were wet and cold. He stretched out his hand for the whiskey bottle. He began to grope about, calmly at first, then wildly.

"Holy God—it's gone," he said at last.

"What's gone?"

"The whiskey."

Murphy reacted automatically by pressing his foot on the brake. They careened from side to side, straightened, swung in a slow circle and, straightening once more, came to rest.

"How could it be gone?"

"It must have fallen when I got out to push you out of the ditch."

"What'll we do?"

"What the hell *can* we do?"

"Nothing, I suppose. We'd never find it now."

"You'd better drive on," Casey said.

As they drove his feet got colder and colder. He no longer gave a damn about the I.R.A. because he felt convinced he was going to die of pneumonia anyway. Once or twice he sneezed. After another half hour, during which they both thought more or less continuously of the whiskey bottle gradually disappearing under the falling snow, a view of the matter occurred to Murphy which he voiced for Casey's consolation.

"Ah well," he said, "thanks be to God it wasn't a full bottle."

At last they crossed the hump-backed bridge on the floor of the valley and swung left to the parking area in front of John Joe Flynn's. The two petrol pumps stood like snowmen, the blinds were down behind the windows, the door shut fast. John Joe could hardly believe his eyes. He dragged them in to the bar and over to the blazing log fire which reflected on the bronze and glass of the bar. Three or four times he repeated:

"Glory be to the Man Above Us, Mr. Casey and Mr. Murphy, well I declare to me daddy."

But he wouldn't let them talk to him until he had poured out a welcome, which he brought over in two well-filled tumblers.

"Get that inside the pair of you now," he said, "and take off the shoes and stockings. Youse must be soaked to the bone." He had a glass in his own hand too, which he raised.

"*Sláinte*," he said.

"*Sláinte Mhór*," they replied.

"You still keep a good drop," Casey approved.

"Hold on there now," John Joe said, "till I get you something to go with it."

He went down into the kitchen and they were alone for a while. Their shoes had left a trail of footprints on the flagged floor, their coats dripped wetly on the hanger. There was a smell of groceries, of drink, of woodsmoke. The oil lamp slung from the centre of the ceiling cast a yellow circle which was edged with black. It made a faint buzzing noise which they found comforting. John Joe returned with a pot of tea and a plate of meat which they dispatched ravenously. They talked of the weather, of mutual friends, of this and that. Then Murphy pushed aside his empty plate and said, deliberately:

"We had a purpose in coming, John Joe."

John Joe smiled and said:

"It occurred to me that it wasn't just to admire the scenery."

They acknowledged the joke. Murphy took the *Daily Echo* from his pocket and spread it on the table.

"As a matter of fact, John Joe, it was this."

"The photograph," he added, when John Joe looked puzzled.

John Joe put on his spectacles and studied the photograph gravely. "Well, I declare to me daddy," he said at last, "that fella was in earnest, after all."

"What fellow?" Murphy asked.

John Joe put his spectacles back in his pocket. They hindered conversation.

"This fellow the other day. He blows in here from nowhere with a bloody big camera and an English accent. He knew me too. 'Are you Mr. John Joe Flynn?' says he. 'That's what the priest called me when he poured on the water anyway,' says I, 'what's your pleasure?' He looked around once or twice as though he felt someone might be listening, *'Dia Dhuit,'* says he. *"Dia's Muire Dhuit,'* says I, surprised to hear an Englishman using the Irish. The next thing was he leaned over and whispered in me ear, 'The Mowsk sent me.'"

"The Mowsk?" Murphy echoed.

"I think that's what it was," John Joe corrected, "but I couldn't be sure. You know the funny bloody way the English has of talking. Anyway I left it at that and your man stayed the night. The next morning after breakfast he told me he was here to get a picture of the I.R.A. drilling."

"What did you say?"

"What would you say to that class of lunatic? I humoured him. I told him it was a bloody serious thing to direct anyone to I.R.A. manoeuvers and asked for time to think it over."

"What did he say to that?"

"What he said before. The Mowsk sent him. He had this Mowsk stuff on the brain. Anyway, half an hour later, just to get shut of him, I told him there might be something stirring if he went down to Fisher's Point at twelve o'clock or thereabouts. And for the love of God, says I to him, don't on any account let yourself be seen.Dammit, but I clean forgot about the boys."

"The boys?" Casey repeated.

"An arrangement the boys had made here a few nights before."

John Joe cocked his ear at the sound of a heavy engine which sent the windows rattling before it churned to a stop. "This'll be Lar Holohan and his helper. Hold on for a minute."

He went over to unlock the door and Murphy exchanged glances with Casey. Both had the feeling of being in the center of a hotbed of illegal activity.

"He means 'The Mask'," Casey whispered. It was quite unnecessary.

"I know," Murphy answered. If anything, the whiskey had made his nerves worse.

The lorry driver and his helper sat down near them while John Joe got tea and bread and meat. It was a fierce night, the lorry driver told them, with a blizzard almost certain. When were they going back?

"Tonight," Murphy said.

The lorry driver addressed his helper.

"They won't get back tonight, will they, Harmless?"

"Not unless they has an airyplane," Harmless confirmed.

"We got ditched twice coming through the pass," the lorry driver said, "it's closed by now."

"Will it be right in the morning?"

"With the class of a night that's in it now, I wouldn't think so. Not for two days at least."

"Three," Harmless corrected.

The food was brought and they attacked it with gusto. When they had finished, John Joe asked Murphy for the *Echo* and spread it in front of the lorry driver.

"Have a look at that, Lar," he invited.

His eyes shone with expectation. Lar exmained it thoroughly.

"Can you guess what it is?" John Joe asked after a while.

The lorry driver stroked his chin.

"It's not the I.R.A. anyway," he said at last. "I recognize Tim Moore and John Feeney."

"So do I," Harmless added. "I wouldn't accuse either of them of ambitions to shed their heart's blood for Ireland. Or anything else."

"I'll tell you," John Joe announced triumphantly, "it's the dog hunt."

The lorry driver guffawed.

"I declare to God," he said, "that's what it is."

"Dog hunt?" Murphy said with a look of enquiry.

"You may remember Matt Kerrigan that lived by himself up the mountain," John Joe began.

Murphy and Casey both remembered him, an old man who was something of a hermit.

"He died a few months ago," John Joe said, "but nothing would induce the bloody oul' mongrel he kept to quit the house."

"A ferocious-looking blackguard of a brute it was too," Harmless assured them. "Not a Christian class of a dog at all."

"That's not a word of a lie," said the lorry driver.

"It stayed on at the house," John Joe continued, "and of course after a while it went wild."

"It was never what you'd call tame," Harmless said. He had a grievance against the dog which had once bitten him.

"It did terrible damage to poultry, and latterly it began to attack the sheep. So when the bad weather came and the boys got together to help bring the flocks down to the lower slopes they thought they'd kill two birds with the one stone and shoot the oul' dog if they could round him up as well. That's why they brought the guns."

"They got it too," Harmless said with relish, "shot it above at Eagle Rock. They said it was mad as well as wild."

"And that's the photograph the journalist got?" Casey asked.

"That's the photograph you see in front of you," John Joe said. "The boys' setting off to get the bowler."

"And he thought it was the I.R.A.," the lorry driver commented, looking at the photograph with renewed relish.

John Joe proceeded to tell the lorry driver why. He described the visit of the journalist and about sending him down to Fisher's Point to get shut of him. Three or four times the lorry driver nearly fell off his stool.

Murphy looked over at Casey. They found it impossible to join in the general laughter. Outside it was snowing hard. A wind had risen which made a deep, rumbling noise in the wide chimney. They thought of the pass filling moment by moment with its barrier of snow.

"We may as well have a drink anyway," Murphy said; "we'll have whiskey all round, John Joe."

The lorry driver stopped laughing in order to hold up his hand and ask him to make his beer, explaining that he and his helper had had a skinful of whiskey already.

"It was when we were struggling with the lorry the second time we got ditched," Harmless explained. "Suddenly my foot kicked something. It was a half bottle of whiskey."

"Someone must have let it fall," said the driver.

"So we polished it off," Harmless concluded and then cocked an ear to the night. He considered carefully.

"At least three days," he added at last, meaning the Pass.

Harmless turned out to be right. Murphy and Casey stayed in John Joe Flynn's. There was nothing else they could do. They telephoned the post office and had a telegram sent on to Hempenstall, explaining that they were weather bound. On the same call John Joe sent a request to the post office to order a dozen copies of the *Daily Echo* and hold them. Every one involved in the dog hunt would want one for himself, he said.

On the third day, while Murphy was gazing out of the window

the thought occurred to him that the telegram they had sent to Hempenstall would bear the name of Slievefada Post Office as its point of origination. This was a fresh complication. It would be difficult to explain to Hempenstall. As he thought about it he grew pale. Even Casey noticed.

"What are you thinking about?" he asked.

Murphy's eyes dwelt in silence for a while on the snow-covered desolation outside. His pallor remained.

"Siberia," he said eventually.

The Martyr's Crown

By Flann O'Brien

Mr. Toole and Mr. O'Hickey walked down the street together in the morning.

Mr. Toole had a peculiarity. He had the habit, when accompanied by another person, of saluting total strangers; but only if these strangers were of important air and costly raiment. He meant thus to make it known that he had friends in high places, and that he himself, though poor, was a person of quality fallen on evil days through some undisclosed sacrifice made in the interest of immutable principle early in life. Most of the strangers, startled out of their private thoughts, stammered a salutation in return. And Mr. Toole was shrewd. He stopped at that. He said no more to his companion, but by some little private gesture, a chuckle, a shake of the head, a smothered imprecation, he nearly always extracted the one question most melodious to his ear: *"Who was that?"*

Mr. Toole was shabby, and so was Mr. O'Hickey, but Mr. O'Hickey had a neat and careful shabbiness. He was an older and a wiser man, and was well up to Mr. Toole's tricks. Mr. Toole at his best, he thought, was better than a play. And he now knew that Mr. Toole was appraising the street with beady eye.

"Gorawars!" Mr. Toole said suddenly.

We are off, Mr. O'Hickey thought.

"Do you see this hop-off-my-thumb with the stick and the hat?" Mr. Toole said.

Mr. O'Hickey did. A young man of surpassing elegance was approaching; tall, fair, darkly dressed; even at fifty yards his hauteur seemed to chill Mr. O'Hickey's part of the street.

"Ten to one he cuts me dead," Mr. Toole said. "This is one of the most extraordinary pieces of work in the whole world."

41

Mr. O'Hickey braced himself for a more than ordinary impact. The adversaries neared each other.

"How are we at all, Sean a chara?" Mr. Toole called out.

The young man's control was superb. There was no glare, no glance of scorn, no sign at all. He was gone, but had left in his wake so complete an impression of his contempt that even Mr. Toole paled momentarily. The experience frightened Mr. O'Hickey.

"Who...who was *that?"* he asked at last.

"I knew the mother well," Mr. Toole said musingly. "The woman was a saint." Then he was silent.

Mr. O'Hickey thought: there is nothing for it but bribery— again. He led the way into a public house and ordered two bottles of stout.

"As you know," Mr. Toole began, "I was Bart Conlon's right-hand man. Bart, of course, went the other way in 'twenty-two."

Mr. O'Hickey nodded and said nothing. He knew that Mr. Toole had never rendered military service to his country.

"In any case," Mr. Toole continued, "there was a certain day early in 'twenty-one and orders come through that there was to be a raid on the Sinn Fein office above in Harcourt Street. There happened to be a certain gawskogue of a cattle jobber from the County Meath had an office on the other side of the street. And he was well in with a certain character be the name of Mick Collins. I think you get me drift?"

"I do," Mr. O'Hickey said.

"There was six of us," Mr. Toole said, "with meself and Bart Conlon in charge. Me man the cattle jobber gets an urgent call to be out of his office accidentally on purpose at four o'clock, and at half-four the six of us is parked inside there with two machine guns, the rifles, and a class of a homemade bomb that Bart used to make in his own kitchen. The military arrived in two lurries on the other side of the street at five o'clock. That was the hour in the orders that come. I believe that man Mick Collins had lads working for him over in the War Office across in London. He was a great stickler for the British being punctual on the dot."

"He was a wonderful organizer," Mr. O'Hickey said.

"Well, we stood with our backs to the far wall and let them have it through the open window and them getting down off the lurries. Sacred godfathers! I never seen such murder in me life. Your men didn't know where it was coming from, and a lot of them wasn't worried very much when it was all over, because there was no heads left in some of them. Bart then gives the order for retreat down the back stairs; in no time we're in the lane, and five minutes more the six of us upstairs in Martin Fulham's pub in Camden Street. Poor Martin is dead since."

"I knew that man well," Mr. O'Hickey remarked.

"Certainly you knew him well," Mr. Toole said, warmly. "The six of us was marked men, of course. In any case, fresh orders come at six o'clock. All hands was to proceed in military formation, singly, be different routes to the house of a great skin in the Cumann na mBan, a widow be the name of Clougherty that lived on the south side. We were all to lie low, do you understand, till there was fresh orders to come out and fight again. Sacred wars, they were very rough days them days; will I ever forget Mrs. Clougherty! She was certainly a marvelous figure of a woman. I never seen a woman like her to bake bread."

Mr. O'Hickey looked up.

"Was she," he said, "was she...all right?"

"She was certainly nothing of the sort," Mr. Toole said loudly and sharply. "By God, we were all thinking of other things in them days. Here was this unfortunate woman in a three-story house on her own, with some quare fellow in the middle flat, herself on the ground floor, and six bloodthirsty pultogues hiding above on the top floor, every manjack ready to shoot his way out if there was trouble. We got feeds there I never seen before or since, and the *Independent* every morning. Outrage in Harcourt Street. The armed men then decamped and made good their escape. I'm damn bloody sure we made good our escape. There was one snag. We couldn't budge out. No exercise at all—and that means only one thing..."

"Constipation?" Mr. O'Hickey suggested.

"The very man," said Mr. Toole.

Mr. O'Hickey shook his head.

"We were there a week. Smoking and playing cards, but when nine o'clock struck, Mrs. Clougherty come up, and, Protestant, Catholic, or Jewman, all hands had to go down on the knees. A very good...strict...woman, if you understand me, a true daughter of Ireland. And now I'll tell you a damn good one. About five o'clock one evening I heard a noise below and peeped out of the window. Sanctified and holy godfathers!"

"What was it—the noise?" Mr. O'Hickey asked.

"What do you think, only two lurries packed with military, with my nabs of an officer hopping out and running up the steps to hammer at the door, and all the Tommies sitting back with their guns at the ready. Trapped! That's a nice word—*trapped!* If there was ever rats in a cage, it was me unfortunate brave men from the battle of Harcourt Street. God!"

"They had you at what we call a disadvantage," Mr. O'Hickey conceded.

"She was in the room herself with the teapot. She had a big silver satteen blouse on her; I can see it yet. She turned on us and gave us all one look that said: *Shut up, ye nervous lousers.* Then she foostered about a bit at the glass and walks out of the room with bang-bang-bang to shake the house going on downstairs. And I see a thing..."

"What?" asked Mr. O'Hickey.

"She was a fine—now you'll understand me, Mr. O'Hickey," Mr. Toole said carefully. "I seen her fingers on the buttons of the satteen, if you follow me, and she leaving the room."

Mr. O'Hickey, discreet, nodded thoughtfully.

"I listened at the stairs. Jakers I never got such a drop in me life. She clatters down and flings open the hall door. This young pup is outside, and asks—awsks—in the law-de-daw voice, 'Is there any men in this house?' The answer took me to the fair altogether. She puts on the guttiest voice I ever heard outside Moor Street and says, 'Sairtintly not at this hour of the night; I wish to God there was. Sure, how could the poor unfortunate women get on without them, officer?' Well lookat. I nearly fell down the stairs on top of the two of them. The next thing I hear is, 'Madam this and madam that' and 'Sorry to disturb and I beg your pardon,' 'I trust this and I trust that,' and then the whispering starts, and at the windup the hall door is closed and into the room off the hall with the pair of them. This young bucko out of the Borderers in a room off the hall with a headquarters captain of the Cumann na mBan! *Give us two more stouts there, Mick!*"

"That is a very queer one, as the man said," Mr. O'Hickey said.

"I went back to the room and sat down. Bart had his gun out, and we were all looking at one another. After ten minutes we heard another noise."

Mr. Toole poured out his stout with unnecessary care.

"It was the noise of the lurries driving away," he said at last. "She'd saved our lives, and when she come up a while later she said 'We'll go to bed a bit earlier tonight, boys; kneel down all.' That was Mrs. Clougherty the saint."

Mr. O'Hickey, also careful, was working at his own bottle, his wise head bent at the task.

"What I meant to ask you was this," Mr. O'Hickey said, "that's an extraordinary affair altogether, but what has that to do with that stuck-up young man we met in the street, the lad with all the airs?"

"Do you not see it, man?" Mr. Toole said in surprise. "For seven hundred year, thousands—no, I'll make it millions—of Irish men and women have died for Ireland. We never rared jibbers; they were glad to do it, and will again. But that young man was *born* for Ireland. There was never anybody else like him. Why wouldn't he be proud?"

"The Lord save us!" Mr. O'Hickey cried.

"A saint I called her," Mr. Toole said, hotly. "What am I talking about—she's a martyr and wears the martyr's crown today!"

Poisson d'Avril

By Sommerville and Ross

The atmosphere of the waiting room set at naught at a single glance the theory that there can be no smoke without fire. The stationmaster, when remonstrated with, stated, as an incontrovertible fact, that any chimney in the world would smoke in a southeasterly wind, and further, said there wasn't a poker, and that if you poked the fire the grate would fall out. He was, however, sympathetic, and went on his knees before the smoldering mound of slack, endeavoring to charm it to a smile by subtle proddings with the handle of the ticket punch. Finally, he took me to his own kitchen fire and talked politics and salmon fishing, the former with judicious attention to my presumed point of view, and careful suppression of his own, the latter with no less tactful regard for my admission that for three days I had not caught a fish, while the steam rose from my wet boots, in witness of the ten miles of rain through which an outside car had carried me.

Before the train was signaled I realized for the hundredth time the magnificent superiority of the Irish mind to the trammels of officialdom, and the inveterate supremacy in Ireland of the Personal Element.

"You might get a foot warmer at Carrig Junction," said a species of lay porter in a knitted jersey, ramming my suitcase upside down under the seat. "Sometimes they're in it, and more times they're not."

The train dragged itself rheumatically from the station, and a cold spring rain—the time was the middle of a most inclement April—smote it in flank as it came into the open. I pulled up both windows and began to smoke; there is, at least a semblance of warmth in a thoroughly vitiated atmosphere.

It is my wife's habit to assert that I do not read her letters, and being now on my way to join her and my family in Gloucestershire, it seemed a sound thing to study again her latest letter of instructions.

"I am starting today, as Alice wrote to say we must be there two days before the wedding, so as to have a rehearsal for the pages. Their dresses have come, and they look too delicious in them—"

(I here omit profuse particulars not pertinent to this tale.)

"—It is sickening for you to have had such bad sport. If the worst comes to the worst couldn't you buy one?—"

I smote my hand upon my knee. I had forgotten the infernal salmon! What a score for Philippa! If these *contretemps* would only teach her that I was not to be relied upon, they would have their uses, but experience is wasted upon her; I have no objection to being called an idiot, but, that being so, I ought to be allowed the privileges and exemptions proper to idiots. Philippa had, no doubt, written to Alice Hervey, and assured her that Sinclair would be only too delighted to bring her a salmon, and Alice Hervey, who was rich enough to find much enjoyment in saving money, would reckon upon it, to its final fin in mayonnaise.

Plunged in morose meditations, I progressed through a country parceled out by shaky and crooked walls into a patch-wood of hazel scrub and rocky fields, veiled in rain. About every six miles there was a station, wet and windswept; at one the sole occurrence was the presentation of a newspaper to the guard by the stationmaster; at the next the guard read aloud some choice excerpts from the same to the porter. The Personal Element was potent on this branch of the Munster and Connaught Railway. Routine, abhorrent to all artistic minds, was sheathed in conversation; even the engine driver, a functionary ordinarily as aloof as the Mikado, alleviated his enforced isolation by sociable shrieks to every level crossing, while the long row of public houses that formed, as far as I could judge, the town of Carrig, received a special and, as it seemed, humorous salutation.

The timetable decreed that we were to spend ten minutes at Carrig Junction; it was fifteen before the crowd of market people on the platform had been assimilated; finally, the window of a neighboring carriage was flung open, and a wrathful English voice asked how much longer the train was going to wait. The stationmaster, who was at the moment engrossed in conversation with the guard and a man who was carrying a long parcel wrapped in newspaper, looked round, and said gravely:

"Well now, that's a mystery!"

The man with the parcel turned away, and convulsively studied a poster. The guard put his hand over his mouth.

The voice, still more wrathfully, demanded the earliest hour at which its owner could get to Belfast.

"Ye'll be asking me next when I take me breakfast," replied the stationmaster, without haste or palpable annoyance.

The window went up again with a bang, the man with the parcel dug the guard in the ribs with his elbow, and the parcel slipped from under his arm and fell on the platform.

"Oh my! oh my! Me fish!" exclaimed the man, solicitously picking up a remarkably good-looking salmon that had slipped from its wrapping of newspaper.

Inspiration came to me, and I, in my turn, opened my window and summoned the stationmaster.

Would his friend sell me the salmon? The stationmaster entered upon the mission with ardor, but without success.

No; the gentleman was only just after running down to the town for it in the delay, but why wouldn't I run down and get one for myself? There was half a dozen more of them below at Coffey's, selling cheap; there would be time enough, the mail wasn't signaled yet.

I jumped from the carriage and doubled out of the station at top speed, followed by an assurance from the guard that he would not forget me.

Congratulating myself on the ascendancy of the Personal Element, I sped through the soapy limestone mud towards the public houses. En route I met a heated man carrying yet another salmon, who, without preamble, informed me that there were three or four more good fish in it, and that he was after running down from the train himself.

"Ye have whips o' time!" he called after me. "It's the first house that's not a public house. Ye'll see boots in the window— she'll give them for tenpence a pound if ye're stiff with her!"

I ran past the public houses.

"Tenpence a pound!" I exclaimed inwardly, "at this time of year! That's good enough."

Here I perceived the house with boots in the window, and dived into its dark doorway.

A cobbler was at work behind a low counter. He mumbled something about Herself, through lengths of waxed thread that hung across his mouth, a fat woman appeared at an inner door, and at that moment I heard, appallingly near, the whistle of the incoming mail. The fat woman grasped the situation in an instant, and with what appeared but one movement, snatched a large fish from the floor of the room behind her and flung a newspaper round it.

"Eight pound weight!" she said swiftly. "Ten shillings!"

A convulsive effort of mental arithmetic assured me that this was more than tenpence a pound, but it was not the moment for stiffness. I shoved a half-sovereign into her fishy hand, clasped my salmon in my arms, and ran.

Needless to say it was uphill, and at the steepest gradient another whistle stabbed me like a spur; above the station roof successive and advancing puffs of steam warned me that the worst had probably happened, but still I ran. When I gained the platform my train was already clear of it, but the Personal Element held good. Every soul in the station, or so it seemed to me, lifted up his voice and yelled. The stationmaster put his fingers in his mouth and sent after the departing train an unearthly whistle, with a high trajectory and a serrated edge. It took effect; the train slackened, I plunged from the platform and followed it up the rails, and every window in both trains blossomed with the heads of deeply interested spectators. The guard met me on the line, very apologetic and primed with an explanation that the gentleman going for the boat train wouldn't let him wait any longer, while from our rear came an exultant cry from the stationmaster.

"Ye *told* him ye wouldn't forget him!"

"There's a few countrywomen in your carriage, sir," said the guard, ignoring the taunt, as he shoved me and my salmon up the side of the train, "but they'll be getting out in a couple of stations. There wasn't another seat in the train for them!"

My sensational return to my carriage was viewed with the utmost sympathy by no less than seven shawled and cloaked

countrywomen. In order to make room for me one of them
seated herself on the floor with her basket in her lap, another,
on the seat opposite to me, squeezed herself under the central
elbow flap that had been turned up to make room. The aromas
of wet cloaks, turf smoke, and salt fish formed a potent blend. I
was excessively hot, and the eyes of the seven women were
fastened upon me with intense and unwearying interest.

"Move west a small piece, Mary Jack, if you please," said a
voluminous matron in the corner, "I declare we're as throng as
three in a bed this minute!"

"Why then, Julia Casey, there's little throubling yourself,"
grumbled the woman under the flap. "Look at the way meself
is! I wonder is it to be putting humps on themselves the gentry
has them things down on top o' them! I'd sooner be carrying a
basket of turnips on me back than to be scrooged this way!"

The woman on the floor at my feet rolled up at me a glance
of compassionate amusement at this rustic ignorance, and
tactfully changed the conversation by supposing that it was at
Coffey's I got the salmon.

I said it was.

There was a silence, during which it was obvious that one
question burnt in every heart.

"I'll go bail she axed him tinpence!" said the woman under
the flap, as one who touches the limits of absurdity.

"It's a beautiful fish!" I said defiantly. "Eight pounds weight.
I gave her ten shillings for it."

What is described in newspapers as "sensation in court"
greeted this confession.

"Look!" said the woman under the flap, darting her head out
of the hood of her cloak, like a tortoise, "tis what it is, ye haven't
as much roguery in your heart as 'd make ye a match for her!"

"Divil blow the ha'penny Eliza Coffey paid for that fish!"
burst out the fat woman in the corner. "Thim lads o' her's had a
creel full o' thim snatched this morning before it was making
day!"

"How would the gentleman be a match for her!" shouted the
woman on the floor through a long-drawn whistle that told of a
coming station. "Sure a Turk itself wouldn't be a match for her!
That one has a tongue that'd clip a hedge!"

At the station they clambered out laboriously, and with

groaning. I handed down to them their monster baskets, laden, apparently, with ingots of lead; they told me in return that I was a fine *grauver* man, and it was a pity there weren't more like me; they wished, finally, that my journey might well thrive with me, and passed from my ken, bequeathing to me, after the agreeable manner of their kind, a certain comfortable mental sleekness that reason cannot immediately dispel. They also left me in possession of the fact that I was about to present the irreproachable Alice Hervey with a contraband salmon.

The afternoon passed cheerlessly into evening, and my journey did not conspicuously thrive with me. Somewhere in the dripping twilight I changed trains, and again later on, and at each change the salmon moulted some more of its damp raiment of newspaper, and I debated seriously the idea of interring it, regardless of consequences, in my portmanteau. A lamp was banged into the roof of my carriage, half an inch of orange flame, poised in a large glass globe, like a goldfish, and of about as much use as an illuminant. Here also was handed in the dinner basket that I had wired for, and its contents, arid though they were, enabled me to achieve at least some measure of mechanical distension, followed by a dreary lethargy that was not far from drowsiness.

At the next station we paused long; nothing whatever occurred, and the rain drummed patiently upon the roof. Two nuns and some schoolgirls were in the carriage next door, and their voices came plaintively and in snatches through the partition; after a long period of apparent collapse, during which I closed my eyes to evade the cold gaze of the salmon through the netting, a voice in the next carriage said resourcefully:

"Oh, girls, I'll tell you what we'll do! We'll say the Rosary!"

"Oh, that will be lovely!" said another voice; "well, who'll give it out? Theresa Condon, you'll give it out."

Theresa Condon gave it out, in a not unmelodious monotone, interspersed with the responses, always in a lower cadence; the words were indistinguishable, but the rise and fall of the western voices was lulling as the hum of bees. I fell asleep.

I awoke in total darkness; the train was motionless, and complete and profound silence reigned. We were at a station, that much I discerned by the light of a dim lamp at the far end of a platform glistening with wet. I struck a match and ascertained that it was eleven o'clock, precisely the hour at which I was to board the mail train. I jumped out and ran down the platform; there was no one in the train; there was no one even on the engine, which was forlornly hissing to itself in the silence. There was not a human being anywhere. Every door was closed, and all was dark. The nameboard of the station was faintly visible; with a lighted match I went along it letter by letter. It seemed as if the whole alphabet were in it, and by the time I had got to the end I had forgotten the beginning. One fact I had, however, mastered, that it was not the junction at which I was to catch the mail.

I was undoubtedly awake, but for a moment I was inclined to entertain the idea that there had been an accident, and that I had entered upon existence in another world. Once more I assailed the station house and the appurtenances thereof, the ticket office, the waiting room, finally, and at some distance, the goods store, outside which the single lamp of the station commented feebly on the drizzle and the darkness. As I approached it a crack of light under the door became perceptible, and a voice was suddenly uplifted within.

"Your best now agin that! Throw down your jack!"

I opened the door with pardonable violence, and found the guard, the stationmaster, the driver, and the stoker seated on barrels round a packing case, on which they were playing a game of cards.

To have too egregiously the best of a situation is not, to a generous mind, a source of strength. In the perfection of their overthrow I permitted the driver and stoker to wither from their places, and to fade away into the outer darkness without any suitable send-off; with the guard and the stationmaster I dealt more faithfully, but the pleasure of throwing water on drowned rats is not a lasting one. I accepted the statements that they thought there wasn't a Christian in the train, that a few minutes here or there wouldn't signify, that they would have me at the junction in twenty minutes, and it was often the mail was late.

Fired by this hope I hurried back to my carriage, preceded at

an emulous gallop by the officials. The guard thrust in with me
the lantern from the card table, and fled to his van.

"Mind the Goods, Tim!" shouted the stationmaster, as he
slammed my door, "she might be coming any time now!"

The answer traveled magnificently back from the engine.

"Let her come! She'll meet her match!" A war whoop upon
the steam whistle fittingly closed the speech, and the train
sprang into action.

We had about fifteen miles to go, and we banged and
bucketed over it in what was, I should imagine, record time.
The carriage felt as if it were galloping on four wooden legs, my
teeth chattered in my head, and the salmon slowly churned its
way forth from its newspaper, and moved along the netting with
dreadfuth stealth.

All was of no avail.

"Well," said the guard, as I stepped forth on to the deserted
platform of Loughranny, "that owld Limited Mail's th'un-
punctualest thrain in Ireland! If you're a minute late she's gone
from you, and maybe if you were early you might be half an
hour waiting for her!"

On the whole the guard was a gentleman. He said he would
show me the best hotel in the town, though he feared I would be
hard set to get a bed anywhere because of the "Feis" (a Feis, I
should explain, is a festival, devoted to competitions in Irish
songs and dances). He shouldered my portmanteau, he even
grappled successfully with the salmon, and, as we traversed the
empty streets, he explained to me how easily I could catch the
morning boat from Rosslare, and how it was, as a matter of fact,
quite the act of providence that my original scheme had been
frustrated.

All was dark at the uninviting portals of the hotel favored by
the guard. For a full five minutes we waited at them, ringing
hard: I suggested that we should try elsewhere.

"He'll come," said the guard, with the confidence of the Pied
Piper of Hamelin, retaining an implacable thumb upon the
button of the electric bell. "He'll come. Sure it rings in his
room!"

The victim came, half awake, half dressed, and with an inch

of dripping candle in his fingers. There was not a bed there, he said, nor in the town neither.

I said I would sit in the dining room till the time for the early train.

"Sure there's five beds in the dining room," replied the boots, "and there's mostly two in every bed."

His voice was firm, but there was a wavering look in his eye.

"What about the billiard room, Mike?" said the guard, in wooing tones.

"Ah, God bless you! we have a mattress on the table this minute!" answered the boots, wearily, "and the fellow that got the First Prize for Reels asleep on top of it!"

"Well, and can't ye put the palliasse on the floor under it, ye omadhawn?" said the guard, dumping my luggage and the salmon in the hall, "sure there's no snugger place in the house! I must run away home now, before Herself thinks I'm dead altogether!"

His retreating footsteps went lightly away down the empty street.

"Annything don't throuble *him!*" said the boots bitterly.

As for me, nothing save the Personal Element stood between me and destitution.

It was in the dark of the early morning that I woke again to life and its troubles. A voice, dropping, as it were, over the edge of some smothering overworld, had awakened me. It was the voice of theFirst Prize for Reels, descending through a pocket of the billiard table.

"I beg your pardon, sir, are ye going on the 5 to Cork?"

I grunted a negative.

"Well, if ye were, ye'd be late," said the voice.

I received this useful information in indignant silence, and endeavored to wrap myself again in the vanishing skirts of a dream.

"I'm going on the 6:30 meself," proceeded the voice, "and it's unknown to me how I'll put on me boots. Me feet is swelled the size o' three-pound loaves with the dint of the little dancing shoes I had on me in the competition last night. Me feet's delicate that way, and I'm a great epicure about me boots."

I snored aggressively, but the dream was gone. So, for all practical purposes was the night.

The First Prize for Reels arose, presenting an astonishing spectacle of grass-green breeches, a white shirt, and pearl-grey stockings, and accomplished a toilet that consisted of removing these and putting on ordinary garments, completed by the apparently excruciating act of getting into his boots. At any other hour of the day I might have been sorry for him. He then removed himself and his belongings to the hall, and there entered upon a resounding conversation with the boots, while I crawled forth from my lair to renew the strife with circumstances and to endeavor to compose a telegram to Alice Hervey of explanation and apology that should cost less than seven and sixpence. There was also the salmon to be dealt with.

Here the boots intervened, opportunely, with a cup of tea, and the intelligence that he had already done up the salmon in straw bottle covers and brown paper, and that I could travel Europe with it if I liked. He further informed me that he would run up to the station with the luggage now, and that maybe I wouldn't mind carrying the fish myself; it was on the table in the hall.

My train went at 6:15. The boots had secured for me one of many empty carriages, and lingered conversationally till the train started; he regretted politely my bad night at the hotel, and assured me that only for Jimmy Durkan having a little drink taken—Jimmy Durkan was the First Prize for Reels—he would have turned him off the billiard table for my benefit. He finally confided to me that Mr. Durkan was engaged to his sister, and was a rising baker in the town of Limerick; "indeed," he said, "any girl might be glad to get him. He dances like whalebone, and he makes grand bread!"

Here the train started.

It was late that night when, stiff, dirty, with tired eyes blinking in the dazzle of electric lights, I was conducted by the Herveys' beautiful footman into the Herveys' baronial hall, and was told by the Herveys' imperial butler that dinner was over, and the gentlemen had just gone into the drawing room. I was in the act of hastily declining to join them there, when a voice cried:

"Here he is!"

And Philippa, rustling and radiant, came forth into the hall, followed in shimmers of satin, and flutterings of lace, by Alice Hervey, by the bride elect, and by the usual festive rout of exhilarated relatives, male and female, whose mission it is to keep things lively before a wedding.

"Is this a wedding present for me, Uncle Sinclair?" cried the bride elect, through a deluge of questions and commiserations, and snatched from under my arm the brown paper parcel that had remained there from force of direful habit.

"I advise you not to open it!" I exlaimed; "it's a salmon!"

The bride elect, with a shriek of disgust, and without an instant of hesitation, hurled it at her nearest neighbor, the head bridesmaid. The head bridesmaid, with an answering shriek, sprang to one side, and the parcel that I had cherished with a mother's care across two countries and a stormy Channel fell, with a crash, on the flagged floor.

Why did it crash?

"A salmon!" screamed Philippa, gazing at the parcel, round which a pool was already forming, "why, that's whiskey! Can't you smell it?"

The footman here respectfully interposed, and kneeling down, cautiously extracted from folds of brown paper a straw bottle cover full of broken glass and dripping with whiskey.

"I'm afriad the other things are rather spoiled, sir," he said seriously, and drew forth, successivley, a very large pair of high-low shoes, two long grey worsted stockings, and a pair of grass-green breeches.

They brought the house down, in a manner doubtless familiar to them when they shared the triumphs of Mr. Jimmy Durkan, but they left Alice Hervey distinctly cold.

"You know, darling," she said to Philippa afterwards, "I don't think it was very clever of dear Sinclair to take the wrong parcel. I *had* counted on that salmon."

Her Trademark

By Julia O'Faolain

The captain—fastidious, with a complexion like raspberry fool—had a smile of great sweetness. From teeth that seemed to have been overlaid with a film of honey. A blond patina—nicotine lichen—clung to his fingers. Hair and moustache were ginger still. A golden lad. He brought scope and a festive dash to the management of local affairs, adoring to organize auctions of garden produce or a charity fête with bunting on his lawns. He treated women with gallantry, called them "the gentle sex," and showed for his own a preference to which scandal did not attach. Neighbours, meeting him with his mother on daily walks, noted that, of the two, she—once toasted at the hunt balls of half Leinster—had now the more military demeanour. Her voice wielded authority, her grip vigour, and she was rarely without an instrument for beheading ragweed blossoms, poking pennyleaves from walls or earthing up wasps' nests.

He retired early to join her on their small estate which he currycombed with fervour. In shining gumboots, shears in hand, he waded through sway-tipped meadows with two handymen at his beck. Like himself, these fellows liked to build pigeon coops, lay stepping-stones or adjust sundials. Between five and six he went in to drink tea—Indian and China—with his mother. Sometimes they tuned to the news, vaguely sipping the aromas of lost empire. Their own concerns absorbed them and it was a shock to find these also threatened. Prices crept up while pensions lagged. The handymen left one day for factory work in Dublin, and professional gardeners, who seemed to be all one could get now, demanded an alarming wage.

Eggs, fruit, tomato plants and dung were offered on a hoarding placed at the lodge gate and sold from the front door as he and his mother, with the ingenuity of their kind, staved off decision. Yet, in the end, like a cosily entrenched weed, he had to tear himself up. He ran an ad in the *Irish Times:* "Retired Brit. Officer (Dunkirk, Tripoli), RC, some French, seeks congenial post. Anything considered."

The solution that turned up was just the ticket. A devout Catholic with an old soldier's savvy and organizing ability was *the* man to guide pilgrimages to Lourdes. The salary was small but the job, being seasonal, allowed him to spend half the year at home with his mother. Then, as he remarked waggishly to her, it would bring him the stir and opportunity for mild military bullying that had been lacking since his retirement.

His parties did not include charity cases or invalids—the nursing Orders saw to them—but paying pilgrims who visited the shrine from piety or to ask for some Intention and were usually of the better type. Less better than the captain himself, they enjoyed and looked up to him. For his part, he took an interest in them and grew good at guessing the rub or worry that lay behind each trip. Some were offering it up for the conversion of a free-thinking relative or an alcoholic. Others were barren wives. Most frequent were the modest but hopeful women civil servants, female bank clerks or school mistresses who were going to ask the Virgin for the husband it was so hard to find in the rural regions to which they were posted. These were toughish, thirty-fivish, die-hard Dianas and, although the captain was in the position of a fox watching preparations for bloodsports, he had to admire their grit. Through living without men they had become mannish, played poker, drank gin together and talked—deplorably—in an endless and anguished gush, as though each were at pains to reconcile the waiting maiden in herself with the harpy she had been obliged to develop in order to protect her. With awe—recalling how often his mother had been photographed just as she was for *Country Life* or *The Irish Tatler and Sketch*—he assisted at their efforts at femininity. Chiffon squares from the Galeries Lafayette wavered on the gaunt masts of their tailor-mades; Rouge Baiser caked off inexpert lips, and the straw hats they bought at the beachwear counter and deposited on their heads for church visiting filled him with such distress that he could have wept for them. He had a flair for clothes himself, having often done wonders with a tablerunner and an old topee at houseparty charades, where his impersonations of well-known female actresses were certs to bring down the house. Yet, from diffidence, he refrained from advising. A full-scale Pygmalion operation could hardly have been conducted within the scope of their ten-day tour. Anything less, he saw, would merely make matters worse. He would have liked to help these lame dogs find and cross their stile, for he had always been a man of quick sympathy, and was touched by the dual glow of hope with which they greeted France: country of the Virgin and of Aphrodite.

"Our Lady doesn't want us to approach her with long faces," he would say in their defence if an older woman made a cutting comment. "We can worship through joy."

After his first season's guiding, he became as much at home with the pious lingo of his parties as he had once been with military jargon. He took to distributing blessed rosaries and pastilles of dehydrated Lourdes water among veteran friends, pulling them out of his waistcoat pocket at dinners with a feeling that this was akin to showing the flag. He had become convinced of the need for propagating the faith by the irreligion he saw in France. "Things look bad on the Continent," he told his mother and her neighbours, returning from his pilgrimages with little bulletins as he had once done from the Front. "Churches empty!" One day, as his touring bus was held up by a demonstration on the Boulevard Antoine in Paris, he surveyed the crowd through his window. "Bally Reds!" he told his pilgrims. "Put on a pretty poor show! Listen: they're singing two different anthems! Still," he peered ardently about, "I see a lot of fine looking young chaps out there! Poor Marianne!" He was glad to get back to Lourdes whose clockwork ceremonies consoled him as did the scale on which it was run. A more efficient army. Still, in the older, "native" part of the town, he could not help noticing a couple of hammers and sickles chalked impertinently on walls. "We need counter publicity," he told his flock. "If we could point to a couple of A1 miracles, it would take those Commies down a peg!"

Two more guiding seasons rattled by with the brisk monotonous rhythm of the touring buses which told on his ankles and, although his spirit did not waver, his breath grew faintly sour. His health suffered from the food in cheap pensions which he was obliged to substitute regularly for the hotels booked by the agency. This was standard practice. Guides were underpaid and the game without perks would simply not have been worth the candle. He disliked such manoeuvres. They, and the expenditure of sympathy required by his interchangeable charges, slowly bled him, so that off-seasons became convalescence periods.

Then his mother began to fail. She withdrew herself so slowly that her death, at the end of his third season, was simply confirmation of a forefelt loss. The house, empty now and more of a problem than ever—since he had only one pension to count on—tormented and distracted him from his mourning so that, feeling guilty, he suffered even more. Yet he could not bear to sell it, although the drains were bad, rewiring urgent, the roof sagged and moss, soft as old silk, was creeping, loop after loop, like a crocheted shawl, over the hump of the gable. He could not afford a caretaker but friends discovered a handsome, deficient young man who, in return for board and lodging, would look after the place. Suddenly shy of his own house, the captain got a job in the next off-season taking ski-ing parties to Switzerland and for eighteen months was hardly home at all. Now and then it occurred to him that, with the young man's help, he could run a chicken farm or take paying guests, save his house and give up the guiding. But each time he thought of it, the young man's mild, beautiful, mad eyes flashed in front of his vision and he rejected the idea.

The last group on the last pilgrimage of his eighteen-month stint was a small one and the captain got to know them better than usual. Three sisters were the core of the party: the Miss Laceys from Sligo with whom he played bridge and pretended to flirt. He could tell that this was as much masculine attention as they had ever commanded, and they had not reached Lourdes at all before he had sensed, loneliness having quickened his apprehension of such things, that they were going to pray for husbands.

"Daddy," Miss Kitty Lacey told him, "died last year."

Frisky as gun dogs at the season's start, they were emerging from a year's mourning.

They lived in deep country, he found, in unrelieved idleness: a bickering family which had carried childhood games into pre-middle age. (They still, they admitted, liked to make toffee and had a Christmas tree with secret presents.) They played tennis and croquet and clock golf on the lawn. Dance? They loved to and had given "hops" in the front room, rolling back the carpet and inviting Daddy and a few of his younger friends—until last year. All three belonged to the local tennis and mountaineering clubs and *all three* took continental holidays together. They even played bridge, as now with the captain, sitting at the same table. What man would have the courage to drive a wedge between them? That none had might be guessed from the unwavering hockey-field voices. They were friendly and crossed muscular legs with nonchalance. Maisie was forty, Kitty thirty-five and Jenny, the baby, thirty-two. It was on their passports. Unabused but a trifle neglected like that of nuns, their skin had the firm, unaromatic texture of linen long preserved in drawers. The captain, who would be free in ten days—after this tour he would have six months in which to tend his estate and decide about his future—watched them with understanding and an occasional stab of horror. (The same sensuous fascination froze him when the post-mistress at home larded his letters with her gummy spittle, rummaging with lubricated finger for the envelope on which a little extra postage must be paid.) The sisters were not identical. The eldest, either more intelligent or merely more resigned, had, visibly, set herself to cultivate inner resources. She had learned French, tutored by an Irish priest who had studied in Belgium, and all through the trip was to be seen, in lounges after dinner, fingering her way down the columns of *France Soir*. The captain, remembering country aunts who had died in maidenly loneliness akin to madness, pitied the Miss Laceys. Kitty and Jenny's noisy laughter—empty vessels—had a desperate note and he had seen them sidle with provocative demureness around French railway officials who responded with icy courtesy.

"Wouldn't you think that trio would have the sense to divide up?" Mrs. O'Keefe, an elderly widow who had been three times to Lourdes—it was the nicest way she knew of taking a holiday—was interested in the Miss Laceys' predicament.

The captain said something about the Miss Laceys being nice girls.

"Isn't that the shame of it!" she agreed with him. She sighed:

"Mind you, three at one go is a tall order even for Our Lady of Lourdes! It'd have to be a real miracle!"

On the return journey, a lightning plane strike stranded the party in Paris. A couple of the older ladies dreaded the crossing by boat and as nobody, it turned out, was pressed for time or money, the group voted to spend a few days at the Hôtel de la Gare.

"Captain! Captain! Maybe we'll have our miracle now!" Mrs. O'Keefe hissed exultantly up the well of the stairs as he descended for dinner. An expert pilgrim, she got dressed faster than anyone and posted herself on the route to the dining-room, ready to pounce on him. "Look! Look!" She nodded at the bar.

The captain saw the three Miss Laceys sitting on high stools, laughing over gin fizzes with two men. He raised his eyebrows. "*Well!* How did that happen?" The men looked nice chaps, and the sisters were chattering nineteen to the dozen. Miss Kitty Lacey's laugh ricocheted across the lounge. "Ca, ca, ca, ca!" High and repetitious like the cry of an anxious cow. Maisie, as if to emphasize a lack of hope, was sitting on the edge and turned half away from the others.

Mrs. O'Keefe had overheard all. She lowered her voice. "They met them," she muttered, "at the tennis tournament at Mount Merrion two years ago. Kitty and Jenny played them in the mixed semi-finals. One's an architect. The other works in a bank. They're staying in the hotel. English!"

The captain's mind raced in unison with hers: "Catholics?" he whispered.

Mrs. O'Keefe drew back in annoyance. "*Captain!* I'm surprised at you! After the present pope's encouragement of mixed marriages! Anyway, they could turn." She leaned forward to his ear. "The drawback is," she whispered, "that there's only *two!*" Again she withdrew herself, this time to give him one of her fixed-eyed, pursed-lipped, slow and ponderous nods.

"Ah!" agreed the captain.

"We," she prompted, "can invite *one* of them to make up a party after dinner. I'll get Miss Taylor to play so we'll only need one to make the fourth. *Maisie,*" she judged. "Then the men can invite the other two out on the tiles." She laughed with the innocent vulgarity to which the captain was becoming used in pious women.

The plan worked. Maisie's sisters took a boisterous, shame-faced leave of her and had not come back with their beaus by the time the bridge party went to bed. It had been a strained little session, for Mrs. O'Keefe, frustrated by Maisie's presence from discussing her sisters' prospects, was too fidgety to concentrate on cards; Maisie played badly too so that by the end of the evening the pair, who were partners, had lost quite a bit.

"Poor me," Maisie lamented as she paid up.

"Ah well! Unlucky in cards you know!" said Miss Taylor abstractedly and was kicked by Mrs. O'Keefe.

The captain's sympathies, repelled by Maisie's play, returned to her on the boomerang of pity. "Well, this has been an agreeable evening indeed!" He drained his glass. "One of the pleasantest on the trip. But all good things and all that. Remember, tomorrow we have to rise early for our tour of the City of Light."

The ladies lumbered upstairs, slowed by drink and con-fidences. Walking behind them—he had paused to say some-thing to the concierge—the captain saw Maisie's box-shaped form tilt towards that of Mrs. O'Keefe. "Oh super! A regular charmer!" Mrs. O'Keefe's hiss floated down the stairs to him. "Isn't it funny, now, he never got married!" He went into his room and locked the door. He polished his shoes, inserted the wooden trees and carefully tied the laces over them. He had a shower, gave himself a friction with eau-de-Cologne and re-membered that the golden rule was to keep things from getting personal. Be *nice* as pie but—off parade, off parade. A bit sticky sometimes. He climbed into bed to read a war memoir in which the human element was considered from a safe, abstracting distance.

Next morning the blue-pennanted busload visited the Sacré Coeur, the Sainte Chapelle, Saint Sulpice and Notre Dame. The pilgrims, weary of churches, gabbled prayers, collected the available indulgences and settled back in their seats with a profane zest when the captain proposed a drive into the country. He took them towards Rambouillet, along roads where mistletoe hung hairy smudges on the limbs of poplars, and sounds were spasms in the air. Returning, they decided to stretch their legs in the Bois de Boulogne and gaped at crisp-figured riders on distant bridle paths. The lake was diamond bright.

"Golly!" Jenny Lacey squeezed old Miss Taylor's arm. "Doesn't it *thrill* you to be here? Doesn't it make your blood run faster?" Heels puncturing the clay, she took off to sniff the passionate humours of the wood.

Kitty Lacey flung out her arms. "I want to hug you captain," she threatened and did so with a buoyant gesture.

"Oho!" Mrs. O'Keefe whispered. "'Tis easy seen a gay old time was had last night!" A conniving elbow stabbed the captain's waistcoat. As they got back into the bus, he noted that Maisie was wearing sensible flat shoes.

The next two days the captain left the group to their own devices until dinner time. He slipped off each morning, avoiding Mrs. O'Keefe who was lurking at loose ends in the lounge, and did not return before seven. He spent one morning looking at pistols in an antique shop, another reading the *Times* in a bar where he partook of a liver paste sandwich and some Beaujolais by the glass, then meandered through grimy streets in the bleak vicinity of the Santé prison, coming in time to the Jardin de l'Observatoire where he sat by the lake and felt lonely for Stephen's Green. At dinner, Mrs. O'Keefe twitted him on his "mysterious double life," remarking that things moved faster when one was abroad, didn't he think?

The two younger Miss Laceys had meanwhile had their hair done. ("Paris, ha, ha," said Miss Taylor, "has gone to their heads!") A sculptural cut, removing the fuzz that had shadowed their faces, revealed hitherto disguised rapacities.

On those two nights the captain played bridge again with Maisie and the two elder women while Jenny and Kitty went dancing with their Englishmen.

"Toodloo!" screamed Kitty, waving an arm bright with a dozen plastic bangles.

"Keep your eye on sis, captain! She'll clean you out!"

"Still waters run deep! She's a cardsharper!"

"And a cannibal man-eater!" They screamed with laughter.

Their sister winced. They were gone.

"Whew!" The captain caught Maisie's embarrassed eye. She laughed back at him and he was pleased that she seemed in better form. Probably decided those young chaps weren't worth being jealous over! He couldn't have agreed more. Anyone who would put up with those screeching termagants.... Well, Mrs. O'Keefe had shown judgment in isolating Maisie from the quartet. She was clearly several cuts above them.... Maisie and Mrs. O'Keefe won back their losses that night.

The next day was to be the pilgrims' last. The strike had been settled and seats were available on a plane the following morning. In the afternoon the hotel was taken over by a provincial wedding party which sang songs that reminded the Irish group of some of their own and struck up a gaiety in which they soon became involved. They were in the thick of it when the captain returned from his stroll. Someone was playing the accordion and a pair of highly liquored Frenchmen—rural types in stiff suits—had threaded arms through the armpits of Maisie and Mrs. O'Keefe and were stamping about to the tune.

"Captain! Come on! Where have you been all day?"

The barman handed him a glass of something and Maisie's partner surrendered her. She was an excellent dancer. Lightfooted.

"I've always said," the captain told her, "the best dancers come from down the country. Where are the other two?"

"They've been out with their fellows since morning," she said, "They're letting the last day be the longest."

"Well so can we," he comforted her and whirled her off again, for the accordionist had started up a waltz. The captain had won prizes for waltzing with his mother and told Maisie about this. "My father was killed when I was twelve. I used to take her to dances from the time I left school, but I never got a look in after the first dance or so. She was so popular."

"And she never remarried?"

"No."

"You must miss her."

"Yes."

The hotel service had been disrupted by the wedding, so guests had to be content with a supper of cold sandwiches, mostly left-overs. They ate them in the pauses between dancing.

"It's mad," Maisie said. "Like an Irish country hotel."

"It's fun," said the captain.

At 2 A.M. he sponged his forehead with a damp handkerchief. "Been overdoing it," he apologized. "If you'll excuse me, I'd better retire. Ladies," he turned towards Maisie who was resting on a couch. He sketched his usual departing bow and toppled into her lap.

There was a snigger from one of the dancing French, too far gone themselves to interpret the situation correctly.

"Captain! Oh! Captain!"

Maisie had been thrown backwards by his impact and now he lay prostrated across her breast. Male smells breathed into her gasping mouth. She tried to lift him but he seemed to have gone rigid and her fingers merely managed to peel his jacket up his back. She probed the intimacy of flesh sweating through his shirt.

"Someone..." she begged. "Please...Mrs. O'Keefe!"

She pulled the flaps of his coat down again. Hugging him violently to her, hands braced beneath his armpits, she got him into a half sitting, half reclining position beside her on the couch. People gathered round at last.

"Captain! Captain!"

"Monsieur le Capitaine! Mais qu'est-ce qu'il a? Il est soûl?"

"No, no, he must be ill!"

"There's a medicine chest in our room! Please, Monsieur, veuillez bien porter le capitaine....Do you mind carrying the captain...."

The accordionist and a friend lugged him up the stairs and along a corridor. His eyes opened, glared. "Just a touch!" he kept gasping out. "Nothing to worry about...passes over...malaria...." O'Keefe and Maisie clucked along behind him. "Mind his head now!" "No, no!" he heard Maisie squawking. "Not here. This is *my* room!" Like one of the three bears. "Mais alors?" the accordionist complained. The captain, the captain thought he understood him to say, was no feather weight. If she didn't want him here, why didn't she speak up sooner? *He* wasn't a paid stretcher bearer. ("Elles en font des manières, ces gonzesses!") A door closed. "Put him on the bed," O'Keefe's voice cut in. "Have sense! The man's ill!" "Yes, yes," the captain tried to shout. "Ill! It'll pass. Only cover me up!" His body was shaking with the cold. He hadn't had a bout like this in years. His teeth, his very bones, were clattering with the cold. "More blankets," he commanded. "Hold my hand. Tightly. More tightly. More blankets. More. It'll pass. It'll pass." He clutched a hand, closed his eyes and heaved like an agonizing fish: his whole body leaping in spasms from the bed. "Just a few minutes. Never takes more," he heard himself say. "Half an hour at most. Hold me, Mummy! Mummy, hold me. Hold me tight. Lie beside me. Keep me warm."

When he awoke from the nightmares that always came with his bouts, he felt her beside him, turned absurdly the other way so that their bottoms bumped and the arm he was clinging to held her pinioned like a clamp. When she felt him stir, she unclenched his fingers and sat up.

"Would you like a cup of tea, captain?" she asked, brushing down her skirt, tidying her blouse. "I have a spirit lamp and tea and sugar." (Wise virgins, they carried plastic-wrapped props against every incursion of the unforeseen.)

"What? What?" the captain groaned, his head throbbing less than he would have liked. There was something to be faced he could already tell. A trifle...what? Unorthodox? He could smell scenty stuff. An animal smell not his. He closed his eyes hopefully. Sleeping dogs. Let lie! The malaria dreams rushed at him.

"Tea!" said Maisie with assurance. "Wake *up*, captain. It will do you good."

He sat up. "Where...your sisters?" The three had shared a room.

"With Mrs. O'Keefe." She was laying out plastic cups. "Feel better? I can see you do!"

"Yes."

"Good!" She plumped his pillow efficiently.

"You gave me some stuff?"

"Quinine."

He laughed. "By golly you're a good nurse. I should marry you!"

She laughed, "crisply," enjoying the rôle.

"And get me cheap? Have you a drop of Scots blood captain?"

Mild whiff of scent from her.

"You called me 'Mummy'," she told him.

He blushed and decided to expire again.

A minute later Mrs. O'Keefe bounced in in a satin kimono to know "how's the patient?"

Maisie told her he was in the best of form. "Been proposing to me," she said. "I think that's a good sign, don't you?"

Mrs. O'Keefe's gargling intake of breath was like the last exodus of water from a bath. "We-el! Of *all* the miracles!" (He opened an eye, saw her fling her arms around Maisie's neck, and closed it quickly.) *"This* is what I've been praying for!" gabbled she. *"Wait* till I tell the others! I can't think of nicer news! I declare I'm happier than yourselves! My heartiest congratulations! I'll say a prayer this minute to Saint Bernadette!"

"Mrs. O'Keefe! We were joking!" He heard Maisie's squawk.

"Joke! After spending the night together! Sure the whole hotel has its eye on the pair of ye!"

The captain trembled.

"We...I..." Maisie strangled.

"You're excited! Shy! *I* understand! Bridal nerves! I'll keep the others away!" The door closed.

The captain opened his eyes again to see Maisie rush to it, lock it, unlock it and sit miserably in an armchair. "I *hate* that woman!" she hissed.

"A monster," the captain agreed timidly.

"We'll straighten things out," she told him, "It's ridiculous! Maybe one day it'll seem funny! Old cat!" She began to cry. "This is nervous! I'm sorry. It's...just that *I'm* never going to hear the end of this! Never! Oh!" She buried her face in a cushion.

"Maybe I should go after her," she said into her cushion. "At once. But they'd all be at me! I couldn't face them this minute. In the morning," she promised. "We'll straighten it out!" She wept.

The captain stared unhappily about him. Charity towards one's neighbours began by leaving them alone. Don't rush in.

Give her time to pick up the shreds. Poor girl! Tough furrow!
Sisters like harpies! Hyenas! Think of them sucking the marrow
from each other's bones for years while he'd been in Egypt,
Burma....Locked up together like inmates of some female
reformatory! He could just see their house in Sligo! Grey—
Connemara stone—with a bumpy tenniscourt—no man to roll
it—wind-bent trees, fringes of nettle and dock. His eye skidded
off the bidet where stockings had been stretched, rose to
observe flies and lees of dust in the ceiling lamp. He felt
depressed. Squashed somehow. Normal enough after an attack.
Drains one. But why the attack? Old age? Ha! No such thing!
The wardrobe looked like a pair of upright coffins with claw
feet. All the better to trail you with. He would be glad to get out
of here.

"I have always tried to be d-d-dignified!" From behind the
cushion.

Poor child! "Now, now!" he comforted. "This could happen
to a bishop. Go on," he advised. "Cry! It'll do you good." But as
she did he added: "What would you say to a walk?"

"Now?" She looked at her watch. "It's 4 A.M."

"Why not? We won't sleep after the tea. Fresh air! Clean the
cobwebs out of our heads. This is Paris. All sorts of things go
on! Let's do a little reconnoitring."

"And your head?"

"Best thing in the world for it. If you're game we'll slip out on
the QT."

They found a taxi rank and the captain, remembering
something he had been told about being able to get a meal at
any hour at Les Halles, asked the driver to take them there.
"Some modest place," he directed. "We didn't get much of a
meal last night," he told Maisie restively. "We can go for a stroll
afterwards and see the dawn maybe over Paris."

The restaurant was shiny and noisy. Nobody looked at
Maisie's red eyes. Over white wine and oysters she grew febrile.

"God!" she groaned. "In this city one could be *alone* or choose
one's company." She watched a well-dressed woman who was
eating a large meal alone with a book. A bottle of wine in front

of her was three-quarters full. "People don't stare and tattle and pity each other's failures.... Oh, what do I know about it? Maybe they do!" She lowered her eyes and ate.

"Couldn't you take a job?" the captain asked. "Break out as it were? Go to Dublin or London...." Shocked at his own indiscretion, he let his voice trail vaguely away. "Lots of women are secretaries, aren't they?" he murmured.

"I'm forty," said Maisie. "And I have had no experience."

At the baldness of that he quivered. The unusual hour, the place, the wine after quinine perhaps, above all her frankness stirred him. The captain had rarely probed beneath the patina of conversational formula. What Maisie had shown of her private self troubled him.

"My dear," he laid down knife and fork, wiped his lips and leaned towards her, "you could come and live with me! Why not? We can work out a *modus vivendi*. That is, if you would not greatly object. I would respect your privacy.... You could depend on that!"

She looked up. "You mean...?"

"Yes, yes!" He smiled in triumph at his own initiative, in assent to the warmth of solidarity, the possibilities that fanned out like fireworks once one removed the lid—the lid of what? The wine danced like a centipede in his throat.

"Marry you?"

"Why not? Why not? Absolutely.... That is to say...." He put down his glass. "In a sense."

"Because of Mrs. O'Keefe? The fuss?"

"Why not," he insisted bravely. "We would be marrying to protect each other. From the others."

"Oh you are *kind!* You want to save my face.... We *could* simply let them go on assuming what they do. For a while."

"No, no, I want you to take the idea seriously! Now that we have it. Unless it strikes you as ludicrous! I think we are compatible!" Over that hurdle, he smiled with his old charm.

"Oh!" she cried. "No! I mean not at all, but, really, I don't know what to think!" Her colour was as high suddenly as the rouge of women at other tables.

He looked at his watch. "We have three hours," he told her shyly, "until we face them."

"Three hours...."

"And we needn't tell *them* the truth even then!"

They laughed, astounded at themselves, and he filled up their glasses. They ate their next course in silence. An old man with a heavily painted face sat weeping in one corner over a plate of choucroute. Their glances shied away from him, back to each other, down to their plates. Workers from the market came in on a gust of cold air smelling of mushrooms and wet dungarees, straw, sooty brick, the night. At the cheese Maisie asked: "Why would you let yourself be rushed into marrying me?" There was coquetry in her tone now. Her eyes were bright. The captain felt he had restored her nerve.

His own wavered forthwith. He patted her hand and an aviary of doubts were flushed up to be shot down like clay pigeons in his head. Pim, pam, poum! They soared again like phoenixes. A wife? Him with a ...? But she was discreet. If any woman was. If, if. The gentle particle furred his inner ear. She was making up now, powdering, toning down her triumphant flush, reddening her lips. She smiled at a flower seller passing their table. He bought her a gardenia and she pinned it on. Bending to smell it with the movement of a cat about to lick its own chest, she said:

"My second gardenia! The first was—oh a long time ago— from a young..."

"Maisie, don't!" The captain stopped her. "Don't tell me now!"

He was astonished by his own agitation. Felt like cavalry surprised in the Russian steppe, congealed in mid-stream by sudden ice. He *must* break out of this!

"My dear," he began. He had cards to be put on the table which he had chested all his life. "Shall we have a liqueur?" As she smiled he guessed she was remembering that recalcitrant Irish swains drink to give themselves courage to make love to their women. Her bosom was swelling; the mounds on either side of the cleft nuzzled the edges of her dress. Had his offer done all this? Turned her into a Juno? He felt himself shrivel. His limbs folded with the dry movement of a scissors. Yet....She would be a splendid businesswoman. They could run a chicken farm together—battery system—they would give up the pilgrimages....Tossing down his drink, he began, "Maisie, do you know my name? Being called 'captain' unnerves me and I have something to tell you."

She laughed a full-throated peal. "Can *I* unnerve you—Edwin?"

This time the coquetry was open. He felt the stiffening in his bones. What did she expect? He glanced at her big moving chest, her voracious mouth.

"You sound ominous!" she teased, her eyes rolling above the rim of her brandy glass. Self-sufficient now as planets; like searchlights, like drills they bored into him. Her lips sipped the fiery liquid. Multimouthed animalitics stirred beneath her skin. Perspiration glittered around her nose.

"Maisie, I..." He eluded her grin.

She stretched out her hand. "You *are* jumpy!" she exclaimed. "Are you worried?" Gently: "You are no more bound than before you know!"

He grasped the hand. "Please try to understand," he gabbled, "that I *have* to tell you this at once. Now! To avoid... ambiguities. Out of consideration for both of us. I am fifty-four. I have lived too long alone to fancy myself able to contract for more. Maisie," he held her hand in both of his, "I am suggesting a...a union of souls, of affection, not....The Church has provision for such limited marriages. In special circumstances." He could feel her hand go limp between his. He did not dare lift his glance to her face. "I think we could make a go of it—if you were to agree. There is so much left. So much of life apart from that side of things. Companionship," he begged, "mutual respect, affection. We would collaborate on the farm. You would be mistress in your own house. It's a nice place, Maisie. You would be your own woman....I think we could help each other...." He stole a glance at her, fell silent, let go her hand.

She was looking through the windows to where artichoke crates had been piled high as the door and at the sky where daylight was unemphatically seeping through, like milk soaking a black cloth. Having delivered himself, he began to feel for her. He guessed her to be reviewing—perhaps closing a final lid on—a vivid hope chest, resigning herself perhaps to the soundness—and damn it, he guaranteed *that*—the drabness of second best. He stretched out a hand. She did not see it. Poor girl! Was she mortified by the eagerness she had displayed?

"Maisie," he whispered, "you needn't say anything now. Let me know later. If...we don't have to meet again. I *had*," he pleaded, "to tell you while I could...."

Or had she understood at all?

She did not look at him again until she had finished her brandy. Her features had contracted. "Perhaps we'd better be getting back," she said.

They walked. Buildings were emerging from the night. Tramps slept on gratings along the pavement, kept alive by a minimal flutter of warmth or the memory of warmth on air unconsidered and exhaled by surrounding houses.

"How do they survive? They must be perished!"

"Would you like my coat?"

"Who's the invalid?"

In the middle of the Pont Neuf, she stopped. "I am going to give you my answer now," she began "I know you to be considerate, kind...."

"Oh," he cried sadly. "This means I've been...that you're going to say 'no'!"

"No! It's 'yes'! Yes, Edwin!"

He took her hands. He was touched and would have liked to say something festive, even tender to her. But he did not dare. Instead, he seized her by the waist and rushed her across the bridge in a kind of dance, an access of exuberance that always accompanied (and saved him from dealing with) feelings of a powerful or uncertain nature. "I'm so glad, Maisie," he told her breathlessly as they paused on the other side. "Old Mrs. O'Keefe is right you know! This—for me—*is* a miracle! A gift. Loneliness you know...."

She gave him her little smile. "The Virgin left her trademark on her gift, didn't she?" she observed. Then, quickly, putting her hand on his sleeve. "But I'm glad too," she said. "Truly."

He seized the hand. "That's right!" he cried. "The Virgin! You've hit the nail on the head! Oh you understand things! I'm sure we shall get on like a house on fire! You'll see!"

They walked on. Quickly. It was late and she had to finish their packing.

The Priest's Housekeeper

By Michael McLaverty

It was young Father Doyle's third change in seven years, and as he wearily watched his furniture being carried into his new quarters he wished with all his might that the bishop would allow him to remain here for the customary six years. He was tired of moving, and even though this new place was never praised by his colleagues still he would make the best of it. It was a lonely place surely, and it was damp into the bargain, and in the evenings mists stole up from the lough and camped in the fields until early morning. And his nearest neighbours, he was told, wouldn't give him any trouble for they were at rest in the graveyard and separated from his house by a few chestnut trees and a thick hawthorn hedge.

His parish priest lived five miles away in a less lonely part of the country, and as the pieces of furniture were carried in Father Doyle went to the phone to ring him up. The old priest wished him well and was about to hang up when Father Doyle asked him about the housekeeper he was to get for him.

"Has she not turned up yet?" the old priest said in surprise. "There was only one reply to my advertisement and I answered at once and told her when to report for duty. That's bad news. But she'll turn up, never fear. Do the best you can in the meantime, and if you ever feel peckish just give me a tinkle and I'll get Bridget to put an extra plate on the table. It'll be no trouble at all, at all. You must guard against malnutrition. One can't pray and work if one's not properly fed."

Father Doyle thanked him and put down the receiver. He didn't like bothering people, not even a priest's housekeeper; he'd be able to manage for a while without one. But the main thing at the moment was to keep warm, and he moved quickly from room to room directing the removers where to place the furniture. And when the last piece was carried in rain fell heavily and he tipped the men generously and apologised for not having a cup of tea ready for them. They thanked him, touched their caps, and climbed into their heavy van. Presently it set off along a road that gleamed like a river in the rain and soon it had disappeared over a hill, leaving nothing behind it except two parallel tracks made by the wheels. Father Doyle shrugged with the cold, turned into the house, and closed the door.

He had two electric heaters and he switched one on in his sitting-room and plugged the other in the kitchen which was as cold as a vault. All his perishable foodstuffs lay on the table: bread, meat, eggs, butter, and a cooked chicken. He had made a list before setting out on his journey and he was pleased he had forgotten nothing, not even a box of matches. He stored most of the things in the fridge and began to light the stove to drive out the cold that had settled in the house.

Wearing his heavy overcoat he made his way upstairs to his bedroom where the furniture removers had screwed up his bed and unrolled his mattress. The window looked out upon the chapel, a rectangular building of grey stone and blue slates, and the rope of an exposed bell hanging down to a ring on the outside wall. Each day he would make sure to ring the Angelus or get the housekeeper to ring it should he be absent. He had great devotion to that prayer since the day a Protestant clergyman praised it as the loveliest of all our Catholic prayers.

The kitchen was filled with smoke when he came downstairs and he opened the draught-door of the stove and heard in a few minutes the healthy roar of the fire. He opened a window and watched the smoke burl out to the cold air. He took a light snack and was making his way to the chapel to read his breviary when a bus stopped at his gate and out of it, stepping backwards, came a solitary passenger. She stood on the roadway, a suitcase in her hand, looked irresolutely about her, and then moved towards the priest's house. Father Doyle walked down to meet her.

"Good evening, Father," she said. "Am I in the right place?"

"You're in the right place, I think. I'm Father Doyle."

"But it was a Father O'Loan I wrote to."

Father Doyle smiled: "It's me that needs you."

She was thin, wore thick spectacles, and her grey hair stuck untidily beneath her hat. She sniffed continually, but whether this was an incipient cold or an ingrained habit he had yet to find out.

He lifted her suitcase and noted that the metal fastenings were unsprung and the case kept closed by two loops of stout string. He'd buy her a new one at Christmas should she turn out to be satisfactory.

"It's a chilly house, Father," she said in a thin, squeaky voice. "I hope I won't get my death."

"I hope you won't," and he checked himself from making a joke about the nearness of the graveyard. At this stage he must be reserved, a bit aloof, until he had found his bearings. He escorted her to her room. It hadn't been touched since her predecessor had vacated it a few days ago. It was narrow, but it was above the kitchen and it should be warm.

"This room's as cold as a railway station," she complained. He explained that no fire had been lighted in the house for the past three days and that he himself had just arrived a short while before her. He placed her case on the only chair in the room.

"I'll bring you an electric heater. I've one in the kitchen and it'll not be needed while the stove's in operation. There's plenty of stuff in the fridge so make yourself a good meal."

"You wouldn't need a fridge in this house, Father," she said, gazing out the window at the wet coal and turf stored in a doorless shed.

He turned from the room without a word. She was going to be a grumbler by all accounts, but as he was glad to get her he wasn't going to cross her if he could help it. More of his weakness, he supposed, more of his misunderstanding of the nature of true meekness.

He crossed to the chapel and finished his office under one light he had switched on near the sanctuary. Darkness had fallen over the country when he came out, stars pincushioned the sky, and lights from the scattered homes shone weakly across the fields. His own house was lighted up like a government office, and he presumed his housekeeper was getting into her stride. There was nothing like bodily activity to keep the circulation in trim this cold weather, he mused.

His car, splashed with mud, was in the yard and he pushed it into the garage out of the cold. A cat meowed at his heels. Parochial property, no doubt; and he went in by the back door to get her a saucerful of milk.

His housekeeper was seated at the stove, the oven door open, and her feet held close to it. She still wore the coat she had travelled in; and the remains of her meal littered the table, and a loaf of bread was cut unevenly as if she had chopped it with a hatchet.

"What's this now your name is? he asked gently.

"Mary. Mary Carroll."

"Well, Mary, there's a cat out there could do with a little nourishment."

"I don't like cats about the place," she said, swiping a finger across each side of her nose and remaining seated.

"I suppose it could take up its quarters in the coal-shed."

"Proper place for it."

He put milk on a saucer and carried it carefully across the yard, the cat following him, its tail erect. He switched on his car lights, and placing the saucer in the driest corner he called the cat and she lowered her tail, put her head to the milk and lapped greedily.

Father Doyle returned to the house by the front door. He crouched close to his electric-heater and filled his pipe. Later he'd have a little of the cold chicken for his supper.

He could hear Mary coughing, the stove being raked, and coal being shovelled on to it. He glanced at the clock on the mantelpiece; it had stopped and he wound it up and set it at the right time by his wristlet watch. It was near eight. He had had a tiresome day and he wouldn't stay up late.

Behind him mist crept round the windows and covered them. He rubbed his hands together and thought of a colleague who warned him that this place would drive anyone to drink. He smiled and stared at his closed cabinet that contained bottles of whiskey, brandy, and sherry—all for passing visitors and old missioners whose blood required a little stimulant. Never copy the Mercy Nuns, he had been warned, for they were the very divils for offering an old priest tea. He hadn't, he knew, offered a glass to the van-men, but that was understandable. Their van was clumsy, the roads narrow, and anything could happen—he needn't accuse himself of lack of hospitality on that score. As for himself, thank God, a craving for drink had never yet possessed him. He had his books, he had his work, and he was content. He had also brought his three hives of bees and they were sheltered now from all winds by the trees and thick hedges in his garden. What would they do, he mused, when the first warm rags of sunlight coaxéd them from their winter sleep. Would they try to make their way back to their old home, over the mountains to the parish in south Down that he had just left? He supposed they hadn't the instinct of homing pigeons and that, like cats, they would speedily adapt themselves to their new surroundings. Attachment to persons was scarcely a characteristic of bees.

The phone rang and he crossed the room to answer it. It was his mother ringing from the city to inquire if he had settled in. Yes, he was nicely settled, he told her. Yes, the housekeeper had arrived. About sixty, he'd say. No, not too robust, but better than nothing.

He paused while his mother took over and launched into her usual litany. He mustn't be too soft with this one, must be strict with her and keep her in her proper place from the word go. She reminded him that he had more than his share of the wrong sort. But it was good to hear that she was an elderly person: she was likely to be a stay-at-home and not a flighty gadabout or one of those harpies that would be demanding half-days off three times a week. But on no account must he keep her if she happened to be an indifferent cook or slatternly in her ways.

"All right, mother. Now don't be worrying." He smiled into the phone. "I've every comfort and I'm in fine form. Good night now, mother.... Good night," and he just had the receiver down when a loud sneeze broke from him. He returned to his armchair, and once again he sneezed, muffling the explosion in his handkerchief. If his mother had heard his sneezes there'd be no peace until she had motored down from the city for a personal inspection.

At nine o'clock Mary came and announced that her poor feet were perished and she was going to bed. She didn't mention his supper and he was too diffident to ask about it.

"Them tea things on the table, Father; I'll wash them up first thing in the morning. It's too cold for me to stand at that sink in the scullery; I'd get a founder. You understand."

Yes, he understood.

"It's a cold snap of a place this," she went on. "There's frost on that window in the scullery and this only the month of November."

"It's nice here in the springtime, I believe."

"That's a long way off."

"It'll not seem so long when you get into your way of going and get to know the people."

"The people! What do I want with people I'd dearly like to know. I'm a person who keeps herself to herself. I mind my own business."

Father Doyle, realising he couldn't make contact with her, began to outline her duties for each day. He would say Mass at eight and would have breakfast at nine, dinner at 1:30, a light snack at 4:30, and supper at eight until further notice. She was to light a fire in the sitting-room each day during the winter months.

"That will be all right, Father. That'll be all right."

"Good night now, Mary."

She closed the door, and he heard her coughing as she ascended the cold stairs.

If she got sick on his hands, he'd be in a nice pickle, he told himself, and turning up the collar of his overcoat he refilled his pipe and pressed his back into the cushions in the arm-chair. Once more the phone rang. His mother, he presumed, remembering some other item on her agenda.

He lifted the receiver. It was Father O'Loan. A sick-call had come through, and as the house was nearer Father Doyle's end of the parish it would be more convenient for him to go. Father O'Loan proceeded to give him precise instructions how to reach the place. He was to set out immediately by the main road and take the second turning on the right. This was a narrow road, pitted with pot-holes like a battlefield, and he was to drive very carefully. He was to close all the car windows because the briars from the hedges hung out like fishing-rods and were apt to scratch the face off him. A mile along that road on his left he would meet two stone pillars but no gate. He was to stop there and sound the horn and wait. Somebody would come forward and pilot him up the stony path that led to the sick-woman's house. This sick-call, Father O'Loan assured him, would give him an opportunity to know his people—the first requisite for any young priest in a new parish.

The night was clear and frosty when he set out, and he had no difficulty in finding the road and no difficulty in finding the gateposts. He sounded the horn, and, as in a fairy tale, a man arrived with a lantern and led him up the narrow, slippery path to the house of the sick-woman.

The house was as warm as an oven. Two oil-lamps hung on the walls and a mound of turf burned in a hearth as wide as a Christmas crib. Three grey-haired women welcomed him, all sisters he discovered when he had introduced himself. A door off the room was open, and the old mother, now in her eighty-eighth year, was in bed, a tiny oil-lamp on a table beyond her reach, and pictures of the Sacred Heart, the Blessed Virgin, and Robert Emmet on the walls. About an hour ago she had taken a terrible fit of coughing and they were sure she was going to go on them, but she rallied, thank God, and was now resting peacefully, her black rosary in her hands. Father Doyle felt her pulse, and holding her hand lightly he sat down on a chair beside the bed and chatted to her.

She had given them all a quare fright, she told him. But, thank God, she was ready to go. Her three daughters were all good girls, she went on, and always did their best for her and never gallivanted about the countryside looking for a husband. And her boy Patrick—the man who led Father Doyle to the house—was a biddable boy, none better in the whole country of Antrim. Oh, a great worker: he could cut and clamp more turf in a week than six strong men could do in a month. There was no need to worry about the girls when they'd Patrick to look after them. She could die in peace.

Yes, Father Doyle thought, they'd all die in peace, and their place would fall in ruins and the briars join fingers across the slippery path and defy all entrance.

After hearing her confession he rested his hand on her forehead and told her he'd call again in the morning and not to worry about anything. She smiled with her lips closed. A lovely young priest, she thought, an ornament to the parish. She wouldn't like to die yet—indeed she would not!

He returned to the kitchen and sat by the fire, glad of the thick warmth that wrapped round him. They made tea for him in a shiny brown teapot that rested on the hot ashes at the side of the hearth. He wanted to take it in his hand by the fire but they insisted on his going to the white-clothed table. And there the tea was served to him in their best china, and the table was laden with home-made bread and jam and salted butter, the measure of their hospitality. The tea warmed him and dispelled a gloom that had come over him whilst talking to the old woman. Good strong daughters and a strong son and not a child amongst them! And yet the old woman would die content!

He took his leave and the son with his lantern helped him to turn his car at the gateposts, and presently he was crunching over the potholes that were paned with ice and arrived back at his own house with the moon shining on it and the windows misted over like tissue paper.

At nine in the morning after he had said Mass, Mary carried in his breakfast. The porridge was lumpy and unsalted, and the fried bacon cracked like a biscuit under his fork and bits fled over the carpet. He told her he'd much prefer cornflakes to porridge if she didn't mind.

"That's all right with me, Father," she agreed. "It'll lighten my work."

And for dinner that day and throughout the whole week, except Friday, she gave him fried steak, potatoes, and onions, and for dessert jelly and milk. Father Doyle, with a certain conscious levity, inquired if she never got tired of steak and onions.

"No, Father, not a bit of me. It's a wholesome dish."

He endured the monotony for another while and recalled how his mother had admonished that he who overcame monotony without complaining had overcome the world. He held his patience. He bought a cookery book, and one night after she had gone to bed he left it on the windowledge in her kitchen. But she didn't change except to substitute sausages for steak. He complained to Father O'Loan and he advised him to get rid of her.

"Yes, get rid of her! Get rid of her!" he thundered. "Yes, young man, have no mistaken notions about the meaning of charity. Give her a fortnight's notice. That's the usual procedure. And stand no blasted nonsense. She might weep, but woman's tears were come-easy, go-easy, and you must not soften at the approach of a deluge."

Neighbours who had brought presents of chickens and eggs to the young priest she turned away. She'd have them all know that neither she nor Father Doyle lived on charity. She made no friends and didn't want any. Even the cat mysteriously disappeared. The people regarded her as odd, and it was whispered to Father Doyle that she was never seen at Mass on a Sunday, neither at first Mass nor at the second. And on days when he wasn't at home she didn't ring the Angelus bell.

She was a failure and Father Doyle waited for an opportunity to give her her notice, and one day when she carried in his plate with the onions still crackling on it (for she had kept it on top of the oven till the last moment) he coughed and said:

"Where's this now you said you were before coming here?"

"I never said I was anywhere, Father."

"I mean, Mary, where were you employed?"

"I was employed in the kitchen of a hospital."

"Cooking?"

"No, Father, washing up."

"Maybe, Mary, you'd like to go back to that work?"

"No, indeed; I like it here, Father. The language in that hospital kitchen was something my ears couldn't stand. My soul would be in jeopardy if I returned."

Father Doyle wished at that moment it were in Picardy or anywhere a hundred miles from his own kitchen, and before he had time to make her realise he wasn't satisfied with her she had glided from the room. However, he had made the first onslaught, and he thought then of bringing in Father O'Loan to give the final push. After all, it was Father O'Loan who had engaged her and by right he should dismiss her. But how was he to suggest such a plan to Father O'Loan. Father O'Loan would probably round on him, scoff at him as a spineless curate, and order him to dismiss her by a certain date. Father Doyle shuddered: it was better to let the hare sit for a while and pretend that there were certain signs of improvement.

Towards the end of February his mother and sister were to visit him and as he told Mary of the impending visit she carefully inquired the day and the time and then announced it would be a convenient opportunity for her to take a day off, reminding him she hadn't taken one solitary day to herself since she came into his employment.

"But what will they do for a meal, Mary? They're motoring all the way from the city."

"They aren't invalids, are they? Surely two able-bodied women can look after themselves for one afternoon."

"But wouldn't it be nice if you gave *them* a free day?"

"The two ladies will understand when you explain how the land lies."

"That's all right, Mary," he said unwittingly plagiarising one of her favourite phrases.

"And that will be all right with me, Father," and left the room.

There and then he resolved that before another week had fled he would get rid of her. And with the days on the turn, the early lambs in the fields, he would have brighter prospects of getting another to take her place. He would discuss all with his mother, and, perhaps, it was better after all that Mary would have that day off.

His mother and sister arrived in the early afternoon. Mary was out and they were free to tour the house from top to bottom. They couldn't believe their eyes. It was like a pig sty. The slut hadn't swept under the beds; there were perfect rectangles of fluff for all who cared to see. One can get accustomed to dirt, unfortunately. And did he not realise he was aiding and abetting in another person's sin—the sin of sloth, one of the deadliest! And how miserable he looked: ill-nourished and pale and gaunt as Lazarus. It wouldn't do. Not another priest in the diocese would tolerate her for a single hour. And how long had he put up with her—fifteen weeks, if you please. Was he trying to practise martyrdom or was this Mary Carroll trying to make a saint out of him! If he didn't act and act quickly she herself, being his mother, would pay a visit to the bishop. Indeed she would! And she besought him, with tears in her eyes, to get rid of this dreadful harridan. He promised he would, and after they had driven away he was so dejected he regretted about having complained so much. But he had promised to get rid of her and get rid of her he would! He would not flinch.

He stiffened himself for Mary's arrival, and as she laid his supper tray on the table he said without looking at her: "Mary, I'm sorry to say you don't suit me. You can take a fortnight's notice or, if you prefer, you can leave tomorrow with a fortnight's wages in advance."

Without a word she left the room. He smiled and congratulated himself. He was a fool not to have spoken bluntly long ago. Polite implication was lost on people like this. The cold truth is the only language they understand.

He turned on the radio. A band was playing a few Irish reels. The mood of revelry appealed to him. The door was knocked on and Mary entered. She stood with her hand on the doorknob. He turned down the radio.

"Father, you said something to me a wee while ago. I came to tell you I'm not leaving. I like it here."

She closed the door before he had time to say a word. He switched off the radio and sat still. His heart was thumping. He began to have doubts about her sanity. There was always something queer about her. There was no doubt about that. She couldn't cook; she was slovenly in her habits; she had alienated the good people of the parish; she had disobeyed his instructions time and time again, and she, a priest's housekeeper, didn't even attend Mass on Sundays or major feast days. The whole set-up was absurd. Was it a case for the bishop? No, the bishop would probably declare it was too localised, too petty, for episcopal interference.

It was better not to decide anything until he had discussed it with Father O'Loan. Father O'Loan was old and he was wise and he was endowed with a voice that would waken the heaviest sleeper from the back of a cathedral. Yes, he would follow Father O'Loan's advice, and the following morning after breakfast he went to see him. He told him how he had given her a fortnight's notice or a fortnight's wages in advance and how she had refused both.

"Perhaps as a last resort I should call in the police?"

"To have her evicted, you mean?" Father O'Loan spluttered. "No, no, that wouldn't do at all. History dies hard in these parts. You'd make a martyr of her in the eyes of the people. They'd become friends of hers as quick as you'd crack your fingers. It would never do to bring in the police. Some quieter method we must pursue. Here today and gone tomorrow like snow off a ditch—that's what we want. It must all go unnoticed, if you know what I mean. Let the hen sit for a day or two."

"Whatever you say," Father Doyle said, only too willing to agree. "I'm sorry for causing this trouble."

"You didn't cause it. She caused it, but I'll end it! Do you know I'm just beginning to enjoy it. Life here can be very dull. This will give me something to think about. I'll call; I'll call tomorrow and I'll make her do the hop-skip-and-jump in true Olympic style."

The following afternoon he called as promised. Father Doyle was alone and he told him that her ladyship was in the kitchen redding up the few dishes.

Father O'Loan coughed loudly: "Just leave her to me and you stay here in the sitting-room."

Father Doyle left the door ajar, and in a few minutes he heard Father O'Loan's voice thunder from the kitchen; then there was silence and a squeaky voice raised to breaking point. There followed a rapid rumbling from Father O'Loan, a deep silence and then his heavy step along the hallway to the sitting-room. He slumped into an armchair.

"That's a dreadful woman, a holy terror! Give me a little spirits to steady my nerves. Never in the long history of the parish did the likes of this ever happen. She won't go! And who is she, may I ask." He took a sip of brandy. "How do you keep your pledge with a woman like that about the place? Drink can be a comfort as well as a curse." He took another sip at his glass, ran a finger round the inside of his collar, and breathed loudly. His face was red. "She won't go, eh! Well, she will go if it's the last thing I do in this mortal life. We could file a lawsuit. No, I'll not do that. That's out of the question." He finished his drink. "I think I'll let her have another broadside before I go. Make it hot and heavy for her and she'll be glad to flee."

"Don't distress yourself any further. I'll put up with her for another while. We'll think of something in due course."

"Not a word to anyone about this. We'd be the laughing-stock of the diocese if it leaked out. Oh, no, not a word about this to a living soul."

But word did leak out amongst the priests of the diocese and each morning Father Doyle had an amusing letter from a colleague; one even sent a postcard with an ink drawing of the house, a plane overhead, an armoured car at the gate, and steel-helmeted soldiers on the lawn. He showed it to Father O'Loan and he, in turn, showed him a piece of satirical verse from an anonymous source. Oh, he had a good idea who composed it though. But he'd end it, and in quick time too.

That night he wrote a long letter to the bishop, explaining in detail the disruption caused by the said Mary Carroll in his little parish, and humbly requesting from his lordship direction in the matter.

At the end of the week the bishop invited him to call, and Father O'Loan finding him in jovial form began to entertain him with dramatic renderings of the whole affair.

With a hand cupped to one ear, because he was discreetly deaf, the bishop listened with controlled amusement.

"Well, my Lord," Father O'Loan concluded, "that's the cleft stick I'm wedged in."

"Well, well," the bishop said slowly. "Most unusual circum-stances. But lift up your heart. For the good of Father Doyle's health and for your peace of mind a change is clearly indicated. You'll be pleased to hear that I am appointing Father Doyle chaplain to the Poor Clare Covent here in the city. He can live with his mother until his health is built up."

"But Mary Carroll, my lord?"

"She comes into the picture too. I am transferring Father Brannigan from Lower Mourne to take his place. He has a faithful housekeeper by all accounts; she is a native, I believe, of your own parish and I'm sure she'll be glad to be amongst her own people again."

"But, my lord, that Mary Carroll one is still in residence."

"Mary Carroll's services, as far as we are concerned, are terminated. You'll find she'll plague you no longer." He looked at Father O'Loan with a knowing smile. "Where you have two women quarrelling at the one sink and quarrelling over the one bed things should end in our favour."

The following morning early Father Doyle's furniture was on the move again—this time to be put in storage in the city. In the afternoon Father Doyle left for his mother's house in the city. He didn't see Mary before he left for she had suddenly turned religious and was up in the chapel saying her prayers. He had already paid her a fortnight's wages in advance and so he could set off with a free heart and leave her to Liza, the new housekeeper to deal with.

They had their first meeting in the kitchen when Mary was seated at the table taking tea and a boiled egg. Without a word Liza took command. She raked the stove vigorously, filled the kettle, and in a firm quick voice told Mary to hurry or she'd miss her bus.

"I like it here and I'm not going on no bus," Mary said.

"I like it here also for I was born and bred here and I'm glad to be back as Father Brannigan's housekeeper. Your duties are ended here and it would be better for you to go to Nazareth House in the city and stay there till work turns up."

"I'm going to no Nazareth House. I'm independent."

"I'm glad to hear it and would dearly like to believe it." She glanced at the clock. "You've exactly fifteen minutes to get ready. Your case is in my room and I'll fetch it for you."

"You'll lay no hand on my case."

"I'll stand no more of your oul guff! Take yourself off quietly before I ring for the police."

"This is Father Doyle's kitchen."

"It was Father Doyle's but he has gone off to live with his mother and sister. The kitchen is now Father Brannigan's and mine, and I must hurry and get the place in order for his arrival." She folded her arms and looked out the window at three people standing at the bus stop. "The bus will be along any minute now. If you miss it you'll have to hoof it—them's my last words to you." Lifting the brush she began to sweep the kitchen, watching Mary out of the corner of her eye.

Suddenly Mary pushed back her chair from the table, squeezed the eggshell in her fist and threw the bits into the fire. She left the kitchen, and in a few minutes Liza heard her pounding across the room above her head.

Liza looked out of the window again. The three people had increased to five.

"Miss Carroll, Miss Carroll," she shouted up the stairs, "hurry like a good woman, the bus will be along any time now."

Mary came downstairs with her case tied with loops of string. She sniffed as if she had a cold, and without a word she slipped out by the side-door.

Liza watched from the window. She saw her mount the bus and saw the bus move off, some withered leaves scampering at its heels.

"Thanks be to God she's gone," and she turned to make herself a cup of tea to steady her nerves.

A Letter to Rome

By George Moore

One morning the priest's housekeeper mentioned, as she gathered up the breakfast things, that Mike Mulhare had refused to let his daughter Catherine marry James Murdoch until he had earned the price of a pig.

"This is bad news," said the priest, and he laid down the newspaper.

"And he waiting for her all the summer! Wasn't it in February last that he came out of the poor-house? And the fine cabin he has built for her! He'll be so lonesome in it that he'll be going—"

"To America!" said the priest.

"Maybe it will be going back to the poor-house he'll be, for he'll never earn the price of his passage at the relief works."

The priest looked at her for a moment as if he did not catch her meaning. A knock came at the door, and he said:

"The inspector is here, and there are people waiting for me." And while he was distributing the clothes he had received from Manchester, he argued with the inspector as to the direction the new road should take; and when he came back from the relief works, his dinner was waiting. He was busy writing letters all the afternoon; and it was not until he had handed them to the post-mistress that he was free to go to poor James Murdoch, who had built a cabin at the end of one of the famine roads in a hollow out of the way of the wind.

From a long way off the priest could see him digging his patch of bog.

And when he caught sight of the priest he stuck his spade in the ground and came to meet him, almost as naked as an animal, bare feet protruding from ragged trousers; there was a shirt, but it was buttonless, and the breast-hair trembled in the wind—a likely creature to come out of the hovel behind him.

"It has been dry enough," he said, "all the summer; and I had a thought to make a drain. But 'tis hard luck, your reverence, and after building this house for her. There's a bit of smoke in the house now, but if I got Catherine I wouldn't be long making a chimney. I told Mike he should give Catherine a pig for her fortune, but he said he would give her a calf when I bought the pig, and I said, 'Haven't I built a fine house, and wouldn't it be a fine one to rear him in?'"

And together they walked through the bog, James talking to the priest all the way, for it was seldom he had anyone to talk to.

"Now I mustn't take you any further from your digging."

"Sure there's time enough," said James. "Amn't I there all day?"

"I'll go and see Mike Mulhare myself," said the priest.

"Long life to your reverence."

"And I will try to get you the price of the pig."

"Ah, 'tis your reverence that's good to us."

The priest stood looking after him, wondering if he would give up life as a bad job and go back to the poor-house; and while thinking of James Murdoch he became conscious that the time was coming for the priests to save Ireland. Catholic Ireland was passing away; in five-and-twenty years Ireland would be a Protestant country if—(he hardly dared to formulate the thought)—if the priests did not marry. The Greek priests had been allowed to retain their wives in order to avert a schism. Rome had always known how to adapt herself to circumstances; there was no doubt that if Rome knew Ireland's need of children she would consider the revocation of the decree of celibacy, and he returned home remembering that celibacy had only been made obligatory in Ireland in the twelfth century.

Ireland was becoming a Protestant country! He drank his tea mechanically, and it was a long time before he took up his knitting. But he could not knit, and laid the stocking aside. Of what good would his letter be? A letter from a poor parish priest asking that one of the most ancient decrees should be revoked! It would be thrown into the waste-paper basket. The cardinals are men whose thoughts move up and down certain narrow ways, clever men no doubt, but clever men are often the dupes of conventions. All men who live in the world accept the conventions as truths. It is only in the wilderness that the truth is revealed to man. "I must write the letter! Instinct," he said, "is a surer guide than logic, and my letter to Rome was a sudden revelation."

As he sat knitting by his own fireside his idea seemed to come out of the corners of the room. "When you were at Rathowen," his idea said, "you heard the clergy lament that the people were leaving the country. You heard the bishop and many eloquent men speak on the subject. Words, words, but on the bog road the remedy was revealed to you.

"That if each priest were to take a wife about four thousand children would be born within the year, forty thousand children would be added to the birthrate in ten years. Ireland can be saved by her priesthood!"

The truth of this estimate seemed beyond question, and yet, Father MacTurnan found it difficult to reconcile himself to the idea of a married clergy. "One is always the dupe of prejudice," he said to himself and went on thinking. "The priests live in the best houses, eat the best food, wear the best clothes; they are indeed the flower of the nation, and would produce magnificent sons and daughters. And who could bring up their children according to the teaching of our holy church as well as priests?"

So did his idea unfold ifself, and very soon he realised that other advantages would accrue, beyond the addition of forty thousand children to the birthrate, and one advantage that seemed to him to exceed the original advantage would be the nationalization of religion, the formation of an Irish Catholicism suited to the ideas and needs of the Irish people.

In the beginning of the century the Irish lost their language, in the middle of the century the characteristic aspects of their religion. It was Cardinal Cullen who had denationalized religion in Ireland. But everyone recognised his mistake. How could a church be nationalised better then by the rescission of the decree of celibacy? The begetting of children would attach the priests to the soil of Ireland; and it could not be said that anyone loved his country who did not contribute to its maintenance. The priests leave Ireland on foreign missions, and every

Catholic who leaves Ireland, he said, helps to bring about the very thing that Ireland has been struggling against for centuries—Protestantism.

His idea talked to him every evening, and, one evening, it said, "Religion, like everything else, must be national," and it led him to contrast cosmopolitanism with parochialism. "Religion, like art, came out of parishes," he said. He felt a great force to be behind him. He must write! He must write....

He dropped the ink over the table and over the paper, he jotted down his ideas in the first words that came to him until midnight; and when he slept his letter floated through his sleep.

"I must have a clear copy of it before I begin the Latin that would come after, very conscious of the fact that he had written no Latin since he had left Maynooth, and that a bad translation would discredit his ideas in the eyes of the Pope's secretary, who was doubtless a great Latin scholar.

"The Irish priests have always been good Latinists," he murmured, as he hunted through the dictionary.

The table was littered with books, for he had found it necessary to create a Latin atmosphere, and one morning he finished his translation and walked to the whitening window to rest his eyes before reading it over. But he was too tired to do any more, and he laid his manuscript on the table by his bedside.

"This is very poor Latin," he said to himself some hours later, and the manuscript lay on the floor while he dressed. It was his servant who brought it to him when he had finished his breakfast, and, taking it from her, he looked at it again.

"It is as tasteless," he said, "as the gruel that poor James Murdoch is eating." He picked up St. Augustine's Confessions. "Here is idiom," he muttered, and he continued reading till he was interrupted by the wheels of a car stopping at his door. It was Meehan! None had written such good Latin at Maynooth as Meehan.

"My dear Meehan, this is indeed a pleasant surprise."

"I thought I'd like to see you. I drove over. But—I am not disturbing you.... You've taken to reading again. St. Augustine! And you're writing in Latin!"

Father James's face grew red, and he took the manuscript out of his friend's hand.

"No, you mustn't look at that."

And then the temptation to ask him to overlook certain passages made him change his mind.

"I was never much of a Latin scholar."

"And you want me to overlook your Latin for you. But why are you writing Latin?"

"Because I am writing to the Pope. I was at first a little doubtful, but the more I thought of this letter the more necessary it seemed to me."

"And what are you writing to the Pope about?"

"You see Ireland is going to become a Protestant country."

"Is it?" said Father Meehan, and he listened, a little while. Then, interrupting his friend, he said:

"I've heard enough. Now, I strongly advise you not to send this letter. We have known each other all our lives. Now, my dear MacTurnan—"

Father Michael talked eagerly, and Father MacTurnan sat listening. At last Father Meehan saw that his arguments were producing no effect, and he said:

"You don't agree with me."

"It isn't that I don't agree with you. You have spoken admirably from your point of view, but our points of view are different."

"Take your papers away, burn them!"

Then, thinking his words were harsh, he laid his hand on his friend's shoulder and said:

"My dear MacTurnan, I beg of you not to send this letter."

Father James did not answer; the silence grew painful, and Father Michael asked Father James to show him the relief works that the Government had ordered.

But important as these works were, the letter to Rome seemed more important to Father Michael, and he said:

"My good friend, there isn't a girl that would marry us; now is there? There isn't a girl in Ireland who would touch us with a forty-foot pole. Would you have the Pope release the nuns from their vows?"

"I think exceptions should be made in favour of those in

Orders. But I think it would be for the good of Ireland if the secular clergy were married."

"That's not my point. My point is that even if the decree were rescinded we shouldn't be able to get wives. You've been living too long in the waste, my dear friend. You've lost yourself in dreams. We shouldn't get a penny. 'Why should we support that fellow and his family?' is what they'd be saying."

"We should be poor, no doubt," said Father James. "But not so poor as our parishioners. My parishioners eat yellow meal, and I eat eggs and live in a good house."

"We are educated men, and should live in better houses than our parishioners."

"The greatest saints lived in deserts."

And so the argument went on until the time came to say good-bye, and then Father James said:

"I shall be glad if you will give me a lift on your car. I want to got to the post-office."

"To post your letter?"

"The idea came to me—it came swiftly like a lightning-flash, and I can't believe that it was an accident. If it had fallen into your mind with the suddenness that it fell into mine, you would believe that it was an inspiration."

"It would take a good deal to make me believe I was inspired," said Father Michael, and he watched Father James go into the post-office to register his letter.

At that hour a long string of peasants returning from their work went by. The last was Norah Flynn, and the priest blushed deeply for it was the first time he had looked on one of his parishioners in the light of a possible spouse; and he entered his house frightened; and when he looked round his parlour he asked himself if the day would come when he should see Norah Flynn sitting opposite to him in his armchair. His face flushed deeper when he looked towards the bedroom door, and he fell on his knees and prayed that God's will might be made known to him.

During the night he awoke many times, and the dream that had awakened him continued when he had left his bed, and he wandered round and round the room in the darkness, seeking a way. At last he reached the window and drew the curtain, and saw the dim dawn opening out over the bog.

"Thank God," he said, "it was only a dream—only a dream."

And lying down he fell asleep, but immediately another dream as horrible as the first appeared, and his housekeeper heard him beating on the walls.

"Only a dream, only a dream," he said.

He lay awake, not daring to sleep lest he might dream. And it was about seven o'clock when he heard his housekeeper telling him that the inspector had come to tell him they must decide what direction the new road should take. In the inspector's opinion it should run parallel with the old road. To continue the old road two miles further would involve extra labour; the people would have to go further to their work, and the stones would have to be drawn further. The priest held that the extra labour was of secondary importance. He said that to make two roads running parallel with each other would be a wanton humiliation to the people.

But the inspector could not appreciate the priest's arguments. He held that the people were thinking only how they might earn enough money to fill their bellies.

"I don't agree with you, I don't agree with you," said the priest. "Better go in the opposite direction and make a road to the sea."

"You see, your reverence, the Government don't wish to engage upon any work that will benefit any special class. These are my instructions."

"A road to the sea will benefit no one....I see you are thinking of the landlord. But there isn't a harbour; no boat ever comes into that flat, waste sea."

"Well, your reverence, one of these days a harbour may be made. An arch would look well in the middle of the bog, and the people wouldn't have to go far to their work."

"No, no. A road to the sea will be quite useless; but its futility will not be apparent—at least, not so apparent—and the people's hearts won't be broken."

The inspector seemed a little doubtful, but the priest assured him that the futility of the road would satisfy English ministers.

"And yet these English ministers," the priest reflected, "are not stupid men; they're merely men blinded by theory and prejudice, as all men are who live in the world. Their folly will be apparent to the next generation, and so on and so on for ever and ever, world without end."

"And the worst of it is," the priest said, "while the people are earning their living on these roads, their fields will be lying idle, and there will be no crops next year."

"We can't help that," the inspector answered, and Father MacTurnan began to think of the cardinals and the transaction of the business in the Vatican; cardinals and ministers alike are the dupes of convention. Only those who are estranged from habits and customs can think straightforwardly.

"If, instead of insisting on these absurd roads, the Government would give me the money, I'd be able to feed the people at a cost of about a penny a day, and they'd be able to sow their potatoes. And if only the cardinals would consider the rescission of the decree on its merits, Ireland would be saved from Protestantism."

Some cardinal was preparing an answer—an answer might be even in the post. Rome might not think his letter worthy of an answer.

A few days afterwards the inspector called to show him a letter he had just received from the Board of Works. Father James had to go to Dublin, and in the excitement of these philanthropic activities the emigration question was forgotten. Six weeks must have gone by when the postman handed him a letter.

"This is a letter from Father Moran," he said to the inspector who was with him at the time. "The Bishop wishes to see me. We will continue the conversation tomorrow. It is eight miles to Rathowen, and how much further is the Palace?"

"A good seven," said the inspector. "You're not going to walk it, your reverence?"

"Why not? In four hours I shall be there." He looked at his boots first, and hoped they would hold together; and then he looked at the sky, and hoped it would not rain.

There was no likelihood of rain; no rain would fall today out of that soft dove-coloured sky full of sun; ravishing little breezes lifted the long heather, the rose-coloured hair of the knolls, and over the cut-away bog wild white cotton was blowing. Now and then a yellow-hammer rose out of the coarse grass and flew in front of the priest, and once a pair of grouse left the sunny hillside where they were nesting with a great whirr; they did not go far, but alighted in a hollow, and the priest could see their heads above the heather watching him.

"The moment I'm gone they'll return to their nest."

He walked on, and when he had walked six miles he sat down and took a piece of bread out of his pocket. As he ate it his eyes wandered over the undulating bog, brown and rose, marked here and there by a black streak where the peasants had been cutting turf. The sky changed very little; it was still a pale, dove colour; now and then a little blue showed through the grey, and sometimes the light lessened; but a few minutes after the sunlight fluttered out of the sky again and dozed among the heather.

"I must be getting on," he said, and he looked into the brown water, fearing he would find none other to slake his thirst. But just as he stooped he caught sight of a woman driving an ass who had come to the bog for turf, and she told him where he would find a spring, and he thought he had never drunk anything so sweet as this water.

"I've got a good long way to go yet," he said, and he walked studying the lines of the mountains, thinking he could distinguish one hill from the other; and that in another mile or two he would be out of the bog. The road ascended, and on the other side there were a few pines. Some hundred yards further on there was a green sod. But the heather appeared again, and he had walked ten miles before he was clear of whins and heather.

As he walked he thought of his interview with the Bishop, and was nearly at the end of his journey when he stopped at a cabin to mend his shoe. And while the woman was looking for a needle and thread, he mopped his face with a great red handkerchief that he kept in the pocket of his threadbare coat— a coat that had once been black, but had grown green with age and weather. He had outwalked himself, and would not be able to answer the points that the Bishop would raise. The woman found him a scrap of leather, and it took him an hour to patch his shoe under the hawthorn tree.

He was still two miles from the Palace, and arrived footsore, covered with dust, and so tired that he could hardly rise from the chair to receive Father Moran when he came into the parlour.

"You seem to have walked a long way, Father MacTurnan."

"I shall be all right presently. I suppose his Grace doesn't want to see me at once."

"Well, that's just it. His Grace sent me to say he would see you at once. He expected you earlier."

"I started the moment I received his Grace's letter. I suppose his Grace wishes to see me regarding my letter to Rome."

The secretary hesitated, coughed, and went out, and Father MacTurnan wondered why Father Moran looked at him so intently. He returned in a few minutes, saying that his Grace was sorry that Father MacTurnan had had so long a walk, and he hoped he would rest awhile and partake of some refreshment.... The servant brought in some wine and sandwiches, and the secretary returned in half an hour. His Grace was now ready to receive him....

Father Moran opened the library door, and Father MacTurnan saw the Bishop—a short, alert man, about fifty-five, with a sharp nose and grey eyes and bushy eyebrows. He popped about the room giving his secretary many orders, and Father MacTurnan wondered if the Bishop would ever finish talking to his secretary. He seemed to have finished, but a thought suddenly struck him, and he followed his secretary to the door, and Father MacTurnan began to fear that the Pope had not decided to place the Irish clergy on the same footing as the Greek. If he had, the Bishop's interest in these many various matters would have subsided: his mind would be engrossed by the larger issue.

As he returned from the door his Grace passed Father MacTurnan without speaking to him, and going to his writing-table he began to search amid his papers. At last Father MacTurnan said:

"Maybe your Grace is looking for my letter to Rome?"

"Yes," said his Grace, "do you see it?"

"It's under your Grace's hand, those blue papers."

"Ah, yes," and his Grace leaned back in his armchair, leaving Father MacTurnan standing.

"Won't you sit down, Father MacTurnan?" he said casually. "You've been writing to Rome, I see, advocating the revocation of the decree of celibacy. There's no doubt the emigration of Catholics is a very serious question. So far you have got the sympathy of Rome, and I may say of myself; but am I to understand that it was your fear for the religious safety of Ireland that prompted you to write this letter?"

"What other reason could there be?"

Nothing was said for a long while, and then the Bishop's meaning began to break in on his mind; his face flushed, and he grew confused.

"I hope your Grace doesn't think for a moment that—"

"I only want to know if there is anyone—if your eyes ever went in a certain direction, if your thoughts ever said, 'Well, if the decree were revoked—'"

"No, your Grace, no. Celibacy has been no burden to me—far from it. Sometimes I feared that it was celibacy that attracted me to the priesthood. Celibacy was a gratification rather than a sacrifice."

"I am glad," said the Bishop, and he spoke slowly and emphatically, "that this letter was prompted by such impersonal motives."

"Surely, your Grace, His Holiness didn't suspect—"

The Bishop murmured an euphonious Italian name, and Father MacTurnan understood that he was speaking of one of the Pope's secretaries.

"More than once," said Father MacTurnan, "I feared if the decree were revoked, I shouldn't have had sufficient courage to comply with it."

And then he told the Bishop how he had met Norah Flynn on the road. An amused expression stole into the Bishop's face, and his voice changed.

"I presume you do not contemplate making marriage obligatory; you do not contemplate the suspension of the faculties of those who do not take wives?"

"It seems to me that exception should be made in favour of

those in Orders, and of course in favour of those who have reached a certain age like your Grace."

The Bishop coughed, and pretended to look for some paper which he had mislaid.

"This was one of the many points that I discussed with Father Michael Meehan."

"Oh, so you consulted Father Meehan," the Bishop said, looking up.

"He came in the day I was reading over my Latin translation before posting it. I'm afraid the ideas that I submitted to the consideration of His Holiness have been degraded by my very poor Latin I should have wished Father Meehan to overlook my Latin, but he refused. He begged of me not to send the letter."

"Father Meehan," said his Grace, "is a great friend of yours. Yet nothing he could say could shake your resolution to write to Rome?"

"Nothing," said Father MacTurnan. "The call I received was too distinct and too clear for me to hesitate."

"Tell me about this call."

Father MacTurnan told the Bishop that the poor man had come out of the workhouse because he wanted to be married, and that Mike Mulhare would not give him his daughter until he had earned the price of a pig. "And as I was talking to him I heard my conscience say, 'No one can afford to marry in Ireland but the clergy.' We all live better than our parishioners.'"

And then, forgetting the Bishop, and talking as if he were alone with his God, he described how the conviction had taken possession of him—that Ireland would become a Protestant country if the Catholic emigration did not cease. And he told how this conviction had left him little peace until he had written his letter.

The priest talked on until he was interrupted by Father Moran.

"I have some business to transact with Father Moran now," the Bishop said, "but you must stay to dinner. You've walked a long way, and you are tired and hungry."

"But, your Grace, if I don't start now, I shan't get home until nightfall."

"A car will take you back, Father MacTurnan. I will see to that. I must have some exact information about your poor people. We must do something for them."

Father MacTurnan and the Bishop were talking together when the car came to take Father MacTurnan home, and the Bishop said:

"Father MacTurnan, you have borne the loneliness of your parish for a long while."

"Loneliness is only a matter of habit. I think, your Grace, I'm better suited to the place than I am for any other. I don't wish any change, if your Grace is satisfied with me."

"No one will look after the poor people better than yourself, Father MacTurnan. But," he said, "it seems to me there is one thing we have forgotten. You haven't told me if you have succeeded in getting the money to buy the pig."

Father MacTurnan grew very red.... "I had forgotten it. The relief works—"

"It's not too late. Here's five pounds, and this will buy him a pig."

"It will indeed," said the priest, "it will buy him two!"

He had left the Palace without having asked the Bishop how his letter had been received at Rome, and he stopped the car, and was about to tell the driver to go back. But no matter, he would hear about his letter some other time. He was bringing happiness to two poor people, and he could not persuade himself to delay their happiness by one minute. He was not bringing one pig, but two pigs, and now Mike Mulhare would have to give him Catherine and a calf; and the priest remembered that James Murdoch had said—"What a fine house this will be to rear them in." There were many who thought that human beings and animals should not live together; but after all, what did it matter if they were happy? And the priest forgot his letter to Rome in the thought of the happiness he was bringing to two poor people. He could not see Mike Mulhare that night; but he drove down to the famine road, and he and the driver called till they awoke James Murdoch. The poor man came stumbling across the bog, and the priest told him the news.

Exile's Return

By Bryan MacMahon

Far away the train whistled. The sound moved in rings through the rain falling on the dark fields. On hearing the whistle the little man standing on the railway bridge gave a quick glance into the up-line darkness and then began to hurry downwards towards the station. Above the metal footbridge the lights came on weak and dim as he hurried onwards. The train beat him to the station; all rattle and squeak and bright playing cards placed in line, it drew in beneath the bridge. At the station's end the engine lurched uneasily: then it puffed and huffed, blackened and whitened, and eventually, after a loud release of steam, stood chained.

One passenger descended—a large man with the appearance of a heavyweight boxer. He was dressed in a new cheap suit and overcoat. A black stubble of beard littered his scowling jowls. The eyes under the cap were black and daft. In his hand he carried a battered attaché case tied with a scrap of rope. Dourly slamming the carriage door behind him, he stood glaring up and down the platform.

A passing porter looked at him, abandoned him as being of little interest, then as on remembrance glanced at him a second time. As he walked away the porter's eyes still lingered on the passenger. A hackney driver, viewing with disgust the serried unprofitable door handles, smiled grimly to himself at the sight of the big fellow. Barefooted boys grabbing cylinders of magazines that came hurtling out of the luggage van took no notice whatsoever of the man standing alone. The rain's falling was visible in the pocking of the cut limestone on the platform's edge.

Just then the little man hurried in by the gateway of the station. His trouser ends were tied over clay-daubed boots above which he wore a cast-off green Army greatcoat. A sweat-soiled hat sat askew on his poll. After a moment of hesitation he hurried forward to meet the swaying newcomer.

"There you are, Paddy!" the small man wheezed brightly, yet not coming too close to the big fellow.

The big fellow did not answer. He began to walk heavily out of the station. The little man moved hoppingly at his side, pelting questions to which he received no reply.

"Had you a good crossing, Paddy?" "Is it true that the Irish Sea is as wicked as May Eve?" "There's a fair share of Irish in Birmingham, I suppose?" Finally, in a tone that indicated that this question was closer to the bone than its fellows: "How long are you away now, Paddy? Over six year, eh?"

Paddy plowed ahead without replying. When they had reached the first of the houses of the country town, he glowered over his shoulder at the humpy bridge that led over the railway line to the open country: after a moment or two he dragged his gaze away and looked at the street that led downhill from the station.

"We'll have a drink, Timothy!" the big man said dourly.

"A drink, Paddy!" the other agreed.

The pub glittered in the old-fashioned way. The embossed wallpaper between the shelving had been painted lime green. As they entered the bar, the publican was in the act of turning with a full pint-glass in his hand. His eyes hardened on seeing Paddy: he delayed the fraction of a second before placing the glass on the high counter in front of a customer.

Wiping his hands in a blue apron, his face working overtime, "Back again, eh, Paddy?" the publican asked, with false cheer. A limp handshake followed.

Paddy grunted, then lurched towards the far corner of the bar. There, sitting on a high stool, he crouched against the counter. Timothy took his seat beside him, seating himself sideways to the counter as if protecting the big fellow from the gaze of the other customers. Paddy called for two pints of porter: he paid for his call from an old-fashioned purse bulky with English treasury notes. Timothy raised his full glass—its size tended to dwarf him—and ventured: "Good health!" Paddy growled a reply. Both men tilted the glasses on their heads and gulped three-quarters of the contents. Paddy set down his glass and looked moodily in front of him. Timothy carefully replaced his glass on the counter, then placed his face closer to the other's ear.

"Yeh got my letter, Paddy?"

"Ay!"

"You're not mad with me?"

"Mad with *you*?" The big man's guffaw startled the bar.

There was a long silence.

"I got yer letter!" Paddy said abruptly. He turned and for the first time looked his small companion squarely in the face. Deliberately he set the big, battered index finger of his right hand inside the other's collar stud. As, slowly, he began to twist his finger, the collarband tightened. When it was taut Paddy drew the other's face close to his own. So intimately were the two men seated that the others in the bar did not know what was going on. Timothy's face changed colour, yet he did not raise his hands to try to release himself.

"Yer swearin' 'tis true?" Paddy growled.

Gaspingly: "God's gospel, it's true!"

"Swear it!"

"That I may be struck down dead if I'm tellin' you a word of a lie! Every mortal word I wrote you is true!"

"Why didn't you send me word afore now?"

"I couldn't rightly make out where you were, Paddy. Only for Danny Greaney comin' home I'd never have got your address. An' you know I'm not handy with the pen."

"Why didn't you let me as I was—not knowin' at all?"

"We to be butties always, Paddy. I thought it a shame you to keep sendin' her lashin's o' money an' she to be like that! You're choking me, Paddy!"

As Paddy tightened still more, the buttonhole broke and the stud came away in the crook of his index finger. He looked at it stupidly. Timothy quietly put the Y of his hand to his chafed neck. Paddy threw the stud behind him. It stuck the timbered encasement of the stairway.

"*Ach!*" he said harshly. He drained his glass and with its heel tapped on the counter. The publican came up to refill the glasses.

Timothy, whispering: "What'll you do, Paddy?"

"What'll I do?" Paddy laughed. "I'll drink my pint," he said. He took a gulp. "Then, as likely as not, I'll swing for her!"

"Sssh!" Timothy counseled.

Timothy glanced into an advertising mirror; behind the picture of little men loading little barrels onto a little lorry he saw the publican with his eyes fast on the pair of them. Timothy warned him off with a sharp look. He looked swiftly around: the backs of the other customers were a shade too tense for his liking. Then suddenly the publican was in under Timothy's guard.

Swabbing the counter: "What way are things over, Paddy?"

"Fair enough!"

"I'm hearin' great accounts of you from Danny Greaney. We were all certain you'd never again come home, you were doin' so well. How'll you content yourself with a small place like this, after what you've seen? But then, after all, home is home!"

The publican ignored Timothy's threatening stare. Paddy raised his daft eyes and looked directly at the man behind the bar. The swabbing moved swiftly away.

"Swing for her, I will!" Paddy said again. He raised his voice. "The very minute I turn my back..."

"Sssh!" Timothy intervened. He smelled his almost empty glass, then said in a loud whisper: "The bloody stout is casky. Let's get away out o' this!"

The word *casky* succeeded in moving Paddy. It also nicked the publican's pride. After they had gone the publican, on the pretense of closing the door, looked after them. He turned and threw a joke to his customers. A roar of laughter was his reward.

Paddy and Timothy were now wandering towards the humpy bridge that led to the country. Timothy was carrying the battered case: Paddy has his arm around his companion's shoulder. The raw air was testing the sobriety of the big fellow's legs.

"Nothin' hasty!" Timothy was advising. "First of all we'll pass out the courage an' go on to my house. You'll sleep with me tonight. Remember, Paddy, that I wrote that letter out o' pure friendship!"

Paddy lifted his cap and let the rain strike his forehead. "I'll walk the gallows high for her!" he said.

"Calm an' collected, that's my advice!"

"When these two hands are on her throat, you'll hear her squealin' in the eastern world!"

"Nothin' hasty, Paddy: nothin' hasty at all!"

Paddy pinned his friend against the parapet of the railway bridge. "Is six years hasty?" he roared.

"For God's sake, let go o' me, Paddy! I'm the only friend you have left! Let go o' me!"

The pair lurched with the incline. The whitethorns were now on each side of them releasing their raindrops from thorn to thorn in the darkness. Far away across the ridge of the barony a fan of light from a lighthouse swung its arc on shore and sea and sky. Wherever there was a break in the hedges a bout of wind mustered its forces and vainly set about capsizing them.

Paddy began to growl a song with no air at all to it.

"Hush, man, or the whole world'll know you're home," Timothy said.

"As if to sweet hell I cared!" Paddy stopped and swayed. After a pause he muttered: "Th' other fellah—is he long gone?"

Timothy whinnied. "One night only it was, like Duffy's Circus." He set his hat farther back on his poll and then, his solemn face tilted to the scud of the moon, said: "You want my firm opinion, Paddy? 'Twas nothin' but a chance fall. The mood an' the man meetin' her. 'Twould mebbe never again happen in a million years. A chance fall, that's all it was, in my considered opinion."

Loudly: "Did you ever know me to break my word?"

"Never, Paddy!"

"Then I'll swing for her! You have my permission to walk into the witness box and swear that Paddy Kinsella said he'd swing for her!"

He resumed his singing.

"We're right near the house, Paddy. You don't want to wake your own children, do you? Your own fine, lawful-got sons! Eh, Paddy? Do you want to waken them up?"

Paddy paused: "Lawful-got is right!—you've said it there!"

"Tomorrow is another day. We'll face her tomorrow and see how she brazens it out. I knew well you wouldn't want to disturb your own sons."

They lurched on through the darkness. As they drew near the low thatched cottage that was slightly below the level of the road, Timothy kept urging Paddy forward. Paddy's boots were more rebellious than heretofore. Timothy grew anxious at the poor progress they were making. He kept saying: "Tomorrow is the day, Paddy! I'll put the rope around her neck for you. Don't wake the lads tonight."

Directly outside the cottage, Paddy came to a halt. He swayed and glowered at the small house with its tiny windows. He drew himself up to his full height.

"She's in bed?" he growled.

"She's up at McSweeney's. She goes there for the sake of company. Half an hour at night when the kids are in bed—you'll not begrudge her that, Paddy?"

"I'll not begrudge her that!" Paddy yielded a single step, then planted his shoes still more firmly on the roadway. He swayed.

"The...?" he queried.

"A girl, Paddy, a girl!"

A growl, followed by the surrender of another step.

"Goin' on six year, is it?"

"That's it, Paddy, six year."

Another step. "Like the ma, or...the da?"

"The ma, Paddy. Mostly all the ma. Come on now, an' you'll have a fine sleep tonight under my roof."

Paddy eyed the cottage. Growled his contempt of it, then spat on the roadway. He gave minor indications of his intention of moving forward. Then unpredictably he pounded off the restraining hand of Timothy, pulled violently away and went swaying towards the passage that led down to the cottage.

After a fearful glance uproad, Timothy wailed: "She'll be back in a minute!"

"I'll see my lawful-got sons!" Paddy growled.

When Timothy caught up with him the big fellow was fumbling with the padlock on the door. As on a thought he lurched aside and groped in vain in the corner of the window sill.

"She takes the key with her," Timothy said. "For God's sake leave it till mornin'."

But Paddy was already blundering on the cobbled pathway that led around by the gable of the cottage. Finding the back door bolted, he stood back from it angrily. He was about to smash it in when Timothy discovered that the hinged window of the kitchen was slightly open. As Timothy swung the window open the smell of turf smoke emerged. Paddy put his boot on an imaginary niche in the wall and dug in the plaster until he gained purchase of a sort. "Gimme a leg!" he ordered harshly.

Timothy began clawing Paddy's leg upwards. Belaboring the small man's shoulders with boot and hand, the big fellow floundered through the open window. Spread-eagled on the kitchen table he remained breathing harshly for a full minute, then laboriously he grunted his way via a *sugan* chair to the floor.

"You all right, Paddy?"

A grunt.

"Draw the bolt of the back door, Paddy."

A long pause followed. At last the bolt was drawn. "Where the hell's the lamp?" Paddy asked as he floundered in the darkness.

"She has it changed. It's at the right of the window now."

Paddy's match came erratically alight. He held it aloft. Then he slewed forward and removed the lamp chimney and placed it on the table. "'Sall right!" he said, placing the match to the wick and replacing the chimney. Awkwardly he raised the wick. He began to look here and there about the kitchen.

The fire was raked in its own red ashes. Two *sugan* chairs stood one on each side of the hearthstone. Delph glowed red, white, and green on the wide dresser. The timber of the chairs and the deal table were white from repeated scrubbings. Paddy scowled his recognition of each object. Timothy stood watching him narrowly.

"See my own lads!" Paddy said, focusing his gaze on the bedroom door at the rear of the cottage.

"Aisy!" Timothy counseled.

Lighting match held aloft, they viewed the boys. Four lads sleeping in pairs in iron-headed double beds. Each of the boys had a mop of black hair and a pair of heavy eyebrows. The eldest slept with the youngest and the two middle-aged lads slept together. They sprawled anyhow in various postures.

Paddy had turned surprisingly sober. "'Clare to God!" he said. "I'd pass 'em on the road without knowin' 'em!"

"There's a flamin' lad!" Timothy caught one of the middle-aged boys by the hair and pivoted the sleep-loaded head.

Transferring his attention to the other of this pair: "There's your livin' spit, Paddy!" Indicating the eldest: "There's your own ould fellah born into the world a second time, devil's black temper an' all!" At the youngest: "Here's Bren—he was crawlin' on the floor the last time you saw him. Ay! Bully pups all!"

"Bully pups all!" Paddy echoed loudly. The match embered in his fingers. When there was darkness: "My lawful-got sons!" he said bitterly.

Timothy was in the room doorway. "We'll be off now, Paddy!" he said. After a growl, Paddy joined him.

Timothy said: "One of us'll have to go out by the window. Else she'll spot the bolt drawn."

Paddy said nothing.

"You'll never manage the window twice."

"I'll be after you," Paddy said.

Timothy turned reluctantly away.

"Where's the...?" Paddy asked. He was standing at the kitchen's end.

"The...?"

"Yeh!"

"She's in the front room. You're not goin' to...?" Paddy was already at the door of the other room.

"She sleeps like a cat," Timothy warned urgently. "If she tells the mother about me, the fat'll be in the fire!"

Paddy opened the door of the front room. Breathing heavily he again began fumbling with the matchbox. Across the window moved the scudding night life of the sky. The matchlight came up and showed a quilt patterned with candlewick. Then abruptly where the bedclothes had been a taut ball there was no longer a ball. As if playing a merry game, the little girl, like Jill-in-the-box, flax-curled and blue-eyed, sprang up.

"Who is it?" she asked fearlessly.

The matchlight was high above her. Paddy did not reply.

The girl laughed ringingly. "You're in the kitchen, Timothy Hannigan," she called out. "I know your snuffle."

"Holy God!" Timothy breathed.

"I heard you talking too, boyo," she said gleefully as the matchlight died in Paddy's fingers.

"'Tis me all right, Maag," said Timmy, coming apologetically to the doorway of the room. "Come on away!" he said in a whisper to Paddy.

"Didn't I know right well 'twas you, boyo!" Maag laughed. She drew up her knees and locked her hands around them in a mature fashion.

Another match sprang alive in Paddy's fingers.

"Who's this fellah?" Maag inquired of Timothy.

Timothy put his head inside the room. "He's your...your uncle!"

"My uncle what?"

"Your uncle...Paddy!"

Paddy and Maag looked fully at one another.

Timothy quavered: "You won't tell your mother I was hear?"

"I won't so!" the girl laughed. "Wait until she comes home!"

Timothy groaned. "C'm'on away to hell outa this!" he said, showing a spark of spirit. Surprisingly enough, Paddy came. They closed the room door behind them.

"Out the back door with you," Timothy said. "I'll manage the lamp and the bolt."

"Out, you!" Paddy growled. He stood stolidly like an ox.

Dubiously: "Very well!"

Timothy went out. From outside the back door he called: "Shoot the bolt quick, Paddy. She'll be back any minute."

Paddy shot the bolt.

"Blow out the lamp, Paddy!" Timothy's head and shoulders were framed in the window.

After a pause Paddy blew out the lamp.

"Hurry, Paddy! Lift your leg!"

No reply.

"Hurry, Paddy, I tell you. What's wrong with you, man?"

Paddy gave a deep growl. "I'm sorry now I didn't throttle you."

"Throttle me! Is that my bloody thanks?"

"It was never in my breed to respect an informer."

"Your breed!" Timothy shouted. "You, with a cuckoo in your nest."

"If my hands were on your throat..."

"Yehoo! You, with the nest robbed."

"Go, while you're all of a piece. The drink has me lazy. I'll give you while I'm countin' five. One, two..."

Timothy was gone.

Paddy sat on the rough chair at the left of the hearth. He began to grope for the tongs. Eventually he found it. He drew the red coals of turf out of the ashes and set them together in a kind of pyramid. The flames came up.

The door of the front bedroom creaked open. Maag was here, dressed in a long white nightdress.

"Were you scoldin' him?"

"Ay!" Paddy answered.

"He wants scoldin' badly. He's always spyin' on my Mom."

After a pause, the girl came to mid-kitchen.

"Honest," she asked, "are you my uncle?"

"In a class of a way!"

"What class of a way?" she echoed. She took a step closer.

"Are you cold, girlie?" Paddy asked.

"I am an' I am not. What class of a way are you my uncle?"

There was no reply.

"Mebbe you're my ould fellah back from England?" she stabbed suddenly.

"Mebbe!"

The girl's voice was shaken with delight. "I knew you'd be back! They all said no, but I said yes—that you'd be back for sure." A pause. A step nearer. "What did you bring me?"

Dourly he put his hand into his pocket. His fingers encountered a pipe, a half-quarter of tobacco, a six-inch nail, a clotted handkerchief, and the crumpled letter from Timothy.

"I left it after me in the carriage," he said limply.

Her recovery from disappointment was swift. "Can't you get it in town o' Saturday?" she said, drawing still closer.

"That's right!" he agreed. There was a short pause. Then: "Come hether to the fire," he said.

She came and stood between his knees. The several hoops of her curls were between him and the firelight. She smelled of soap. His fingers touched her arms. The mother was in her surely. He knew it by the manner in which her flesh was sure and unafraid.

They remained there without speaking until the light step on the road sent her prickling alive. "Mom'll kill me for bein' out of bed," she said. Paddy's body stiffened. As the girl struggled to be free, he held her fast. Of a sudden she went limp, and laughed: "I forgot!" she whispered. "She'll not touch me on account of you comin' home." She rippled with secret laughter. "Wasn't I the fooleen to forget?"

The key was in the padlock. The door moved open. The woman came in, her shawl down from her shoulders. "Maag!" she breathed. The girl and the man were between her and the firelight.

Without speaking the woman stood directly inside the door. The child said nothing but looked from one to the other. The woman waited for a while. Slowly she took off her shawl, then closed the door behind her. She walked carefully across the kitchen. A matchbox noised. She lighted the warm lamp. As the lamplight came up Paddy was seen to be looking steadfastly into the fire.

"You're back, Paddy?"

"Ay!"

"Had you a good crossin'?"

"Middlin'!"

"You hungry?"

"I'll see...soon!"

There was a long silence. Her fingers restless, the woman stood in mid-kitchen.

She raised her voice: "If you've anything to do or say to me, Paddy Kinsella, you'd best get it over. I'm not a one for waitin'!"

He said nothing. He held his gaze on the fire.

"You hear me, Paddy? I'll not live cat and dog with you. I know what I am. Small good your brandin' me when the countryside has me well branded before you."

He held his silence.

"Sayin' nothin' won't get you far. I left you down, Paddy. Be a man an' say it to my face!"

Paddy turned: "You left me well down," he said clearly. He turned to the fire and added, in a mutter: "I was no angel myself!"

Her trembling lips were unbelieving. "We're quits, so?" she ventured at last.

"Quits!"

"You'll not keep firin' it in my face?"

"I'll not!"

"Before God?"

"Before God!"

The woman crossed herself and knelt on the floor. "In the presence of my God," she said, "because you were fair to me, Paddy Kinsella, I'll be better than three wives to you. I broke my marriage-mornin' promise, but I'll make up for it. There's my word, given before my Maker!"

Maag kept watching with gravity. The mother crossed herself and rose.

Paddy was dourly rummaging in his coat pocket. At last his fingers found what he was seeking. "I knew I had it some-where!" he said. He held up a crumpled toffee-sweet. "I got it from a kid on the boat."

Maag's face broke in pleasure: "'Twill do—till Saturday!" she said.

The girl's mouth came down upon the striped toffee. Then, the sweet in her cheek, she broke away and ran across the kitchen. She flung open the boy's bedroom.

"Get up outa that!" she cried out. "The ould fellah is home!"

The Can with the Diamond Notch

By Seamus O'Kelly

1

Festus Clasby, the name stood out in chaste white letters from the black background of the signboard. Indeed the name might be said to spring from the landscape, for this shop jumped from its rural setting with an air of aggression. It was a commercial oasis on a desert of grass. It proclaimed the clash of two civilizations. There were the hills, pitched round it like the galleries of some vast amphitheatre, rising tier upon tier to the blue of the sky. There was the yellow road, fantastic in its frolic down to the valley. And at one of its wayward curves was the shop, the shop of Festus Clasby, a foreign growth upon the landscape, its one long window crowded with sombre merchandise, its air that of established, cob-web respectability.

Inside the shop was Festus Clasby himself, like some great masterpiece in its ancient frame. He was the product of the two civilizations, a charioteer who drove the two fiery steeds of Agricolo and Trade with a hand of authority. He was a man of lands and of shops. His dark face, framed in darker hair and beard, was massive and square. Behind the luxurious growth of hair the rich blood glowed on the clear skin. His chest had breadth, his limbs were great, showing girth at the hips and power at the calves. His eyes were large and dark, smouldering in soft velvety tones. The nose was long, the nostrils expressive of a certain animalism, the mouth looked eloquent.

His voice was low, of an agreeable even quality, floating over the boxes and barrels of his shop like a chant. His words never jarred, his views were vaguely comforting, based on accepted

114

conventions, expressed in round, soft, lulling platitudes. His manner was serious, his movements deliberate, the great bulk of the shoulders looming up in unconscious but dramatic poses in the curiously uneven lighting of the shop. His hands gave the impression of slowness and a moderate skill; they could make up a parcel on the counter without leaving ugly laps; they could perform a minor surgical operation on a beast in the fields without degenerating to butchery; and they would always be doing something, even if it were only rolling up a ball of twine. His clothes exuded a faint suggestion of cinnamon, nutmeg and caraway seeds.

Festus Clasby would have looked the part in any notorious position in life; his shoulders would have carried with dignity the golden chain of office of the mayorality of a considerable city; he would have looked a perfect chairman of a jury at a Coroner's inquest; as the Head of a pious Guild in a church he might almost be confused with the figures of the stained glass windows; marching at the head of a brass band he would have reconciled one to death. There was no technical trust which men would not have reposed in him, so perfectly was he wrought as a human casket. As it was, Festus Clasby filled the most fatal of all occupations to dignity without losing his tremendous illusion of respectability. The hands which cut the bacon and the tobacco turned the taps over pint measures, scooped bran and flour into scales, took herrings out of their barrels, rolled up sugarsticks in shreds of paper for children, were hands whose movements the eyes of no saucy customer dared follow with a gleam of suspicion. Not once in a lifetime was that casket tarnished; the nearest he ever went to it was when he bought up very cheaply as was his custom—a broken man's insurance policy a day after the law made such a practice illegal. There was no haggling at Festus Clasby's counter. There was only conversation, agreeable conversation about things which Festus Clasby did not sell, such as the weather, the diseases of animals, the results of races, and the scandals of the Royal Families of Europe. These conversations were not hurried or yet protracted. They came to a happy ending at much the same moment as Festus Clasby made the knot of the twine of your parcel. But to stand in the devotional light in front of his counter, wedged in between divisions and sub-divisions of his boxes and barrels, and to scent the good scents which exhaled from his shelves, and to get served by Festus Clasby in person, was to feel that you had been indeed served.

The small farmers and herds and the hardy little dark mountainy men had this reverential feeling about the good man and his shop. They approached the establishment as holy pilgrims might approach a shrine. They stood at his counter with the air of devotees. Festus Clasby waited on them with patience and benignity. He might be some warm-blooded god handing gifts over the counter. When he brought forth his great account book and entered up their purchases with a carpenter's pencil—having first moistened the tip of it with his flexible lips—they had strongly, deep down in their souls, the conviction that they were then and for all time debtors to Festus Clasby. Which, indeed and in truth, they were. From year's end to year's end their accounts remained in that book; in the course of their lives various figures rose and faded after their names, recording the ups and downs of their financial histories. It was only when Festus Clasby had supplied the materials for their wakes that the great pencil, with one mighty stroke of terrible finality, ran like a sword through their names, wiping their very memories from the hillsides. All purchases were entered up in Festus Clasby's mighty record without vulgar discussions as to price. The business of the establishment was conducted on the basis of a belief in the man who purchased. The customers of Festus Clasby would as soon have thought of questioning his prices as they would of questioning the right of the earth to revolve round the sun. Festus Clasby was the planet around which this constellation of small farmers, herds, and hardy little dark mountainy men revolved; from his shop they drew the light and heat and food which kept them going. Their very emotions were registered at his counter. To the man with a religious turn he was able at a price to hand down from his shelves the *Key of Heaven;* the other side of the box he comforted the man who came panting to his taps to drown the memory of some chronic impertinence. He gave a very long credit, and a very long credit, in his philosophy, justified a very, very long profit. As to security, if Festus Clasby's customers had not a great deal of money they had grass which grew every year, and the beasts which Festus Clasby fattened and sold at the fairs had sometimes to eat his debtors out of his book. If his bullocks were not able to do even this, then Festus Clasby talked to the small farmer about a mortgage on the land, so that now and again small farmers became herds for Festus Clasby. In this way was he able to maintain his position with his back to the hills and his toes in the valley, striding his territory like a Colossus. When you saw his name on the signboard standing stark from the landscape, and when you saw Festus Clasby behind his counter, you knew instinctively that both had always stood for at least twenty shillings in the pound.

2

Now, it came to pass that on a certain day Festus Clasby was passing through the outskirts of the nearest country town on his homeward journey, his cart laden with provisions. At the same moment the spare figure of a tinker whose name was Mac-an-Ward, the Son of the Bard, veered around the corner of a street with a new tin can under his arm. It was the Can with the Diamond Notch.

Mac-an-Ward approached Festus Clasby, who pulled up his cart. "Well, my good man?" queried Festus Clasby, a phrase usually addressed across his counter, his hands outspread, to longstanding customers.

"The last of a rare lot," said Mac-an-Ward, deftly poising the tin can on the top of his fingers, so that it stood level with Festus Clasby's great face. Festus Clasby took this as a business proposition, and the soul of the trader revolved within him. Why not buy the tin can from this tinker and sell it at a profit across his counter, even as he would sell the flitches of bacon that were wrapped in sacking upon his cart? He was in mellow mood, and laid down the reins in the cart beside him.

"And so she is the last?" he said, eyeing the tin can.

"She is the Can with the Diamond Notch."

"Odds and ends go cheap," said Festus Clasby.

"She is the last, but the flower of the flock."

"Remnants must go as bargains or else remain as remnants."

"My wallet!" protested Mac-an-Ward, "you wound me. Don't speak as if I picked it off a scrap heap."

"I will not but I will say that being a tail end and an odd one it must go at a sacrifice."

The Son of the Bard tapped the side of the can gently with his knuckles.

"Listen to him, the hard man from the country! He has no regard for my feelings. I had the soldering iron in my hand in face of it before the larks stirred this morning. I had my back to the East, but through the bottom of that can there I saw the sun rise in its glory. The brightness of it is as the harvest moon."

"I don't want it for its brightness."

"Dear heart, listen to the man who would not have brightness. He would pluck the light from the moon, quench the heat in the heart of the sun. He would draw a screen across the aurora borealis and paint out the rainbow with lamp black. He might do such things, but he cannot deny the brightness of this can. Look upon it! When the world is coming to an end it will shine up at the sky and it will say! 'Ah, where are all the great stars now that made a boast of their brightness?' And there will be no star left to answer. They will all be dead things in the heaven buried in the forgotten graves of the skies."

"Don't mind the skies. Let me see if there may not be a leakage in it." Festus Clasby held the can between his handsome face and the bright sky.

"Leakages!" exclaimed Mac-an-Ward.

"A leakage in a can that I soldered as if with my own heart's blood. Holy Kilcock, what a mind has this man from the country! He sees no value in its brightness; now he will tell me that there is no virtue in its music."

"I like music," said Festus Clasby. "No fiddler has ever stood at my door but had the good word to say of me. Not one of them could ever say that he went thirsty from my counter."

Said the Son of the Bard: "Fiddlers, what are fiddlers? What sound have they like the music of the sweet milk going into that can from the yellow teats of the red cow? Morning and evening there will be a hymn played upon it in the haggard. Was not the finest song ever made called *Cailin deas cruidhte na mbo*? Music!

Do you think that the water in the holy well will not improve in its sparkle to have such a can as this dipped into it? It will be welcome everywhere for its clearness and its cleanness. Heavenly Father, look at the manner in which I rounded the edge of that can with the clippers! Cut clean and clever, soldered at the dawn of day, the dew falling upon the hands that moulded it, the parings scattered about my feet like jewels. And now you would bargain over it. I will not sell it to you at all. I will put it in a holy shrine."

Festus Clasby turned the can over in his hands, a little bewildered. "It looks an ordinary can enough," he said.

"It is the Can with the Diamond Notch," declared Mac-an-Ward.

"Would it be worth a shilling now?"

"He puts a price upon it! It is blasphemy. The man has no religion; he will lose his soul. The devils will have him by the heels. They will tear his red soul through the roof. Give me the can; don't hold it in those hands any longer. They are coarse; the hair is standing about the purple knuckles like stubbles in an illcut meadow. That can was made for the hands of a delicate woman or for the angels that carry water to the Court of Heaven. I saw it in a vision the night before I made it; it was on the head of a maiden with golden hair. Her feet were bare and like shells. She walked across a field where daisies rose out of young grass; she had the can resting on her head like one coming from the milking. So I rose up then and said, 'Now, I will make a can fit for this maiden's head.' And I made it out of the rising sun and the falling dew. And now you ask me if it is worth a shilling."

"For all your talk, it is only made of tin, and not such good tin."

"Not good tin! I held it in my hand in the piece before ever the clippers was laid upon it. I bent it and it curved, supple as a young snake. I shook it, and the ripples ran down the length of it like silver waves in a little lake. The strength of the ages was in its voice. It has gathered its power in the womb of the earth. It was smelted from the precious metal taken from the mines of the Peninsula of Malacca, and it will have its gleam when the sparkle of the diamond is spent."

"I'll give you a shilling for it, and hold your tongue."

"No! I will not have it on my conscience. God is my judge, I will break it up first. I will cut it into pieces. From one of them will yet be made a breastplate, and in time to come it will be nailed to your own coffin, with your name and your age and the date of your death painted upon it. And when the paint is faded it will shine over the dust of the bone of your breast. It will be dug up and preserved when all graveyards are abolished. They will say, 'We will keep this breastplate, for who knows but that it bore the name of the man who refused to buy the Can with the Diamond Notch.' "

"How much will you take for it?"

"Now you are respectful. Let me put a price upon it, for it was I who fashioned it into this shape. It will hold three gallons and a half from now until the time that swallows wear shoes. But for all that I will part with it, because I am poor and hungry and have a delicate wife. It breaks my heart to say it but pay into my hands two shillings and it is yours. Pay quickly or I may repent. It galls me to part with; in your charity pay quickly and begone."

"I will not. I will give you one-and-six."

"Assassin! You stab me. What a mind you have! Look at the greed of your eyes; they would devour the grass of the fields from this place up to the Devil's Bit. You would lock up the air and sell it in gasping breaths. You are disgusting. But give me the one-and-six and to Connacht with you! I am damning my soul standing beside you and your cart, smelling its contents. How can a man talk with the smell of fat bacon going between him and the wind? One-and-six and the dew that fell at the making hardly dry upon my hands yet. Farewell, a long farewell, my Shining One; we may never meet again."

The shawl of Mac-an-Ward's wife had been blowing around the nearby corner while this discussion had been in progress. It flapped against the wall in the wind like a lose sail in the rigging. The head of the woman herself came gradually into view, one eye spying around the masonry, half-closing as it measured the comfortable proportions of Festus Clasby seated upon his cart. As the one-and-six was counted out penny by penny into the palm of the brown hand of the Son of the Bard, the figure of his wife floated out on the open road, tossing and tacking and undecided in its direction to the eye of those who understood not the language of gestures and motions. By a series of giddy evolutions she arrived at the cart as the last of the coppers was counted out.

"I have parted with my inheritance," said Mac-an-Ward. "I have sold my soul and the angels have folded their wings, weeping."

"In other words, I have bought a tin can," said Festus Clasby, and his frame and the entire cart shook with his chuckling.

The tinker's wife chuckled with him in harmony. Then she reached out her hand with a gesture that claimed a sympathetic examination of the purchase. Festus Clasby hesitated, looking into the eyes of the woman. Was she to be trusted? Her eyes were clear, grey and open, almost babyish in their rounded innocence. Festus Clasby handed her the tin can and she examined it slowly.

"Who sold you the Can with the Diamond Notch?" she asked.

"The man standing by your side."

"He has wronged you. The can is not his."

"He says he made it."

"Liar! He never curved it in the piece."

"I don't much care whether he did or not. It is mine now anyhow."

"It is my brother's can. No other hand made it. Look! Do you see this notch on the piece of sheet iron where the handle is fastened to the sides?"

"I do."

"Is it not shaped like a diamond?"

"It is."

"By that mark I identify it. My brother cuts that diamond-shaped notch in all the work he puts out from his hands. It is his private mark. The shopkeepers have knowledge of it. There is a value on the cans with that notch shaped like a diamond. This man here makes cans when he is not drunk, but the notch to them is square. The shopkeepers have knowledge of them too for they do not last. The handles fall out of them. He has never given his time to the art, and so does not know how to rivet them."

"She vilifies me," said Mac-an-Ward, *sotto voce.*

"Then I am glad he has not sold me one of his own," said Festus Clasby. "I have a fancy for the lasting article."

"You may be able to buy it yet," said the woman. "My brother is lying sick of the fever, and I have his right to sell the Can with the Diamond Notch on the handles where they are riveted."

"But I have bought it already."

"This man," said the damsel, in a tone which discounted the husband, "had no right to sell it. If it is not his property, but the property of my brother, won't you say that he nor no other man has a right to sell it?"

Festus Clasby felt puzzled. He was unaccustomed to dealing with people who raised questions of title. His black brows knit.

"How can a man who doesn't own a thing sell a thing?" she persisted. "Is it a habit of yours to sell that which you do not own?"

"It is not," Festus Clasby said, feeling that an assault had been wantonly made on his integrity as a trader. "No one could ever say that of me. Honest value was ever my motto."

"And the motto of my brother who is sick with the fever. I will go to him and say, 'I met the most respectable-looking man in all Europe, who put a value on your can because of the diamond notch.' I will pay into his hands the one-and-six which is its price."

Festus Clasby had, when taken out of his own peculiar province a heavy mind and the type of mind that will range along side-issues and get lost in them if they are raised often enough and long enough. The diamond notch on the handle, the brother who was sick of the fever, the alleged non-title of Mac-an-Ward, the interposition of the woman, the cans with the handles which fall out, and the cans with the handles which do not fall out, the equity of selling that which does not belong to you—all these things chased each other across Festus Clasby's mind. The Son of the Bard stood silent by the car, looking away down the road with a passive look on his long, narrow face.

"Pay me the one-and-six to put into the hands of my brother," the woman said.

Festus Clasby's mind was brought back at once to his pocket. "No," he said, "but this man can give you my money to pay into the hand of your brother."

"This man," she said airily, "has no interest for me. Whatever took place between the two of you in regard to my brother's can I will have nothing to say to."

"Then if you won't," said Festus Clasby, "I will have nothing to do with you. If he had no right to the can you can put the police onto him; that's what police are for."

"And upon you," the woman added. "The police are also for that."

"Upon me?" Festus Clasby exclaimed, his chest swelling. "My name has never crossed the mind of a policeman, except, maybe for what he might owe me at the end of the month for pig's heads. I never stood in the shadow of the law. And to this man standing by your side I have nothing to say."

"You have. You bought from him that which did not belong to him. You received and the receiver is as bad as the rogue. So the law has it. The shadow of the law is great."

Festus Clasby came down from his car, his face troubled. "I am not used to this," he said.

"You are a handsome man, a man thought well of. You have great provisions upon your cart. This man has nothing but the unwashed shirt which hangs on his slack back. It will not become you to march handcuffed with his like, going between two policeman to the bridewell."

"What are you saying of me, woman?"

"It will be no token of business to see your cart and the provisions it contains driven into the yard of the barracks. All the people of this town will see it, for they have many eyes. The people of trade will be coming to their doors, speaking of it. 'A man's property was molested,' they will say. 'What property?' will be asked. 'The Can with the Diamond Notch,' they will answer; 'the man of substance conspired with the thief to make away with it.' These are the words that will be spoken in the streets."

Festus Clasby set great store on his name, the name he had got painted for the eye of the country over his door.

"I will be known to the police as one extensive in my dealings," he said.

"They will not couple me with this man who is known as one living outside of the law."

"It is not for the Peelers to put the honest man on one side and the thief on the other. That will be for the court. You will stand with him upon my charge. The Peelers will say to you, 'We know you to be a man of great worth, and the law will uphold you.' But the law is slow and a man's good name goes fast."

Festus Clasby fingered his money in his pocket and the touch of it made him struggle. "The can may be this man's for all I know. You have no brother and I believe you to be a fraud."

"That too will be for the law to decide. If I have a brother the law will produce him when his fever is ended. If I have no brother the law will so declare it. If my brother did not make a Can with the Diamond Notch you will know me as one deficient in truth. There is no point under the stars that the law cannot be got to declare upon. But as is right, the law is slow, and will wait for a man to come out of his fever. Before it can decide another man's good name, like a little cloud riding across the sky is gone from the memory of the people and will not come riding back upon the crest of any wind."

"It will be a great price to be paying for a tin can," said Festus Clasby. He was turning around with his fingers the coins in his pocket.

The woman put the can on her arm, then covered it up with her shawl, like a hen taking a chick under the protection of her wing.

"I have given you many words," she said, "because you are a man sizeable and good to the eye of a foolish woman. If I had not a sick brother I might be induced to let slip his right in the Can with the Diamond Notch for the pleasure I have found in the look of your face. When I saw you on the cart I said, 'There is the build of a man which is to my fancy.' When I heard your voice I said, 'That is good music to the ear of a woman.' When I saw your eye I said, 'There is danger to the heart of a woman.' When I saw your beard I said, 'There is great growth from the strength of a man.' When you spoke to me and gave me your laugh I said, 'Ah, what a place that would be for a woman to be seated, driving the roads of the country on a cart laden with provisions beside one so much to the female liking.' But my sick brother waits, and now I go to that which may make away with the goodness of your name. I must seek those who will throw the shadow of the law over many."

She moved away, sighing a quick sigh, as one might who was setting out on a disagreeable mission. Festus Clasby called to her and she came back, her eyes pained as they sought his face. Festus Clasby paid the money, a bright shilling and two three-penny bits, into her hand, wondering vaguely, but virtuously, as he did so, what hardy little dark mountainy man he would later charge up the can to at the double price.

"Now," said the wife of Mac-an-Ward, putting the money away, "you have paid me for my brother's can and you would be within your right in getting back your one-and-six from this bad man." She hitched her shawl contemptuously in the direction of Mac-an-Ward.

Festus Clasby looked at the Son of the Bard with his velvety soft eyes. "Come, sir," said he, his tone a little nervous.

Mac-an-Ward hitched his trousers at the hips like a sailor, spat through his teeth, and eyed Festus Clasby through a slit in his half-closed eyes. There was a little patter of the feet on the road on the part of Mac-an-Ward, and Festus Clasby knew enough of the world and its ways to gather that these were scientific movements invented to throw a man in a struggle. He did not like the look of the Son of the Bard.

"I will go home and leave him to God," he said. "Hand me the can and I will be shortening my road."

At this moment three small boys, ragged, eager, their faces hard and weather-beaten, bounded up to the cart. They were breathless and they stood about the woman.

"Mother!" they cried in chorus. "The man in the big shop; he is looking for a can."

"What can?" cried the woman.

The three young voices rose like a great cry: "The Can with the Diamond Notch."

The woman caught her face in her hands as if some terrible thing had been said. She stared at the youngsters intently.

"He wants one more to make up an order," they chanted. "He says he will pay—"

The woman shrank from them with a cry. "How much?" she asked.

"Half-a-crown!"

The wife of Mac-an-Ward threw out her arms in a wild

gesture of despair. "My God!" she cried. "I sold it. I wronged my sick brother."

"Where did you sell it, mother?"

"Here, to this handsome dark man."

"How much did he pay?"

"Eighteen-pence."

The three youngsters raised a long howl, like beagles who had lost their quarry.

Suddenly the woman's face brightened. She looked eagerly at Festus Clasby, then laid the hand of friendship, of appeal, on his arm.

"I have it!" she cried, joyfully.

"Have what?" asked Festus Clasby.

"A way out of the trouble," she said. "A means of saving my brother from wrong. A way of bringing him his own for the Can with the Diamond Notch."

"What way might that be?" asked Festus Clasby, his manner growing skeptical.

"I will go to the shopman with it and get the half-crown. Having got the half-crown I will hurry back here—or you can come with me—and I will pay you back your one-and-six. In that way I will make another shilling and do you no wrong. Is that agreed?"

"It is not agreed," said Festus Clasby. "Give me out the tin can, I am done with you now."

"It's robbery!" cried the woman, her eyes full of a blazening sudden anger.

"What is robbery?" asked Festus Clasby.

"Doing me out of a shilling. Wronging my sick brother out of his earnings. A man worth hundreds, maybe thousands, to stand between a poor woman and a shilling. I am deceived in you."

"Out with the can," said Festus Clasby.

"Let the woman earn her shilling," said Mac-an-Ward. His voice came from behind Festus Clasby.

"Our mother must get her shilling," cried the three youngsters.

Festus Clasby turned about to Mac-an-Ward, and as he did so

he noticed that two men had come and set their backs against a wall hard by; they leaned limply, casually, against it, but they were, he noticed, of the same tribe as the Mac-an-Wards.

"It was always lucky, the Can with the Diamond Notch," said the woman. "This offer of the man in the big shop is a sign of it. I will not allow you to break my brother's luck and he lying in his fever."

"By heaven!" cried Festus Clasby. "I will have you all arrested. I will have the law on you now."

He wheeled about the horse and cart, setting his face for the police barrack, which could be seen shining in the distance in the plumage of a magpie. The two men who stood by came over, and from the other side another man and three old women. With Mac-an-Ward, Mrs. Mac-an-Ward, and the three young Mac-an-Wards, they grouped themselves around Festus Clasby, and he was vaguely conscious that they were grouped with some military art. A low murmur of a dispute arose among them, rising steadily. He could only hear snatches of their words: "Give it back to him," "He won't get it," "How can he be travelling without the Can with the Diamond Notch?" "Is it the Can with the Diamond Notch?" "No," "Maybe it is, maybe it is not," "Who knows that?" "I say yes," "Hold your tongue," "Be off, you slut," "Rattle away."

People from the town were attracted to the place. Festus Clasby, the dispute stirring something in his own blood, shook his fist in the long narrow face of Mac-an-Ward. As he did so he got a tip on the heels and a pressure upon the chest sent him staggering a fews steps back. One of the old women held him up in her arms and another old woman stood before him, striking her breast. Festus Clasby saw the wisps of hair hanging about the bony face and froth on the corners of her mouth. Vaguely he saw the working of the bones of her wasted neck, and below it a long V-shaped gleam of the yellow tanned breast, which she thumped with her fist. Afterwards the memory of this ugly old trollop remained with him. The youngsters were shooting in and out through the group, sending up unearthly shrieks. Two of the men peeled off their coats and were sparring at each other wickedly, shouting all the time, while Mac-an-Ward was making a tumultuous peace. The commotion and the strife, or the illusion of strife, increased. "Oh," an onlooker cried, "the tinkers are murdering each other!"

The patient horse at last raised its head with a toss and then wheeled about to break away. With the instinct of his kind, Festus Clasby rushed to the animal's head and held him. As he did so the striped petticoats and the tossing shawls of the women flashed about the shafts and the body of the cart. The men raised a hoarse roar.

A neighbour of Festus Clasby driving up the street at this moment, was amazed to see the great man of lands and shops in the midst of the wrangling tinkers. He pulled up, marvelling, then went to him.

"What is this Festus?" he asked.

"They have robbed me," cried Festus Clasby.

"Robbed you?"

"Ay, of money and property."

"Good God! How much money?"

"I don't rightly know—I forget—some shillings, maybe."

"Oh! And of property?"

"No matter. It is only one article, but property."

"Come home, Festus; in the name of God get out of this," advised the good neighbour.

But Festus Clasby was strangely moved. He was behaving like a man who had taken drink. Something had happened wounding to his soul. "I will not go," he cried. "I must have back my money."

The tinkers had now ceased disputing among themselves. They were grouped about the two men as if they were only spectators of an interesting dispute.

"Back I must have my money," cried Festus Clasby, his great hand going up in a mighty threat. The tinkers clicked their tongues on the roofs of their mouths in a sound of amazement, as much as to say, "What a terrible thing! What a wonderful and a mighty man!"

"I advise you to come," persuaded his neighbour.

"Never! God is my judge, never!" cried Festus Clasby.

Again the tinkers clicked their tongues, looked at each other in wonder.

"You will be thankful you brought your life out of this," said the neighbour. "Let it not be said of you on the countryside that you were seen wrangling with the tinkers in this town."

"Shame! Shame! Shame!" broke out like a shocked murmur among the attentive tinkers. Festus Clasby faced his audience in all his splendid proportions. Never was he seen so moved. Never had such a great passion seized him. The soft tones of his eyes were no longer soft. They shone in fiery wrath. "I will at least have that which I bought twice over!" he cried. "I will have my tin can!"

Immediately the group of tinkers broke up in the greatest disorder. Hoarse cries broke out among them. They behaved like people upon whom some fearful doom had been suddenly pronounced. The old women threw themselves about, racked with pain and terror. They beat their hands together, threw wild arms in despairing gestures to the sky, raising a harrowing lamentation. The men growled in sullen gutturals. The youngsters knelt on the road, giving out the wild beagle-like howl. Voices cried above the uproar: "Where is it? Where is the can with the Diamond Notch? Get him the Can with the Diamond Notch! He must have the Can with the Diamond Notch! How can he travel without the Can with the Diamond Notch? He'll die without the Can with the Diamond Notch!"

Festus Clasby was endeavoring to deliver his soul of impassioned protests when his neighbour, assisted by a bystander or two, forcibly hoisted him up on his cart and he was driven away amid a great howling from the tinkers.

It was twilight when he reached his place among the hills, and the good white letters under the thatch showed clear in his eyes. Pulling himself together he drove with an air about the gable and into the wide open yard at the back, fowls clearing out of his way, a sheep-dog coming to welcome him, a mewing mournfully over the half-door of a stable. Festus Clasby was soothed by this homely, worshipful environment, and got off the cart with a sigh. Inside the kitchen he could hear the faithful women trotting about preparing the great master's meal. He made ready to carry the provisions into the shop. When he unwrapped the sacking from the bacon, something like a sudden stab went through his breast. Perspiration came out on his forehead.

Several large long slices had been cut off in jagged slashes from the flitches. They lay like wounded things on the body of the cart. He pulled down the other purchases feverishly, horror in his face. How many loaves had been torn off his batch of bread? Where were all the packets of tea and sugar, the currants and raisins, the flour, the tobacco, the cream-of-tartar, the caraway seeds, the nutmeg, the lemon peel, the hair oil, the—

Festus Clasby wiped the perspiration from his forehead. He stumbled out of the yard, sat up on a ditch, and looked across the silent, peaceful, innocent country. How good it was! How lovely were the beasts grazing, fattening, in the fields! His soft velvety eyes were suddenly flooded with a bitter emotion and he wept.

The loaves of bread were under the shawl of the woman who had supported Festus Clasby when he stumbled; the bacon was under another bright shawl; the tobacco and flour fell to the lot of her whose yellow breast showed the play of much sun and many winds; the teas and sugar and the nutmeg and caraway seeds were under the wing of the wife of the Son of the Bard in the Can with the Diamond Notch.

The Anticlerical Pup

By Hugh Leonard

Our dog, Jack, was anti-clerical. That was the opinion of Mr. Quirk who lived next door, but my father clung to the theory that the dog simply detested the colour black: which did not explain why postmen were allowed to pass unmolested, but let a priest or a brace of nuns appear on our road and Jack's mane rose like the quills on a porcupine. In a moment he would be in front of them, a veritable Petain of a dog, determined that they should not pass. He growled, snarled and bayed at them, his hindquarters in the air, his forelegs flat on the pavement, his teeth inches away from the hem of a robe or the turn-up of a trousers leg. His victims were not to know that he was a fraud—the one time he caught a rabbit he tossed the unfortunate animal into the air with his snout, then held it down gently with one paw until to his puzzlement it died of fright—but one look at those slavering jaws must have convinced many a Little Sister of the Poor that her martyrdom was at hand. What made it worse was that he positively fawned on the Protestant minister, whose black suit had a white pin-stripe.

My mother was scandalized. Her neighbour, Mrs. Kinsella—whose addiction to malicious gossip and a protruding lower jaw had earned her the nickname of Mary Plock—had hinted that the dog's militant bigotry was symptomatic of a hidden God-lessness in our house. She sat on a flat granite boulder, less seat than throne, outside her front door where nothing escaped her unblinking eye: she could, so my father insisted, see a midge on the Hill of Howth. Whenever Jack bared his fangs at the approach of clerical broadcloth she would suck on a lone sentinel of a tooth and observe with relish: "The dog didn't learn *that* be hisself!" Once, I made friends with a boy named Stan Slonom, and it was Mary Plock who told me that he was a

Jew and it was a sin to talk to him because the Jews had crucified Our Lord.

At last the inevitable happened and Jack picked on the wrong nun. She fetched him a blow between the eyes with her reticule, whereupon he seized her sleeve between his teeth and shook her arm so vigorously from side to side that she seemed to be imparting a blessing to the entire neighbourhood. When she managed, quite literally, to tear herself loose she made straight for the police station, while the dog trotted proudly back to our doorstep, bearing in his jaws the enemy's colours.

My mother feared two kinds of people: the clergy and policemen. The only honourable circumstance in which the former might cross one's threshold was when death was imminent: otherwise their presence signalled your shame to the world, for it proclaimed apostacy, wifebeating, infidelity or a child gone to the bad. A visitation by a policeman was as degrading: a summons for pilfering firewood might be nothing to write home about in the moral sense, but thereafter it was unwise to brandish your respectability at a neighbour. In fact, at your great-grandchild's wedding breakfast sixty years in the future, a guest would be sure to remark on how warm the room was, adding with a leer and a wink: "But then the family never went short of firewood!" So my mother was shamed twice over to be in trouble with the police as the result of a complaint made by a nun.

That same day at tea time a civic guard came stooping through our front door, which was high enough for an ordinary Christian, but not for him. He was the "Cat" McDonald, so named because he had once leaped from a ten-foot wall to catch an apple-thief. Later, when I read *Les Misérables,* Javert's face was his. He had pale eyes, with the bluish tint of sun on ice. There was long dark hair on his cheekbones, and he craved to be feared the way other men need to be liked. His children played alone. One night I saw the glint of his peaked cap while I was wheeling an unlit bicycle. At once I hoisted it on my shoulder so that it ceased to be a vehicle, and he stalked me for three miles, whispering threats and insults while I staggered under the weight. But I was younger—perhaps ten—the evening he came to the house.

Another guard would have been red-faced and apologetic, singing hosannas to our world-wide reputation as decent people. The "Cat" came in with the face of a public hangman, his eyes ransacking the room for a sign of unlawful affluence. My father, who knew him for a gouger who would begrudge you the time of day, stared sullenly at him, the egg yolk dribbling from his spoon on to the sheet of newspaper we used as a tablecloth. My mother, lost to all shame, was doggedly flirtatious: in moments of desperation she believed, like my grandmother, that she could charm songs from a cow. She shoved a chair against Guard McDonald's unyielding knees, declared that he would have a cup of tea with us ("In your hand, just…you will, you will!") and implied with a nudge of her eyes that his steeliness was a sham. Only the whiteness of her face showed how afraid she was. The "Cat" bided his time until her voice became small and ran down like a clock-work toy. When he spoke, the words were baton blows. He was a great man for phrases. We were the custodians of a dangerous animal. A complaint had been lodged. An attack upon the person of a religious. Intimation of prosecution was hereby given. Good day to us.

At the door he turned to regard my father, who was still eyeing him malevolently, the egg yolk now congealed. My mother was cringing piteously, but perhaps the "Cat" was not content until my father, too, had been brought to heel.

"Listen here to me, my good man." For some unexplained reason all Irish policemen have bass voices but his could rattle the windows. "This matter is coming to court. If you want a lenient view to be taken you will destroy that animal without more ado. There is a gun below in the barracks for such purposes and any one of the guards will put a bullet into him. If you'll be guided by my advice it may go easy with you."

He was a clever one. I knew by my mother's face that she would grab at the straw, and he knew it, too. My father might strut and bluster, but it was she who ruled the roost. Her terror of the law went far deeper than a two-pound fine and our names in the *Evening Herald:* it was an almost primeval fear, beyond argument or reason, akin to the dread evoked by the *terra incognita* on ancient maps, and in a panic she could no more think or behave sanely than rain could fall upwards. As the "Cat" turned on his heel to leave, he fetched my father a quick pitying glance to let him know who had the upper hand.

In bed that night I heard my parents whispering in the other room. My father sighed "I dunno" a couple of times, then was silent as she railed on at him. I lifted the window blind and could make out the dog, exiled in disgrace to the back yard. The next day at breakfast time I said: "You won't kill Jack, mammy, sure you won't?" She was silent, and my father said: "Not at all. Don't mind her." Over my Saturday comic I saw her look at him angrily.

I stayed close to the house all that day, not daring to go to the corner for fear I might see the "Cat" reappear, this time with a gun in his hand. Towards tea time my father was no sooner home from work than I was sent on a message to Toole's shop. Hurrying back, I caught sight of him turning out of our lane and leading the dog by a length of rope tied to his collar, which in itself was unusual because Jack had always been allowed to run free. I knew straight off that the errand was a red herring and that my father was on his way to the harbour to drown the dog.

I know that my parents were not cruel; in fact I often heard my father inveigh against people who got rid of unwanted animals by taking them into the country and losing them. He believed drowning to be a humane death. Call it ignorance, or say that life had hardened him or that he simply lacked the imagination to feel in his mind the panic, the struggle for breath and the bursting of lungs. And out of bull-headedness he would not give the "Cat" the satisfaction of seeing Jack die with a police bullet in his brain. At any rate, watching him and the dog disappear down Victoria Road towards the sea, I began to bawl, hating my mother and despising my da for his weakness in not defying her. It was in my nature to slouch off in solitary misery, and I would be lying if I pretended, more than thirty years later, to know why I followed my father to the harbour instead, running to catch up and howling as I ran; but what happened there is branded on my mind as if by lightning.

It was October and a gale was roaring in from the north east: the kind of once-in-ten-years gale that in a night turned the beach at the White Rock from fine sand to pebbles. There was a flood tide and the sea itself seemed to come driving into the harbour, surging over the piers, not in waves but in a great maddened swell which boiled around the boats high on the slipway, then retreated for a new onslaught, turning the stone steps into cataracts. A lobster pot, caught by the wind, went bowling along the road. The air was filled with flying leaves and twigs. The sea thundered, and I felt spray on my face all the way along Coliemore Road. There are two piers, one a stub of granite jutting out from the land, the other at a right angle to it. This second pier catches the full force of the sea and there is a protecting wall running the length of its seaward edge. When I reached the top of the slipway, half-blinded by spray, I saw my father crouched beneath the wall. He was holding the dog steady between his knees and tying one end of the rope he had used as a lead around what looked like a concrete block. I ran towards him along the pier. I cried out, but the wind shouted harder, and before I could reach him he had gathered up the dog and the concrete in his arms and dropped them over the wall into the sea.

I stopped dead a few yards from him. He said afterwards that my wailing was like the moan of a banshee. He was hanging on to the wall to avoid being blown into the harbour, and I have never seen such a stricken look on a human face as when he turned and saw me. The sea roared, white gobs of foam spat around his boots and Dalkey Island was at his back like a sinking ship. Then another green wall of water came rushing in between the piers, and I saw Jack, unbelievably on its crest, his paws flailing like paddle-wheels.

The sea bore him into the harbour like matchwood, threatening to dash him against the pier. Less from bravery than impulse, I started down the steps cut into the granite. My father shouted out "Jack!", but I never knew whether he meant me or the dog. Unknowingly, I was running down into the trough of the previous wave, and before I had time to be amazed the sea rose from nowhere: it was around my waist, my chest, and then had swallowed me. The steps were no longer under my feet. I opened my mouth to gasp and was breathing sea water. Then I felt a tug; my own heaviness and the agony of being yanked upwards by my hair. I was hauled back up the steps to the accompaniment of a volley of curses and dumped like Monday's washing on the pier. I choked and retched, and the wind knifed through my wet clothes. I was missing a shoe. After a moment I could make out the blurred figure of my father below me on the steps. He was hanging on to an iron mooring ring with one hand and reaching out for the dog with the other, yelling: "You cur, you whelp, you whoor's melt, will you come here to me!" He stooped to grab him by the collar, an after-wave broke over him, and then the dog was on the steps, scrabbling with his paws to hold on, for the concrete block was still tied to the rope. My father carried it as if it were a bridal train, and cut it loose when they were safely on the pier. He sat in a pool of water from his own clothes and looked at me and the dog, who was shaking himself nonchalantly. His whiskers dripped. His hat was bobbing below us in the harbour. "Amn't I the misfortunate poor divil," he moaned, "with the pair of yous?"

I should have danced for joy at the dog's reprieve, but my wet clothes and chattering teeth kept my delight within bounds. While I turned blue with cold my father took an oar from the boat-house and fished out his hat. Then the three of us set off for home, my one shoe squelching water, his wet trousers snapping like a whip in the wind, the dog leading the way, tail high, with every appearance of having enjoyed his swim. "She'll murder us," my father said. "The woman will ate us." The litany of his woes embraced my missing shoe, our ruined clothes, unavoidable pleurisy for himself, certain consumption for me, and his utter failure to drown the dog. Identifying Jack as the architect of his misfortunes, he snarled: "I'll learn you to swim with a ton weight of concrete tied to you!", and made a sudden frenzied kick at him. As the dog bounded effortlessly out of range, my father's sodden boot took leave of his foot and sailed into a garden.

Further up the road, the cup of his mortification brimmed over when we met our neighbour, Tweedy Costello, who kept hens and, in fact, had the beaky profile of a Wyandotte. "Fine fresh evening," my father said to him, as if, far from there being aught amiss, it was his daily custom to take a child swimming, fully clothed in a Force Nine gale. Mr. Costello made it a point of pride never to seem astonished, except when there was no reason for astonishment, but on this occasion he turned so sharply to look at us that one of the bicycle clips he wore whether awheel or on foot shot off his ankle and sang in mid-air. My father kept walking, and when our house came into view a moment later he could not have looked more despairing had it been a gibbet.

As soon as he opened the door the dog squirmed past him, through the front room and into the lighted kitchen. We followed him, expecting to hear his survival greeted with shrieks and execrations; instead, we saw my mother on her knees. Tears were streaming down her face and her arms were wrapped around the dog's neck. "God love him, he came back to me," she paeaned, while Jack, gratified by his welcome, gave her face a lick and looked around for his supper. "Ah, he's wet, the creature. Did they try to drown him?" she asked with a fawning shamelessness that made us reel. Her delirium knew no bounds. She fondled his brown head. Then her eyes strayed from him to two spreading pools of water on the linoleum, and she looked up and saw my father and me.

The prosecution never materialized. Perhaps the local sergeant, in whose side the "Cat" was a long-festering thorn, simply ran his pen through an entry in the summons book, and that was that. Nonetheless, my father bought a muzzle for the dog in a spirit of appeasement, but that canine Houdini managed to escape from it on the first day and chewed it to pieces. He lived, persecuting the clergy, for another nine years.

The Boarding House

By James Joyce

Mrs. Mooney was a butcher's daughter. She was a woman who was quite able to keep things to herself: a determined woman. She had married her father's foreman and opened a butcher's shop near Spring Gardens. But as soon as his father-in-law was dead Mr. Mooney began to go to the devil. He drank, plundered the till, ran headlong into debt. It was no use making him take the pledge: he was sure to break out again a few days after. By fighting his wife in the presence of customers and by buying bad meat he ruined his business. One night he went for his wife with the cleaver and she had to sleep in a neighbour's house.

After that they lived apart. She went to the priest and got a separation from him with care of the children. She would give him neither money nor food nor house-room; and so he was obliged to enlist himself as a sheriff's man. He was a shabby stooped little drunkard with a white face and a white moustache and white eyebrows, pencilled above his little eyes, which were pink-veined and raw; and all day long he sat in the bailiff's room, waiting to be put on a job. Mrs. Mooney, who had taken what remained of her money out of the butcher business and set up a boarding house in Hardwicke Street, was a big imposing woman. Her house had a floating population made up of tourists from Liverpool and the Isle of Man and, occasionally, *artistes* from the music halls. Its resident population was made up of clerks from the city. She governed the house cunningly and firmly, knew when to give credit, when to be stern and when to let things pass. All the resident young men spoke of her as *The Madam*.

Mrs. Mooney's young men paid fifteen shillings a week for board and lodgings (beer or stout at dinner excluded). They shared in common tastes and occupations and for this reason they were very chummy with one another. They discussed with one another the chances of favourites and outsiders. Jack Mooney, the Madam's son, who was clerk to a commission agent in Fleet Street, has the reputation of being a hard case. He was fond of using soldiers' obscenities: usually he came home in the small hours. When he met his friends he had always a good one to tell them and he was always sure to be on to a good thing— that is to say, a likely horse or a likely *artiste*. He was also handy with the mits and sang comic songs. On Sunday nights there would often be a reunion in Mrs. Mooney's front drawing-room. The music-hall *artistes* would oblige; and Sheridan played waltzes and polkas and vamped accompaniments. Polly Mooney, the Madam's daughter, would also sing. She sang:

> *I'm a ... naughty girl.*
> *You needn't sham:*
> *You know I am.*

Polly was a slim girl of nineteen; she had light soft hair and a small full mouth. Her eyes, which were grey with a shade of green through them, had a habit of glancing upwards when she spoke with anyone, which made her look like a little perverse madonna. Mrs. Mooney had first sent her daughter to be a typist in a corn-factor's office but, as a disreputable sheriff's man used to come every other day to the office, asking to be allowed to say a word to his daughter, she had taken her daughter home again and set her to do housework. As Polly was very lively the intention was to give her the run of the young men. Besides, young men like to feel that there is a young woman not very far away. Polly, of course, flirted with the young men but Mrs. Mooney, who was a shrewd judge, knew that the young men were only passing the time away: none of them meant business. Things went on so for a long time and Mrs. Mooney began to think of sending Polly back to typewriting when she noticed that something was going on between Polly and one of the young men. She watched the pair and kept her own counsel.

Polly knew that she was being watched, but still her mother's persistent silence could not be misunderstood. There had been no open complicity between mother and daughter, no open understanding but, though people in the house began to talk of the affair, still Mrs. Mooney did not intervene. Polly began to grow a little strange in her manner and the young man was evidently perturbed. At last, when she judged it to be the right moment, Mrs. Mooney intervened. She dealt with moral problems as a cleaver deals with meat: and in this case she had made up her mind.

It was a bright Sunday morning of early summer, promising heat, but with a fresh breeze blowing. All the windows of the boarding house were open and the lace curtains ballooned gently towards the street beneath the raised sashes. The belfry of George's Church sent out constant peals and worshippers, singly or in groups, traversed the little circus before the church, revealing their purpose by their self-contained demeanour no less than by the little volumes in their gloved hands. Breakfast was over in the boarding house and the table of the breakfast-room was covered with plates on which lay yellow streaks of eggs with morsels of bacon-fat and bacon-rind. Mrs. Mooney sat in the straw arm-chair and watched the servant Mary remove the breakfast things. She made Mary collect the crusts and pieces of broken bread to help to make Tuesday's bread-pudding. When the table was cleared, the broken bread collected, the sugar and butter safe under lock and key, she began to reconstruct the interview which she had had the night before with Polly. Things were as she had suspected: she had been frank in her questions and Polly had been frank in her answers. Both had been somewhat awkward, of course. She had been made awkward by her not wishing to receive the news in too cavalier a fashion or to seem to have connived and Polly had been made awkward not merely because allusions of that kind always made her awkward but also because she did not wish it to be thought that in her wise innocence she had divined the intention behind her mother's tolerance.

Mrs. Mooney glanced instinctively at the little gilt clock on the mantelpiece as soon as she had become aware through her revery that the bells of George's Church had stopped ringing. It was seventeen minutes past eleven: she would have lots of time to have the matter out with Mr. Doran and then catch short twelve at Marlborough Street. She was sure she would win. To begin with she had all the weight of social opinion on her side: she was an outraged mother. She had allowed him to live beneath her roof, assuming that he was a man of honour, and he had simply abused her hospitality. He was thirty-four or thirty-five years of age, so that youth could not be pleaded as his excuse; nor could ignorance be his excuse since he was a man who had seen something of the world. He had simply taken advantage of Polly's youth and inexperience: that was evident. The question was: What reparation would he make?

There must be reparation made in such case. It is all very well for the man: he can go his ways as if nothing had happened, having had his moment of pleasure, but the girl has to bear the brunt. Some mothers would be content to patch up such an affair for a sum of money; she had known cases of it. But she would not do so. For her only one reparation could make up for the loss of her daughter's honour: marriage.

She counted all her cards again before sending Mary up to Mr. Doran's room to say that she wished to speak with him. She felt sure she would win. He was a serious young man, not rakish or loud-voiced like the others. If it had been Mr. Sheridan or Mr. Meade or Bantam Lyons her task would have been much harder. She did not think he would face publicity. All the lodgers in the house knew something of the affair; details had been invented by some. Besides, he had been employed for thirteen years in a great Catholic wine-merchant's office and publicity would mean for him, perhaps, the loss of his job. Whereas if he agreed all might be well. She knew he had a good screw for one thing and she suspected he had a bit of stuff put by.

Nearly the half-hour! She stood up and surveyed herself in the pier-glass. The decisive expression of her great florid face satisfied her and she thought of some mothers she knew who could not get their daughters off their hands.

Mr. Doran was very anxious indeed this Sunday morning. He had made two attempts to shave but his hand had been so unsteady that he had been obliged to desist. Three days' reddish beard fringed his jaws and every two or three minutes a mist gathered on his glasses so that he had to take them off and polish them with his pocket-handkerchief. The recollection of his confession of the night before was a cause of acute pain to him; the priest had drawn out every ridiculous detail of the affair and in the end had so magnified his sin that he was almost thankful at being afforded a loophole of reparation. The harm was done. What could he do now but marry her or run away? He could not brazen it out. The affair would be sure to be talked of and his employer would be certain to hear of it. Dublin is such a small city: everyone knows everyone else's business. He felt his heart leap warmly in his throat as he heard in his excited imagination old Mr. Leonard calling out in his rasping voice: "Send Mr. Doran here, please."

All his long years of service gone for nothing! All his industry and diligence thrown away! As a young man he had sown his wild oats, of course; he had boasted of his free-thinking and denied the existence of God to his companions in public-houses. But that was all passed and done with...nearly. He still bought a copy of *Reynolds's Newspaper* every week but he attended to his religious duties and for nine-tenths of the year lived a regular life. He had money enough to settle down on; it was not that. But the family would look down on her. First of all there was her disreputable father and then her mother's boarding house was beginning to get a certain fame. He had a notion that he was being had. He could imagine his friends talking of the affair and laughing. She *was* a little vulgar; some times she said "I seen" and "If I had've known." But what would grammar matter if he really loved her? He could not make up his mind whether to like her or despise her for what she had done. Of course he had done it too. His instinct urged him to remain free, not to marry. Once you are married you are done for, it said.

While he was sitting helplessly on the side of the bed in shirt and trousers she tapped lightly at his door and entered. She told him all, that she had made a clean breast of it to her mother and that her mother would speak with him that morning. She cried and threw her arms round his neck, saying:

"O Bob! Bob! What am I to do? What am I to do at all?"

She would put an end to herself, she said.

He comforted her feebly, telling her not to cry, that it would be all right, never fear. He felt against his shirt the agitation of her bosom.

It was not altogether his fault that it had happened. He remembered well, with the curious patient memory of the celibate, the first casual caresses her dress, her breath, her fingers had given him. Then late one night as he was undressing for bed she had tapped at his door, timidly. She wanted to relight her candle at his for hers had been blown out by a gust. It was her bath night. She wore a loose open combing-jacket of printed flannel. Her white instep shone in the opening of her furry slippers and the blood glowed warmly behind her perfumed skin. From her hands and wrists too as she lit and steadied her candle a faint perfume arose.

On nights when he came in very late it was she who warmed up his dinner. He scarcely knew what he was eating feeling her beside him alone, at night, in the sleeping house. And her thoughtfulness! If the night was anyway cold or wet or windy there was sure to be a little tumbler of punch ready for him. Perhaps they could be happy together....

They used to go upstairs together on tiptoe, each with a candle, and on the third landing exchange reluctant goodnights. They used to kiss. He remembered well her eyes, the touch of her hand and his delirium....

But delirium passes. He echoed her phrase, applying it to himself: *"What am I to do?"* The instinct of the celibate warned him to hold back. But the sin was there; even his sense of honour told him that reparation must be made for such a sin.

While he was sitting with her on the side of the bed Mary came to the door and said that the missus wanted to see him in the parlour. He stood up to put on his coat and waistcoat, more helpless than ever. When he was dressed he went over to her to comfort her. It would be all right, never fear. He left her crying on the bed and moaning softly: *"O my God!"*

Going down the stairs his glasses became so dimmed with moisture that he had to take them off and polish them. He longed to ascend through the roof and fly away to another country where he would never hear again of his trouble, and yet a force pushed him downstairs step by step. The implacable faces of his employer and of the Madam stared upon his discomfiture. On the last flight of stairs he passed Jack Mooney who was coming up from the pantry nursing two bottles of Bass. They saluted coldly; and the lover's eyes rested for a second or two on a thick bulldog face and a pair of thick short arms. When he reached the foot of the staircase he glanced up and saw Jack regarding him from the door of the return-room.

Suddenly he remembered the night when one of the music-hall *artistes*, a little blond Londoner, had made a rather free allusion to Polly. The reunion had been almost broken up on account of Jack's violence. Everyone tried to quiet him. The music-hall *artiste*, a little paler than usual, kept smiling and saying that there was no harm meant: but Jack kept shouting at him that if any fellow tried that sort of a game on with his sister he'd bloody well put his teeth down his throat, so he would.

Polly sat for a little time on the side of the bed, crying. Then she dried her eyes and went over to the looking glass. She dipped the end of the towel in the water-jug and refreshed her eyes with the cool water. She looked at herself in profile and readjusted a hairpin above her ear. Then she went back to the bed again and sat at the foot. She regarded the pillows for a long time and the sight of them awakened in her mind secret, amiable memories. She rested the nape of her neck against the cool iron bed-rail and fell into a reverie. There was no longer any perturbation visible on her face.

She waited on patiently, almost cheerfully, without alarm, her memories gradually giving place to hopes and visions of the future. Her hopes and visions were so intricate that she no longer saw the white pillows on which her gaze was fixed or remembered that she was waiting for anything.

At last she heard her mother calling. She started to her feet and ran to the banisters.

"Polly! Polly!"

"Yes, mamma?"

"Come down, dear. Mr. Doran wants to speak to you."

Then she remembered what she had been waiting for.

A Voice from the Dead (A Monologue)

By Mary Lavin

The Misses Coniffe, not being married, were unsparing of their services to the Ladies Altar Society of Castlerampart, the town of their birth. It was they who undertook the laundering of altar linens, communion cloths and surplices, the polishing of the brass candelabra and altar vases, as well as the disposal of withered flowers, ferns and pot plants. They also undertook the recruitment of fresh flowers from all gardens in the town other than their own, which understandably produced few blooms. However, in consequence of this dedication, Miss Theresa and her sister Sara had come to enjoy a privilege previously accorded only to old Luke Humphries, the sacristan, the privilege of staying behind in the chapel after evening devotions when the rest of the congregation had been herded out into the chapel yard and the votive candles quenched. Then, the chapel door firmly bolted, Miss Theresa withdrew to the sacristy, there to attend to the numerous tasks awaiting her, medals to be sewn to Confirmation rosettes, candle-grease to be removed from the various articles, rents to be repaired in sodality banners. Sara, on the other hand, remained in the body of the chapel to tiptoe about with old Luke, peering under kneelers and pews in search of any mortuary cards, rosary beads or other pious items let fall by the religious in the fervour of prayer. Such items if found were, by tradition, placed on the ledge of the nearest window, where they lay until such time as they were espied, identified and repossessed by their owners.

Except for the occasional grating noise of a pew being straightened, a respectful silence was observed by all. However, one evening in early Spring, a second after the doors were bolted, there was a loud and sudden rapping on a side-aisle door, and a peremptory voice called out for admittance.

"Let me in, Luke Humphries! Let me in! Do you hear? It's me, Mrs. Mulloy." To the elder Miss Coniffe, in the sacristy, the voice was sufficiently indistinct to be ignored, and assuming that old Luke would turn a deaf ear to the unseemly clamour, she went on with her stitching. But in the darkening body of the church Mrs. Mulloy's every word was heard with the compulsive force of a voice from the pulpit. "Listen to me, Luke Humphries. I've lost my cousin Lottie's mortuary card. It must have fallen out of my prayer book. Let me in at once. I want to look for it."

Sara, who happened to be standing just under the sanctuary lamp, in the pool of its red light, could only marvel that Mrs. Mulloy had detected so quickly the loss of one mortuary card among the hundreds that swelled her prayer book to the size of another woman's handbag. "I'll look for it, Luke?" Sara whispered. "When I find it, you can hand it out to her?" But Luke, having feigned deafness to the clamour of Mrs. Mulloy, could hardly betray that he had heard Miss Sara's timid whisper. Instead he stomped over to a confessional box and began to open and close the doors, for no good reason that Sara could see.

The voice came again.

"The poor soul would turn in her grave if she thought I'd left my only memento of her lying all night on the window-ledge of a cold, empty church!"

"Oh, Luke," Sara wailed so piteously Luke stomped back and opened up the great oak door.

Next minute Mrs. Mulloy was sailing down the centre aisle towards the pew she habitually occupied, and standing up on the seat, she groped along the window ledge. "Don't tell me it's not there," she cried, in stricken tones, which however, gave way to loud thanksgivings as, grovelling on her hands and knees, she recovered her lost property a mortuary card lavishly edged with black paper lace, and so monumental in size it had had to be folded in two to fit into a prayer book. "I would not have wished for all the world to lose it—because of a solemn promise I made to Lottie" she said, addressing herself to Sara, who, unlike Luke, had lacked the presence of mind to vanish. Then, as a draught caused the sanctuary light to sway and its ruby rays to tremble, Mrs. Mulloy lowered her voice, though it was not certain whether this was in deference to the Perpetual Presence or in awe of her own promise to the dead. She held up the card. "The strange thing is that I missed it before I got as far as the chapel gates. And I want to tell you, Sara, there is very little doubt in my mind that, this night, I have been in the presence of a force beyond my own poor earthly power to fathom." Here, without further preamble, she launched into her story. "I was just about to leave the chapel yard, and go about my business as I've done all my life, when I noticed that the chapel gates, and for that matter the chapel railings as well, were shockingly in need of a coat of paint. Now, considering it must be seven years since they were painted, isn't it a strange thing it was on this night of all others I noticed the condition of those gates? And from noticing it, I naturally went on to thinking it our duty as parishioners to point out to Father Drew what ought to be done, the person undertaking this duty not, of course, being myself, seeing as how my daughter is married to a painter. I know only too well, and so do you, Sara, the odd constructions that can be put on an innocent word in this town. Indeed some of us might have been better to have had our mouth sewn up, a thing my own mother was always threatening to get done to me when I was a child—God rest her soul—as well as that of Lottie." Pausing to cross herself, Mrs. Mulloy here permitted herself a slight digression. "Though mind you, Sara, when it comes to putting in a word in praise of our own, more can often times be lost than gained, by refraining. If we don't praise them, are there many likely to praise them for us?" She sadly shook her head. "Few. Very few. Furthermore, I trust you won't mind my saying this, Sara, but if your own mother, who is dead and gone now with Lottie and the rest, God grant eternal peace to all their souls, if your mother had not been so behind-hand in coming forward with a hint, in certain well-chosen quarters, of the fortune that you and your sisters would inherit—I mean before it was too late—there's no knowing but you and Theresa might both be married now, and your money not lying in a bank useless to everyone—including yourselves. Not but I've heard whispers, Sara, that there won't be much of that fortune left if your young sister Lily's husband is let get his hands on it. That, of course, is no business of mine. And, I will say this, he's a good-looking man. Lily was lucky to collar him. Don't we all know it's better for a woman to marry any sort of man, than no man at all. Are you listening to me, Sara?"

"You were telling me about your cousin Lottie," Sara said faintly.

"Ah, yes, poor Lottie. The minute I noticed the condition of those gates—"

"Yes? What happened?" Sara asked less faintly.

"I am trying to tell you, Sara. I wish you'd stop interrupting me," Mrs. Mulloy said. "When I saw the rust on those gates, and decided something should be done about the matter, I got to thinking how bright and shiny they used to be when I was a child. In those days, the chapel and the chapel-yard were considered the safest places for children to play. On wet days we ran about inside the chapel, playing hide and seek in the confessional boxes and behind the statues. On fine days we stayed outside in the chapel-yard, jumping over the graves, or chasing an odd rat, with no one to complain about us shrieking and screaming. You realise of course, Sara, that I'm not speaking of the new cemetery? I never approved of that new place being opened so far outside of town. To be honest I never thought people would permit themselves to be put down in it. I have to allow though that it's well populated now. It will soon be as overcrowded as the old place, but at least here the plots are roomy, with plenty of space for all the family. Even distant connections can be fitted in, if they have no place of their own to go. We children knew the name of every living soul under the sod here, because, when we'd get tired of playing we used to pull up fistfuls of grass and rub the moss off the headstones to show up the lettering. We kept the place as clean as our own back yards. The older people used to laugh at us—all except Lottie. When Lottie passed and saw us cleaning up a grave she used to call me over and whisper to me that, after she was dead, if a bird should happen to fall his dirty droppings on her grave-stone she hoped I'd wipe off the mess. Poor Lottie, she was always brooding over her final end, certain each moment would be her last. She often brought me into her house to show me the shroud she'd bought a few days after she married Matty. You

remember Matty? The Lord have mercy on him too, poor man.
From the start Matty took a poor view of her purchase. He
hated the sight of that shroud. In fact, Sara, between ourselves,
he went on a batter every time she took it out to air it, which she
did regularly on a fine Spring day like today. She used to throw
it over a bush in the garden to take out the creases and make
sure that moths would not consume it before its time. Matty
couldn't really be blamed for his carry-on, I suppose, seeing he
was a good ten years older than Lottie, and seeing they didn't
get on too well together from the start. Though, mind you,
some people thought he ought to have been glad of a reminder
of the day she'd take her departure, which they felt might be
sooner than you'd have believed from the look of her, a stout
woman with a good, strong colour in her face. But no! Matty
took a poor view of her preparations for the next world. And
such preparations! The shroud was only the beginning. The
next thing she did was get a cardboard box fitted up with all the
necessities for Extreme Unction in case of her call coming when
there was no one around who knew the lay-out of the house.
She had the oil and the blessed candle, the crucifix, the rosary
beads and the bottle of holy water, as well as a square of linen as
stiff as a board for under her chin when she'd be getting
communion. Not to mention a towel and a bowl for water for
the priest to wash his hands when all would be over. She was
bent on ordering her coffin too, I believe, and storing it under
the stairs, but Matty put his foot down on the coffin. Although
again you'd think he'd welcome the sight of it coming into the
house, to put him in mind of the day he'd be shouldering it out
again. But he had a long wait, God help him. Poor Lottie, in
spite of her prophecies, wasn't called to her reward for thirty-
seven years, in spite of having her bag packed, as you might put
it. And by that time the very people who used to be tittering at
her in her lifetime had the mortification of seeing better grave-
cloths on the corpse than they had on their own beds, and better
worsted in her shroud than in the clothes on their own backs.
But that was nothing. When they opened her closet what did
they find but a stack of mortuary cards, all printed with her
name and her picture, as nice a picture as she'd ever had taken,
when she was a young girl, standing by a rosebush in her garden

at home before she ever laid eyes on Matty, much less married
him. Mrs. Mulloy produced a card. Just look at that. The best of
paper! And where would you get paper lace now, except
perhaps on doyleys, or Valentines, and *they're* not black. There's
no date on it, of course, but Lottie was never over-anxious to
disclose her age. Anyway, I recall her saying once that such
details didn't matter. All that mattered was to get as many
indulgenced prayers as possible on to a card—as many as it
could hold—each prayer carrying nothing less than three
hundred days' indulgence. She never could make any sense—
and neither could I—of people wasting their time saying
prayers that earned them only a hundred days, when there were
other prayers the same length that could get them three
hundred. She was always a great one for good value. She had all
the envelopes addressed and stamped ready to be dropped in
the post. I suppose she wanted to make sure they'd be sent to
those she could rely on for prayers. The only flaw in the poor
creature's plan was that most of those to whom the envelopes
were addressed were dead long before herself, and those
envelopes had to be thrown in the fire. Matty, I'm glad to say,
had the wit to steam off the stamps, and I was given to
understand he sold them for a nice penny. The rest of us got the
shock of our lives when we got our card in the handwriting of
the corpse we'd just seen coffined. I have to tell you, Sara, there
was a great commotion in some houses when the postman
delivered the cards. One particular person, whose name cannot
be revealed because there was talk at the time of a law case being
taken against poor Matty, but this particular person, who was ill
at the time, hadn't been told that Lottie was no more, and this
person took such a turn at the sight of a card in the hand of the
corpse, she fell in a faint and hit her head off the brass bed-head
in her own room. She was buried the day after Lottie. Poor
Lottie! She didn't get many prayers from that source. But of
course Lottie couldn't have held it against that person like she
could have held it against me, if I failed her. You see, Lottie
made me give my solemn promise never to look at that
mortuary card, without saying a prayer for her immortal soul.
And I kept that promise faithfully up until yesterday, when the
prayer book I've had all my life finally fell apart, and I had to

buy a new one. Things not being done nowadays on the same scale as in Lottie's day, my new prayer book is in no way to be compared with my old one. Lottie's card wouldn't fit into it without me folding it in two, as you can see. Unfortunately, and in order to protect her photograph, I folded it so the picture was on the inside, which meant of course that Lottie could not, as you might say, keep her eye on me. And I didn't always know it was Lottie I was looking at when I turned the page, and so if I'd left it sticking out, the edges would have frayed away to nothing, but Lottie would have fared better, and not have been put to such lengths as she was tonight to communicate with me. You are of course aware, Sara, of what I'm driving at? Ever since I bought the new prayer book, poor Lottie must have been trying to get in touch with me. She must have known I'd break my promise, which I did! But Lottie was always a determined woman. It must have been her who saw to it that my prayer book fell on the floor tonight and the contents were strewn about, and all this without me being nudged or jostled by anyone. Then when I picked them all up, as I thought I had done, unbeknownst to me I had left Lottie's card behind. Then when devotions ended and Luke began quenching the candles— although it can't be said I'm the first to jump up when the priest leaves the altar—I have to admit to having a sensitive nose and I can't stand the smell of guttering-out candles, and I went out of the chapel as quietly as I could and poor Lottie would not have got a prayer out of me from that time until such time as Father Drew takes it into his head to have the church decorated, which won't be for many a day, I'd be bound, him being a bit of a miser, priest or no priest. But lo and behold, when I reached the chapel gates and saw the rust on them, I was put in mind of how spick and span they used to be when I was a child. And from that I was put in mind of how we used to play in the chapel-yard. Of course, from that, it was only a hop, a step and a jump to remembering the promise Lottie extracted from me. There and then I stopped dead in my tracks in tending to fold her mortuary card the other way around with the face looking at me. And then what? Well, I shouldn't have to tell you! But I will. I opened the prayer book and saw at once there was no sign of Lottie's card. That was when I ran back and banged on the door to be let in to look for it. You know the rest? There it was on the floor. Did you ever hear anything stranger than that? Oh, some say the dead are dead. But after tonight I'll never be persuaded that they haven't a way of getting through to us if they are determined on it."

Suddenly Mrs. Mulloy stopped short. "Good Heavens, I still haven't said a prayer for her. Excuse me Sara!" Going down on one knee she speedily dispatched her duty to the dead and scrambled to her feet again. And, realising the time she'd wasted on the one person in the town who had little or no conversation with which to repay the prodigality of those who had, after a brisk good night to Sara, she let herself out into the fresh, night air.

A Rest and a Change

By Honor Tracy

The view across the bay to the soft blue hills beyond was one
of the finest in Ireland. Traveled people would often say it was
one of the finest in Europe, if not in the world. They stopped
their motor-cars on the excellent road provided by the government and got out to enjoy it better. In their rapture, they would
call to anyone of the country who happened to pass.

"A wonderful place you have!"

"D'ye think so?" The reply was always the same, and the
speaker never looked round. Sometimes, when it was a man, he
spat.

"Marvelous! A fairyland! Oh, you're lucky!"

"D'ye think so?"

The people who lived on the shores of the bay were mostly
old or very young. The rest were there because they had small
children or ailing parents to mind. These, in the local expression, were "stuck." Everyone who could went to work in
England, sending home money week by week, returning once in
the year to help with the turf, the potatoes, or the hay. In the
summer months, you often saw the old ones crying by the
roadside, and you knew the morning bus had taken their sons
and daughters off.

Not one had a good word for the country; yet all were
mysteriously bound to it. They wished their children to grow up
here, and themselves came back to die; out-and-out emigration
was rare. If one was killed abroad, his mates collected to send
the body home, and the people walked miles inland to meet the
coffin on its journey from Dublin. They never talked of their
feelings or complained of their lives, but when tourists prattled
to them of luck, they were angry.

Not every traveler flitted straight through. Artists would come to paint, and students spent weeks in search of the Gaelic way of life. These, who bought butter and eggs and milk for cash as well as providing themes for talk, were welcome. Apart from wakes and funerals, the one diversion the people had was the endless talk, talk, talk that went on steady as August rain; if somebody only crossed the road, they had to go into his reasons for it.

Now they had a visitor that no one could fathom at all. He was English but did not look it, with a mane of kinky white hair and eyes like two black plums with purple shadows round them. His name was Julius Fountain, and shoals of letters came for him every day. Young Paddy Doyle said his motor-car was a Rolls-Bentley and cost three thousand pounds—there was little Paddy didn't know. He just drove up in it one day and inquired for an empty cottage to rent, with only the barest of furnishing. Everything else he had brought, even pots and pans, like a tinker. Niall Tuohy's cabin was going since Niall died, and this, for a staggering sum, Niall's brother offered to let. Mr. Fountain declared himself enchanted.

When the people could bear the mystery no longer, they charged the postman to make inquiries.

"You never were here before," Milo began, delicately feeling his way.

"No," Mr. Fountain agreed. His manner was cordial enough, but his voice sounded tired. "I go somewhere new every year, for a rest and a change. Above all, for a change." And he smiled in a peculiar way he had, a smile for himself alone.

"You'll be working hard at home, I dare say."

Mr. Fountain saw into Milo's mind and hastened to inform him, "Very much so. I have a business in London, with my brother," he said. "We buy diamonds and sell them."

"Diamonds, God help us!" Milo was awestruck. "You'd be looking at Inish Bay a while before you found diamonds there."

Mr. Fountain smiled again. "Diamonds are not what I want from all of you." He put out a smooth, pale hand with a Greek intaglio ring on the little finger and took his letters. "A telegram, ah. I expected one yesterday."

"And 'twas yesterday that this came," said Milo with pride. "But we thought we should rest it, after it traveled the long way from New York."

"A decent, poor, simple man," he reported back to his friends.

"I wonder now," he opened next day, primed with their further instructions, "a gentleman like yourself would ever hear of a place like this one."

Mr. Fountain responded as helpfully as before. "I read a piece about it by your Irish writer Mat O'Sullivan," he said.

"That scoundrel, is it?" exclaimed Milo. No Inish man could bear to think of O'Sullivan. "'Twas on all the Dublin papers and the radio and TV itself how he took our name away!"

The writing fellow, the city slicker, came there with his elegant clothes and his oily manners to make money instead of spending it. Such tales as they spun him! They pulled his leg till it might nearly come off. And the cram of it was how they directed him into a bog and stung him nicely after, when they salvaged his car. It was their pleasure and pride to cheat the men of the city. It showed they were quicker and sharper than people of money or class; it fed their self-esteem and assuaged their envy a little. But Mat O'Sullivan—don't mind his solemn face and professions of gratitude, he hadn't been fooled a minute. Off he went and wrote them up in a foreign paper, putting their names in and all for the world to laugh at. The very thought of it set them writhing still.

"But he made you appear so charming," Mr. Fountain drawled with his smile.

"Arrah, he'd best not show himself here again."

When the men of Inish heard of this they held a council of war. In the evening, old Ted Doyle, acknowledged the master mind, dressed in his Sunday black and paid a call. He walked straight in with his hat on his head and, seating himself by the fire, inquired ceremoniously after the Englishman's health.

Mr. Fountain had rods and lines strewn over the floor and seemed glad of the visit. "You can probably help me," he said in his weary voice. "How is the fishing here? I very much want to try it."

There was a pause of about five seconds while Doyle laid and developed a plan. "Round here it's no good at all, then," he said. "The stream do all be fished out. But a small way off there's a lough that's teeming. You'll want a permit, mind you; it belongs to his lordship. But we'll manage it for you."

"I'm sure you are very good."

"And when we have you the permit fixed, me son will run you to the lough in the old jalopy I have," Doyle went on. "You'd never risk your car on our mountain roads."

"Now, isn't your son called Paddy?" Mr. Fountain asked, looking amused. "For I think you must be Mr. Edward Doyle."

"He is. I am." Doyle remembered O'Sullivan's remarks about him and spoke abruptly. "I'll say goodnight to you, so. His lordship's factor's above, and we must beg the permit for you. There'll be a small, little sum to pay."

Alone in the cottage Mr. Julius Fountain smiled.

In Twomey's that night, they had an uproarious time of it, faking a permit for the phantom rights of the imaginary earl. The schoolmaster drafted it in Irish and Twomey, whose bar was the Post Office too, put the postmark at the top and, to make it legally watertight, a five-shilling stamp at the foot. Then Doyle wrote "Lord Clare" with a flourish across the stamp and early next morning sent Paddy up with the finished article. Mr. Fountain got into the ancient car, from which the windscreen was missing, and the pair of them bounced and rattled away to the lough.

The lough was just the other side of the hill, and Mr. Fountain could have reached it on foot in half an hour. To drive him over the country first at a shilling the mile was Paddy's own unaided idea.

"A great boy, a great boy surely," Doyle murmured when they told him of this, and tears of love and pride came into his eyes.

Mr. Fountain went fishing every day after that and once caught three little trout. "Take care of these, won't you my dear?" he said to Mary Kilbane when she came in to cook his supper. "They cost nine pounds, seventeen shillings, and sixpence each."

Mary talked to her mother that night about the English fellow's creepy smile.

A spell of dry weather was setting in, and the people took the chance of cutting and making the hay. Only Doyle left his to stand, risking the year's crop so Paddy was free while Mr. Fountain wanted him. These days, the father was sunk in beautiful dreams. Paddy was grown now and, once the hay was saved, would have to cross the water to work with the rest. He would have to join one of the Irish gangs that labored on building sites or mended roads—unless a man of influence would help him to better things. But such a man was there on the spot, the very same fool that Paddy was after stinging and bleeding! The sheer knavery of it set his peasant mind aglow.

On the evening before Mr. Fountain left, Doyle washed and shaved and put on his Sunday clothes. Once in the cottage, he even took off his hat, a thing so rarely done that his upper forehead was pale like a mackerel's belly. With the boy's future at stake, he was tongue-tied, ill at ease, and the Englishman did nothing to help him. He was holding the fake permit and smiling over it in what, to Doyle's guilty mind, seemed an offensively pointed way. At last, sighing, he folded it with tender care and put it away in his wallet and urbanely inquired what he might do for Mr. Doyle.

"I'm hoping, sir, our Paddy didn't annoy you?" the father mumbled.

"Dear me, no," Mr. Fountain replied. His manner tonight was strange, he was offhand, abstracted, as if in spirit he had left Inish behind already. "On the contrary, he made the holiday for me. I'm only so sorry it has to end."

The gratified parent took heart at these words. "He'll be away to England now, and him seventeen," he said eagerly. "There's no work at all for the young ones here, not a tap. At election time, the deputy fellas come running to promise the moon and the stars, but that's the last of it once they're in."

"Politicians are the same everywhere," Mr. Fountain remarked. He took a letter from a pile on the table and began reading it as if no one else were there.

"He'll have to go for a common laborer," Doyle went on, raising his voice a little. "Him, that's the brightest in the land!"

"I should think he will make his way. He is clever enough, all right."

Mr. Fountain said this like a man putting the final word to a discussion of little importance. He finished reading the letter and tore it up. Then he got to his feet and stared about the room, as people with much on hand will do when trying to make a start. Doyle felt the dismissal implied and inwardly seethed with anger.

"I said to the mother, if you couldn't give him a bit of a hand?" he pleaded roughly. "If you couldn't take him to London now, with yourself? With the head he has on him, he'd make a fortune for you!"

Mr. Fountain looked at him absently, as if wondering who he was. Then a spark of merriment flickered in the languid eyes and went out. "You are not serious, I imagine," he replied, sitting down to his papers again.

"Why wouldn't I be?" Doyle was panting a little now.

The Englishman read and destroyed more letters before exerting himself to reply. "I beg your pardon," he murmured. "I thought you were joking."

"And isn't he good enough for you, then?" cried Doyle, trembling with passion. "Hasn't he brains as good as your own?"

The mortification, the disappointment were greater than he could bear. Paddy's clothes were packed up ready to go, and now this simpleton, this idiot, the butt and laughing-stock of them all, dared to reject him! Throwing caution to the winds he yelled, "He'd make a ring round the London men, all the same!"

Mr. Fountain heaved a sigh. "That is just it," he said. Now he turned from the raging peasant and looked through the cracked, little window to the wild, blue mountains beyond the bay. He was thinking ruefully of all the years of honest transactions, of scruple, of probity, that had gone to make Fountain & Fountain the leading small firm of the world: the dull, barren, wasting years that had left him old before his time.

"Your son was a tonic to me," he said kindly, as man to man. "It was a real pleasure to meet him. But, you see, he is so immensely clever. To do any good in diamonds, alas, one has to be very stupid indeed."

Doyle rushed from the cottage, swearing and stamping and calling to heaven to avenge his wrongs.

Mr. Fountain continued to sort out his correspondence, looking tired and sad. Late in the evening he went for a last little walk, over the hill to Paddy's lough. It was bright and heavy like a pool of silver, the mountains were black, a full yellow moon rode over the sea. A long while he stood there, resting his eyes on the scene and smiling his peculiar smile as if in a parting benediction. Then he strolled back to the cottage again and sat by the fire till it died.

Death in Jerusalem

By William Trevor

"Till then," Father Paul said, leaning out of the train window. "Till Jerusalem, Francis."

"Please God, Paul." As he spoke the Dublin train began to move and his brother waved from the window and he waved back, a modest figure on the platform. Everyone said Francis might have been a priest as well, meaning that Francis's quietness and meditative disposition had an air of the cloister about them. But Francis contented himself with the running of Daly's hardware business, which his mother had run until she was too old for it. "Are we game for the Holy Land next year?" Father Paul had asked that July. "Will we go together, Francis?" He had brushed aside all Francis's protestations, all attempts to explain that the shop could not be left, that their mother would be confused by the absence of Francis from the house. Rumbustiously he'd pointed out that there was their sister Kitty, who was in charge of the household of which Francis and their mother were part and whose husband, Myles, could surely be trusted to look after the shop for a single fortnight. For thirty years, ever since he was seven, Francis had wanted to go to the Holy Land. He had savings which he'd never spent a penny of: you couldn't take them with you, Father Paul had more than once stated that July.

On the platform Francis watched until the train could no longer be seen, his thoughts still with his brother. The priest's ruddy countenance smiled again behind cigarette smoke; his bulk remained impressive in his clerical clothes, the collar pinching the flesh of his neck, his black shoes scrupulously polished. There were freckles on the backs of his large, strong hands; he had a fine head of hair, grey and crinkly. In an hour and a half's time the train would creep into Dublin, and he'd take a taxi. He'd spend a night in the Gresham Hotel, probably falling in with another priest, having a drink or two, maybe playing a game of bridge after his meal. That was his brother's way and always had been—an extravagant, easy kind of way, full of smiles and good humour. It was what had taken him to America and made him successful there. In order to raise money for the church that he and Father Steigmuller intended to build before 1980 he took parties of the well-to-do from San Francisco to Rome and Florence, to Chartres and Seville and the Holy Land. He was good at raising money, not just for the church but for the boys' home of which he was president, and for the Hospital of Our Saviour, and for St. Mary's Old People's Home on the west side of the city. But every July he flew back to Ireland, to the town in Co. Tipperary where his mother and brother and sister still lived. He stayed in the house above the shop which he might have inherited himself on the death of his father, which he'd rejected in favour of the religious life. Mrs. Daly was eighty now. In the shop she sat silently behind the counter, in a corner by the chicken-wire, wearing only clothes that were black. In the evenings she sat with Francis in the lace-curtained sitting-room, while the rest of the family occupied the kitchen. It was for her sake most of all that Father Paul made the journey every summer, considering it his duty.

Walking back to the town from the station, Francis was aware that he was missing his brother. Father Paul was fourteen years older and in childhood had often taken the place of their father, who had died when Francis was five. His brother had possessed an envied strength and knowledge; he'd been a hero, quite often worshipped, an example of success. In later life he had become an example of generosity as well: ten years ago he'd taken their mother to Rome, and their sister Kitty and her husband two years later; he'd paid the expenses when their sister Edna had gone to Canada; he'd assisted two nephews to make a start in America. In childhood Francis hadn't possessed his brother's healthy freckled face, just as in middle age he didn't have his ruddy complexion and his stoutness and his easiness with people. Francis was slight, his sandy hair receding, his face rather pale. His breathing was sometimes laboured because of wheeziness in the chest. In the ironmonger's shop he wore a brown cotton coat.

"Hullo, Mr. Daly," a woman said to him in the main street of the town. "Father Paul's gone off, has he?"

"Yes, he's gone again."

"I'll pray for his journey so," the woman promised, and Francis thanked her.

A year went by. In San Francisco another wing of the boys' home was completed, another target was reached in Father Paul and Father Steigmuller's fund for the church they planned to have built by 1980. In the town in Co. Tipperary there were baptisms and burial services and First Communions. Old Loughlin, a farmer from Bansha, died in Flynn's grocery and bar, having gone there to celebrate a good price he'd got for a heifer. Clancy, from behind the counter in Doran's drapery, married Maureen Talbot; Mr. Nolan's plasterer married Miss Driscoll; Johneen Lynch married Seamus in the chip shop, under pressure from her family to do so. A local horse, from the stables on the Limerick road, was said to be an entry for the Fairyhouse Grand National, but it turned out not to be true. Every evening of that year Francis sat with his mother in the lace-curtained sitting-room above the shop. Every weekday she sat in her corner by the chicken-wire, watching while he counted out screws and weighed staples, or advised about yard brushes or tap-washers. Occasionally, on a Saturday, he visited the three Christian Brothers who lodged with Mrs. Shea and afterwards he'd tell his mother about how the authority was slipping these days from the nuns and the Christian Brothers, and how Mrs. Shea's elderly maid, Agnes, couldn't see to cook the food any more. His mother would nod and hardly ever speak. When he told a joke—what young Hogan had said when he'd found a nail in his egg or how Agnes had put mint sauce into a jug with milk in it—she never laughed and looked at him in surprise when he laughed himself. But Dr. Grady said it was best to keep her cheered up.

All during that year Francis talked to her about his forthcoming visit to the Holy Land, endeavouring to make her understand that for a fortnight next spring he would be away from the house and the shop. He'd been away before for odd days, but that was when she'd been younger. He used to visit an aunt in Tralee, but three years ago the aunt had died and he hadn't left the town since.

Francis and his mother had always been close. Before his birth two daughters had died in infancy, and his very survival had often struck Mrs. Daly as a gift. He had always been her favourite, the one among her children whom she often considered least able to stand on his own two feet. It was just like Paul to have gone blustering off to San Francisco instead of remaining in Co. Tipperary. It was just like Kitty to have married a useless man. "There's not a girl in the town who'd touch him," she'd said to her daughter at the time, but Kitty had been headstrong and adamant, and there was Myles now, doing nothing whatsoever except cleaning other people's windows for a pittance and placing bets in Donovan's the turf accountant's. It was the shop and the arrangement Kitty had with Francis and her mother that kept her and the children going, three of whom had already left the town, which in Mrs. Daly's opinion they mightn't have done if they'd had a better type of father. Mrs. Daly often wondered what her own two babies who'd died might have grown up into, and imagined they might have been like Francis, about whom she'd never had a moment's worry. Not in a million years would he give you the feeling that he was too big for his boots, like Paul sometimes did with his lavishness and his big talk of America. He wasn't silly like Kitty, or so sinful you couldn't forgive him, like you couldn't forgive Edna, even though she was dead and buried in Toronto.

Francis understood how his mother felt about the family. She'd had a hard life, left a widow early on, trying to do the best she could for everyone. In turn he did his best to compensate for the struggles and disappointments she'd suffered, cheering her in the evenings while Kitty and Myles and the youngest of their children watched the television in the kitchen. His mother had ignored the existence of Myles for ten years, ever since the day he'd taken money out of the till to pick up the odds on Gusty Spirit at Phoenix Park. And although Francis got on well enough with Myles he quite understood that there should be a long aftermath to that day. There'd been a terrible row in the kitchen, Kitty screaming at Myles and Myles telling lies and Francis trying to keep them calm, saying they'd give the old woman a heart attack.

She didn't like upsets of any kind, so all during the year before he was to visit the Holy Land Francis read the New Testament to her in order to prepare her. He talked to her about Bethlehem and Nazareth and the miracle of the loaves and fishes and all the other miracles. She kept nodding, but he often wondered if she didn't assume he was just casually referring to episodes in the Bible. As a child he had listened to such talk himself, with awe and fascination, imagining the walking on the water and the temptation in the wilderness. He had imagined the cross carried to Calvary, and the rock rolled back from the tomb, and the rising from the dead on the third day. That he was now to walk in such places seemed extraordinary to him, and he wished his mother was younger so that she could appreciate his good fortune and share it with him when she received the postcards he intended, every day, to send her. But her eyes seemed always to tell him that he was making a mistake, that somehow he was making a fool of himself by doing such a showy thing as going to the Holy Land. *I have the entire itinerary mapped out,* his brother wrote from San Francisco. *There's nothing we'll miss.*

It was the first time Francis had been in an aeroplane. He flew by Aer Lingus from Dublin to London and then changed to an El Al flight to Tel Aviv. He was nervous and he found it exhausting. All the time he seemed to be eating, and it was strange being among so many people he didn't know. "You will taste honey such as never before," an Israeli businessman in the seat next to his assured him. "And Galilean figs. Make certain to taste Galilean figs." Make certain too, the businessman went on, to experience Jerusalem by night and in the early dawn. He urged Francis to see places he had never heard of, the Yad Va-Shem, the treasures of the Shrine of the Book. He urged him to honour the martyrs of Masada and to learn a few words of Hebrew as a token of respect. He told him of a shop where he could buy mementoes and warned him against Arab street traders.

"The hard man, how are you?" Father Paul said at Tel Aviv airport, having flown in from San Francisco the day before. Father Paul had had a drink or two and he suggested another when they arrived at the Plaza Hotel in Jerusalem. It was half-past nine in the evening. "A quick little nightcap," Father Paul insisted, "and then hop into bed with you, Francis." They sat in an enormous open lounge with low, round tables and square modern armchairs. Father Paul said it was the bar.

They had said what had to be said in the car from Tel Aviv to Jerusalem. Father Paul had asked about their mother, and Kitty and Myles. He'd asked about other people in the town, old Canon Mahon and Sergeant Malone. He and Father Steigmuller had had a great year of it, he reported: as well as everything else, the boys' home had turned out two tip-top footballers. "We'll start on a tour at half-nine in the morning," he said. "I'll be sitting having breakfast at eight."

Francis went to bed and Father Paul ordered another whisky, with ice. To his great disappointment there was no Irish whisky in the hotel so he'd had to content himself with Haig. He fell into conversation with an American couple, making them promise that if they were ever in Ireland they wouldn't miss Co. Tipperary. At eleven o'clock the barman said he was wanted at the reception desk and when Father Paul went there and announced himself he was given a message in an envelope. It was a telegram that had come, the girl said in poor English. Then she shook her head, saying it was a telex. He opened the envelope and learnt that Mrs. Daly had died.

Francis fell asleep immediately and dreamed that he was a boy again, out fishing with a friend whom he couldn't now identify.

On the telephone Father Paul ordered whisky and ice to be brought to his room. Before drinking it he took his jacket off and knelt by his bed to pray for his mother's salvation. When he'd completed the prayers he walked slowly up and down the length of the room, occasionally sipping at his whisky. He argued with himself and finally arrived at a decision.

For breakfast they had scrambled eggs that looked like yellow ice cream, and orange juice that was delicious. Francis wondered about bacon, but Father Paul explained that bacon was not readily available in Israel.

"Did you sleep all right?" Father Paul enquired. "Did you have the jet-lag?"

"Jet-lag?"

"A tiredness you get after jet flights. It'd knock you out for days."

"Ah, I slept great, Paul."

"Good man."

They lingered over breakfast. Father Paul reported a little more of what had happened in his parish during the year, in particular about the two young footballers from the boys' home. Francis told about the decline in the cooking at Mrs. Shea's boarding-house, as related to him by the three Christian Brothers. "I have a car laid on," Father Paul said, and twenty minutes later they walked out into the Jerusalem sunshine.

The hired car stopped on the way to the walls of the old city. It drew into a lay-by at Father Paul's request and the two men got out and looked across a wide valley dotted with houses and olive trees. A road curled along the distant slope opposite. "The Mount of Olives," Father Paul said. "And that's the road to Jericho." He pointed more particularly. "You see that group of eight big olives? Just off the road, where the church is?"

Francis thought he did, but was not sure. There were so many olive trees, and more than one church. He glanced at his brother's pointing finger and followed its direction with his glance.

"The Garden of Gethsemane," Father Paul said.

Francis did not say anything. He continued to gaze at the distant church, with the clump of olive trees beside it. Wild flowers were profuse on the slopes of the valley, smears of orange and blue on the land that looked poor. Two Arab women herded goats.

"Could we see it closer?" he asked, and his brother said that definitely they would. They returned to the waiting car and Father Paul ordered it to the Gate of St. Stephen.

Tourists heavy with cameras thronged the Via Dolorosa. Brown, bare-foot children asked for alms. Stall-keepers pressed their different wares, cotton dresses, metal-ware, mementoes, sacred goods. "Get out of the way," Father Paul kept saying to them, genially laughing to show he wasn't being abrupt. Francis wanted to stand still and close his eyes, to visualise for a moment the carrying of the Cross. But the ceremony of the Stations, familiar to him for as long as he could remember, was unreal. Try as he would, Christ's journey refused to enter his imagination, and his own plain church seemed closer to the heart of the matter than the noisy lane he was now being jostled on. "God damn it, of course it's genuine," an angry American voice proclaimed, in reply to a shriller voice which insisted that cheating had taken place. The voices argued about a piece of wood, neat beneath plastic in a little box, a sample or not of the cross that had been carried.

They arrived at the Church of the Holy Sepulchre, and at the Chapel of the Nailing to the Cross, where they prayed. They passed through the Chapel of the Angel, to the tomb of Christ. Nobody spoke in the marble cell, but when they left the church Francis overheard a quiet man with spectacles saying it was unlikely that a body would have been buried within the walls of the city. They walked to Hezekiah's Pool and out of the old city at the Jaffa Gate, where their hired car was waiting for them. "Are you peckish?" Father Paul asked, and although Francis said he wasn't they returned to the hotel.

Delay funeral till Monday was the telegram Father Paul had sent. There was an early flight on Sunday, in time for an afternoon one from London to Dublin. With luck there'd be a late train on Sunday evening and if there wasn't they'd have to fix a car. Today was Tuesday. It would give them four and a half days. *Funeral eleven Monday* the telegram at the reception desk now confirmed. "Ah, isn't that great?" he said to himself, bundling the telegram up.

"Will we have a small one?" he suggested in the open area that was the bar. "Or better still a big one." He laughed. He was in good spirits in spite of the death that had taken place. He gestured at the barman, wagging his head and smiling jovially.

His face had reddened in the morning sun; there were specks of sweat on his forehead and his nose. "Bethlehem this afternoon," he laid down. "Unless the jet-lag...?"

"I haven't got the jet-lag."

In the Nativity Boutique Francis bought for his mother a small metal plate with a fish on it. He had stood for a moment, scarcely able to believe it, on the spot where the manger had been, in the Church of the Nativity. As in the Via Dolorosa it had been difficult to rid the imagination of the surroundings that now were present, of the exotic Greek Orthodox trappings, the foreign-looking priests, the oriental smell. Gold, frankincense and myrrh, he'd kept thinking, for somehow the church seemed more the church of the kings than of Joseph and Mary and their child. Afterwards they returned to Jerusalem, to the Tomb of the Virgin and the Garden of Gethsemane. "It could have been anywhere," he heard the quiet, bespectacled sceptic remarking in Gethsemane. "They're only guessing."

Father Paul rested in the late afternoon, lying down on his bed with his jacket off. He slept from half-past five until a quarter-past seven and awoke refreshed. He picked up the telephone and asked for whisky and ice to be brought up and when it arrived he undressed and had a bath, relaxing in the warm water with the drink on a ledge in the tiled wall beside him. There would be time to take in Nazareth and Galilee. He was particularly keen that his brother should see Galilee because Galilee had atmosphere and was beautiful. There wasn't, in his own opinion, very much to Nazareth but it would be a pity to miss it all the same. It was at the Sea of Galilee that he intended to tell his brother of their mother's death.

We've had a great day, Francis wrote on a postcard that showed an aerial view of Jerusalem. *The Church of the Holy Sepulchre, where Our Lord's tomb is, and Gethsemane and Bethlehem. Paul's in great form.* He addressed it to his mother, and then wrote other cards, to Kitty and Myles and to the three Christian Brothers in Mrs. Shea's, and to Canon Mahon. He gave thanks that he was privileged to be in Jerusalem. He read St. Mark and some of St. Matthew. He said his rosary.

"Will we chance the wine?" Father Paul said at dinner, not that wine was something he went in for, but a waiter had come up and put a large padded wine-list into his hand.

"Ah, no, no," Francis protested, but already Father Paul was running his eye down the listed bottles.

"Have you local wine?" he enquired of the waiter. "A nice red one?"

The waiter nodded and hurried away, and Francis hoped he wouldn't get drunk, the red wine on top of the whisky he'd had in the bar before the meal. He'd only had the one whisky, not being much used to it, making it last through his brother's three.

"I heard some gurriers in the bar," Father Paul said, "making a great song and dance about the local red wine."

Wine made Francis think of the Holy Communion, but he didn't say so. He said the soup was delicious and he drew his brother's attention to the custom there was in the hotel of a porter ringing a bell and walking about with a person's name chalked on a little blackboard on the end of a rod.

"It's a way of paging you," Father Paul explained. "Isn't it nicer than bellowing out some fellow's name?" He smiled his easy smile, his eyes beginning to water as a result of the few drinks he'd had. He was beginning to feel the strain: he kept thinking of their mother lying there, of what she'd say if she knew what he'd done, how she'd savagely upbraid him for keeping the fact from Francis. Out of duty and humanity he had returned each year to see her because, after all, you only had the one mother. But he had never cared for her.

Francis went for a walk after dinner. There were young soldiers with what seemed to be toy guns on the streets, but he knew the guns were real. In the shop windows there were television sets for sale, and furniture and clothes, just like anywhere else. There were advertisements for some film or other, two writhing women without a stitch on them, the kind of thing you wouldn't see in Co. Tipperary. "You want something, sir?" a girl said, smiling at him with broken front teeth. The siren of a police car or an ambulance shrilled urgently near by. He shook his head at the girl. "No, I don't want anything," he said, and then realised what she had meant. She was small and very dark, no more than a child. He hurried on, praying for her.

When he returned to the hotel he found his brother in the lounge with other people, two men and two women. Father Paul was ordering a round of drinks and called out to the barman to bring another whisky. "Ah, no, no," Francis protested, anxious to go to his room and to think about the day, to read the New

Testament and perhaps to write a few more postcards. Music was playing, coming from speakers that could not be seen.

"My brother Francis," Father Paul said to the people he was with, and the people all gave their names, adding that they came from New York. "I was telling them about Tipp," Father Paul said to his brother, offering his packet of cigarettes around.

"You like Jerusalem, Francis?" one of the American women asked him, and he replied that he hadn't been able to take it in yet. Then, feeling that that didn't sound enthusiastic enough, he added that being there was the experience of a lifetime.

Father Paul went on talking about Co. Tipperary and then spoke of his parish in San Francisco, the boys' home and the two promising footballers, the plans for the new church. The Americans listened and in a moment the conversation drifted on to the subject of their travels in England, their visit to Istanbul and Athens, an argument they'd had with the Customs at Tel Aviv. "Well, I'm for the hay-pile," one of the men announced eventually, standing up.

The others stood up too and so did Francis. Father Paul remained where he was, gesturing again in the direction of the barman. "Sit down for a nightcap," he urged his brother.

"Ah, no, no—" Francis began.

"Bring us two more of those," the priest ordered with a sudden abruptness, and the barman hurried away. "Listen," said Father Paul. "I've something to tell you."

After dinner, while Francis had been out on his walk, before he'd dropped into conversation with the Americans, Father Paul had said to himself that he couldn't stand the strain. It was the old woman stretched out above the hardware shop, as stiff as a board already, with the little lights burning in her room: he kept seeing all that, as if she wanted him to, as if she was trying to haunt him. Nice as the idea was, he didn't think he could continue with what he'd planned, with waiting until they got up to Galilee.

Francis didn't want to drink any more. He hadn't wanted the whisky his brother had ordered him earlier, nor the one the Americans had ordered for him. He didn't want the one that the barman now brought. He thought he'd just leave it there, hoping his brother wouldn't see it. He lifted the glass to his lips, but he managed not to drink any.

"A bad thing has happened," Father Paul said.

"Bad? How d'you mean, Paul?"

"Are you ready for it?" He paused. Then he said, "She died."

Francis didn't know what he was talking about. He didn't know who was meant to be dead, or why his brother was behaving in an odd manner. He didn't like to think it but he had to: his brother wasn't fully sober.

"Our mother died," Father Paul said. "I'm after getting a telegram."

The huge area that was the lounge of the Plaza Hotel, the endless tables and people sitting at them, the swiftly moving waiters and barmen, seemed suddenly a dream. Francis had a feeling that he was not where he appeared to be, that he wasn't sitting with his brother, who was wiping his lips with a handkerchief. For a moment he appeared in his confusion to be struggling his way up the Via Dolorosa again and then in the Nativity Boutique.

"Take it easy, boy," his brother was saying. "Take a mouthful of whisky."

Francis didn't obey that injunction. He asked his brother to repeat what he had said, and Father Paul repeated that their mother had died.

Francis closed his eyes and tried as well to shut away the sounds around them. He prayed for the salvation of his mother's soul. "Blessed Virgin, intercede," his own voice said in his mind. "Dear Mary, let her few small sins be forgiven."

Having rid himself of his secret, Father Paul felt instant relief. With the best of intentions in the world it had been a foolish idea to think he could maintain the secret until they arrived in a place that was perhaps the most suitable in the world to hear about the death of a person who'd been close to you. He took a gulp of his whisky and wiped his mouth with his handkerchief again. He watched his brother, waiting for his eyes to open.

"When did it happen?" Francis asked eventually.

"Yesterday."

"And the telegram only came—"

"It came last night, Francis. I wanted to save you the pain."

"Save me? How could you save me? I sent her a postcard, Paul."

"Listen to me, Francis—"

"How could you save me the pain?"

"I wanted to tell you when we got up to Galilee."

Again Francis felt he was caught in the middle of a dream. He couldn't understand his brother: he couldn't understand what he meant by saying a telegram had come last night, why at a moment like this he was talking about Galilee. He didn't know why he was sitting in this noisy place when he should be back in Ireland.

"I fixed the funeral for Monday," Father Paul said.

Francis nodded, not grasping the significance of this arrangement. "We'll be back there this time tomorrow," he said.

"No need for that, Francis. Sunday morning's time enough."

"But she's dead—"

"We'll be there in time for the funeral."

"We can't stay here if she's dead."

It was this, Father Paul realised, he'd been afraid of when he'd argued with himself and made his plan. If he'd have knocked on Francis's door the night before, Francis would have wanted to return immediately without seeing a single stone of the land he had come so far to be moved by.

"We could go straight up to Galilee in the morning," Father Paul said quietly. "You'll find comfort in Galilee, Francis."

But Francis shook his head. "I want to be with her," he said.

Father Paul lit another cigarette. He nodded at a hovering waiter, indicating his need of another drink. He said to himself that he must keep his cool, an expression he was fond of.

"Take it easy, Francis," he said.

"Is there a plane out in the morning? Can we make arrangements now?" He looked about him as if for a member of the hotel staff who might be helpful.

"No good'll be done by tearing off home, Francis. What's wrong with Sunday?"

"I want to be with her."

Anger swelled within Father Paul. If he began to argue his words would become slurred: he knew that from experience. He must keep his cool and speak slowly and clearly, making a few simple points. It was typical of her, he thought, to die inconveniently.

"You've come all this way," he said as slowly as he could without sounding peculiar. "Why cut it any shorter than we need? We'll be losing a week anyway. She wouldn't want us to go back."

"I think she would."

He was right in that. Her possessiveness in her lifetime would have reached out across a dozen continents for Francis. She'd known what she was doing by dying when she had.

"I shouldn't have come," Francis said. "She didn't want me to come."

"You're thirty-seven years of age, Francis."

"I did wrong to come."

"You did no such thing."

The time he'd taken her to Rome she'd been difficult for the whole week, complaining about the food, saying everywhere was dirty. Whenever he'd spent anything she'd disapproved. All his life, Father Paul felt, he'd done his best for her. He had told her before anyone else when he'd decided to enter the priesthood, certain that she'd be pleased. "I thought you'd take over the shop," she'd said instead.

"What difference could it make to wait, Francis?"

"There's nothing to wait for."

As long as he lived Francis knew he would never forgive himself. As long as he lived he would say to himself that he hadn't been able to wait a few years, until she'd passed quietly on. He might even have been in the room with her when it happened.

"It was a terrible thing not to tell me," he said. "I sat down and wrote her a postcard, Paul. I bought her a plate."

"So you said."

"You're drinking too much of that whisky."

"Now, Francis, don't be silly."

"You're half drunk and she's lying there."

"She can't be brought back no matter what we do."

"She never hurt anyone," Francis said.

Father Paul didn't deny that, although it wasn't true. She had hurt their sister Kitty, constantly reproaching her for marrying the man she had, long after Kitty was aware she'd made a mistake. She'd driven Edna to Canada after Edna, still unmarried, had had a miscarriage that only the family knew about. She had made a shadow out of Francis although Francis didn't know it. Failing to hold on to her other children, she had grasped her last-born to her, as if she had borne him to destroy him.

"It'll be you'll say a mass for her?" Francis said.

"Yes, of course it will."

"You should have told me."

Francis realised why, all day, he'd been disappointed. From the moment when the hired car had pulled into the lay-by and his brother had pointed across the valley at the Garden of Gethsemane he'd been disappointed and had not admitted it. He'd been disappointed in the Via Dolorosa and in the Church of the Holy Sepulchre and in Bethlehem. He remembered the bespectacled man who'd kept saying that you couldn't be sure about anything. All the people with cameras made it impossible to think, all the jostling and pushing was distracting. When he'd said there'd been too much to take in he'd meant something different.

"Her death got in the way," he said.

"What d'you mean, Francis?"

"It didn't feel like Jerusalem, it didn't feel like Bethlehem."

"But it is, Francis, it is."

"There are soldiers with guns all over the place. And a girl came up to me on the street. There was that man with a bit of the Cross. There's you, drinking and smoking in this place—"

"Now, listen to me, Francis—"

"Nazareth would be a disappointment. And the Sea of Galilee. And the Church of the Loaves and Fishes." His voice had risen. He lowered it again. "I couldn't believe in the Stations this morning. I couldn't see it happening the way I do at home."

"That's nothing to do with her death, Francis. You've got a bit of jet-lag, you'll settle yourself up in Galilee. There's an. atmosphere in Galilee that nobody misses."

"I'm not going near Galilee." He struck the surface of the table, and Father Paul told him to contain himself. People turned their heads, aware that anger had erupted in the pale-faced man with the priest.

"Quieten up," Father Paul commanded sharply, but Francis didn't.

"She knew I'd be better at home," he shouted, his voice shrill and reedy. "She knew I was making a fool of myself, a man out of a shop trying to be big—"

"Will you keep your voice down? Of course you're not making a fool of yourself."

"Will you find out about planes tomorrow morning?"

Father Paul sat for a moment longer, not saying anything, hoping his brother would say he was sorry. Naturally it was a shock, naturally he'd be emotional and feel guilty, in a moment it would be better. But it wasn't and Francis didn't say he was sorry. Instead he began to weep.

"Let's go up to your room," Father Paul said, "and I'll fix about the plane."

Francis nodded but did not move. His sobbing ceased, and then he said, "I'll always hate the Holy Land now."

"No need for that, Francis."

But Francis felt there was and he felt he would hate, as well, the brother he had admired for as long as he could remember. In the lounge of the Plaza Hotel he felt mockery surfacing everywhere. His brother's deceit, and the endless whisky in his brother's glass, and his casualness after a death seemed like the scorning of a Church which honoured so steadfastly the mother of its founder. Vivid in his mind, his own mother's eyes reminded him that they'd told him he was making a mistake, and upbraided him for not heeding her. Of course there was mockery everywhere, in the splinter of wood beneath plastic, and in the soldiers with guns that were not toys, and the writhing nakedness in the Holy City. He'd become part of it himself, sending postcards to the dead. Not speaking again to his brother, he went to his room to pray.

"Eight A.M., sir," the girl at the reception desk said, and Father Paul asked that arrangements should be made to book two seats on the plane, explaining that it was an emergency, that a death had occurred. "It will be all right, sir," the girl promised.

He went slowly downstairs to the bar. He sat in a corner and lit a cigarette and ordered two whiskies and ice, as if expecting a companion. He drank them both himself and ordered more. Francis would return to Co. Tipperary and after the funeral he would take up again the life she had ordained for him. In his brown cotton coat he would serve customers with nails and hinges and wire. He would regularly go to Mass and to Confession and to Men's Confraternity. He would sit alone in the lace-curtained sitting-room, lonely for the woman who had made him what he was, married forever to her memory.

Father Paul lit a fresh cigarette from the butt of the last one. He continued to order whisky in two glasses. Already he could sense the hatred that Francis had earlier felt taking root in himself. He wondered if he would ever again return in July to Co. Tipperary, and imagined he would not.

At midnight he rose to make the journey to bed and found himself unsteady on his feet. People looked at him, thinking it disgraceful for a priest to be drunk in Jerusalem, with cigarette ash all over his clerical clothes.

A Journey to the Seven Streams

By Benedict Kiely

My father, the heavens be his bed, was a terrible man for telling you about the places he had been and for bringing you there if he could and displaying them to you with a mild and gentle air of propriertorship. He couldn't do the showmanship so well in the case of Spion Kop where he and the fortunate ones who hadn't been ordered up the hill in the ignorant night had spent a sad morning crouching on African earth and listening to the deadly Boer guns that, high above the plain, slaughtered their hapless comrades. Nor yet in the case of Halifax nor the Barbadoes where he had heard words of Gaelic from coloured girls who were, he claimed, descended from the Irish transported into slavery in the days of Cromwell. The great glen of Aherlow, too, which he had helped to chain for His Majesty's Ordnance Survey, was placed inconveniently far to the South in the mystic land of Tipperary, and Cratloe Wood, where the fourth Earl of Leitrim was assassinated, was sixty miles away on the winding Donegal fjord called Mulroy Bay. But townlands like Corraheskin, Drumlish, Cornavara, Dooish, The Minnieburns and Claramore, and small towns like Drumquin and Dromore were all within a ten-mile radius of our town and something of moment or something amusing had happened in every one of them.

The reiterated music of their names worked on him like a charm. They would, he said, take faery tunes out of the stone fiddle of Castle Caldwell; and indeed it was the night he told us the story of the stone fiddle and the drowned fiddler, and recited for us the inscription carved on a fiddle in memory of the fiddler, that he decided to hire a hackney car, a rare and daring thing to do in those days, and bring us out to see in one round trip those most adjacent places of his memories and dreams.

—In the year 1770 it happened, he said. The landlord at the time was Sir James Caldwell, Baronet. He was also called the Count of Milan, why, I never found anybody to tell me. The fiddler's name was Dennis McCabe and by tradition the Mc-Cabes were always musicians and jesters to the Caldwells. There was festivity at the Big House by Lough Erne Shore and gentry there from near and far, and out they went to drink and dance on a raft on the lake, and wasn't the poor fiddler so drunk he fiddled himself into the water and drowned.

—Couldn't somebody have pulled him out, Da?

—They were all as drunk as he was. The story was that he was still sawing away with the bow when he came up for the third time. The party cheered him until every island in Lough Erne echoed and it was only when they sobered up they realised they had lost the fiddler. So the baronet and Count of Milan had a stone fiddle taller than a man made to stand at the estate gate as a monument to Dennis McCabe and as a warning for ever to fiddlers either to stay sober or to stay on dry land.

—Ye fiddlers beware, ye fiddler's fate, my father recited. Don't attempt the deep lest ye repent too late. Keep to the land when wind and storm blow, but scorn the deep if it with whisky flow. On firm land only exercise your skill; there you may play and safely drink your fill.

Travelling by train from our town to the seaside you went for miles along the green and glistening Erne shore but the train didn't stop by the stone fiddle nor yet at the Boa island for the cross-roads' dances. Always when my father told us about those dances, his right foot rhythmically tapped and took music out of the polished steel fireside fender that had Home Sweet Home lettered out on an oval central panel. Only the magic motor, bound to no tracks, compelled to no fixed stopping places, could bring us to the fiddle or the crowded cross-roads.

—Next Sunday then, he said, as certain as the sun sets and rises, we'll hire Hookey and Peter and the machine and head for Lough Erne.

—Will it hold us all, said my mother. Seven of us and Peter's big feet and the length of the driver's legs.

—That machine, he said, would hold the twelve apostles, the Connaught Rangers and the man who broke the bank at Monte Carlo. It's the size of a hearse.

—Which is just what it looks like, said the youngest of my three sisters who had a name for the tartness of her tongue.

She was a thin dark girl.

—Regardless of appearance, he said, it'll carry us to the stone fiddle and on the way we'll circumnavigate the globe: Clanabogan, and Cavanacaw, Pigeon Top Mountain and Corraduine, where the barefooted priest said Mass at the Rock in the penal days and Corraheskin where the Muldoons live...

—Them, said the third sister.

She had had little time for the Muldoons since the day their lack of savoir faire cost her a box of chocolates. A male member, flaxen-haired, pink-cheeked, aged sixteen, of those multitudinous Muldoons had come by horse and cart on a market day from his rural fastnesses to pay us a visit. Pitying his gaucherie, his shy animal-in-a-thicket appearance, his outback ways and gestures, she had grandly reached him a box of chocolates so as to sweeten his bitter lot with one honeyed morsel or two, or, at the outside three; but unaccustomed to towny ways and the mores of built-up areas the rural swain had appropriated the whole box.

—He thought, she said, I was a paleface offering gifts to a Comanche.

—But by their own hearth, said my father, they're simple hospitable people.

—And Cornavara, he said, and Dooish and Carrick Valley and your uncle Owen, and the two McCannys the pipers, and Claramore where there are so many Gormleys every family has to have its own nickname, and Drumquin where I met your mother, and Dromore where you (pointing to me) were born and where the mail train was held up by the I.R.A. and where the three poor lads were murdered by the Specials when you (again indicating me) were a year old, and the Minnieburns where the seven streams meet to make the head waters of the big river. Hookey and Peter and the machine will take us to all those places.

—Like a magic carpet, said my mother—with just a little dusting of the iron filings of doubt in her voice.

Those were the days, and not so long ago, when cars were rare and every car, not just every make of car, had a personality of its own. In our town with its population of five thousand, not counting the soldiers in the barracks, there were only three cars for hire and one of them was the love-child of the pioneer passion of Hookey Baxter for the machine. He was a long hangle of a young fellow, two-thirds of him made up of legs, and night and day he was whistling. He was as forward-looking as Lindbergh and he dressed like Lindbergh, for the air, in goggles, leather jacket and helmet; an appropriate costume, possibly, considering Hookey's own height and the altitude of the driver's seat in his machine. The one real love of his young heart was the love of the born tinkerer, the instinctive mechanic, for that hybrid car: the child of his frenzy, the fruit of days spent deep in grease giving new life and shape to a wreck he had bought at a sale in Belfast. The original manufacturers, whoever they had been, would have been hard put to it to recognise their altered offspring.

—She's chuman, Peter Keown would say as he patted the sensitive quivering bonnet.

Peter meant human. In years to come his sole recorded comment on the antics of Adolf Hitler was that the man wasn't chuman.

—She's as nervous, he would say, as a thoroughbred.

The truth was that Peter, Hookey's stoker, grease-monkey and errand boy, was somewhat in awe of the tall rangy metal animal yet wherever the car went, with the tall goggled pilot at the wheel, there the pilot's diminutive mate was also sure to go. What living Peter earned he earned by digging holes in the street as a labouring man for the town council's official plumber so that, except on Sundays and when he motored with Hookey, nobody in the town ever saw much of him but the top of his cloth cap or his upturned face when he'd look up from the hole in the ground to ask a passer-by the time of day. Regularly once a year he spent a corrective month in Derry Jail, because his opportunities as a municipal employee and his weakness as a kleptomaniac meant that good boards, lengths of piping, coils of electric wire, monkey wrenches, spades, and other movable properties faded too frequently into thin air.

—A wonderful man, poor Peter, my father would say. That cloth cap with the turned up peak. And the thick-lensed, thin-rimmed spectacles—he's half-blind—and the old tweed jacket too tight for him, and the old Oxford-bag trousers too big for him, and his shrill voice and his waddle of a walk that makes him look always like a duck about to apologise for laying a hen-egg. How he survives is a miracle of God's grace. He can resist the appeal of nothing that's portable.

—He's a dream, said the third sister. And the feet are the biggest part of him.

—The last time he went to Derry, said my brother, all the old women from Brook Street and the lanes were at the top of the Courthouse Hill to cheer him as he passed.

—And why not, said my mother. They're fond of him and they say he's well-liked in the jail. His heart's as big as his feet. Everything he steals he gives away.

—Robin Hood, said the third sister. Robbing the town council to pay Brook Street.

—The Council wouldn't sack him, said my eldest sister, if he stole the town.

—At the ready, roared my father. Prepare to receive cavalry.

In the street below the house there was a clanking, puffing, grinding tumult.

—God bless us look at Peter, said my father. Aloft with Hookey like a crown prince beside a king. Are we all ready? Annie, Ita, May, George, yourself ma'am, and you the youngest of us all. Have we the sandwiches and the flasks of tea and the lemonade? Forward.

A lovelier Sunday morning never shone. With the hood down and the high body glistening after its Saturday wash and polish, the radiator gently steaming, the car stood at the foot of the seven steps that led down from our door. The stragglers coming home from early mass, and the devout setting off early for late mass had gathered in groups to witness our embarkation. Led by my father and in single file, we descended the steps and ascended nearly as high again to take our lofty places in the machine.

There was something of the Citroen in the quivering mongrel, in the yellow canvas hood now reclining in volu-minous ballooning folds, in the broad back-seat that could hold five fair-sized people. But to judge by the radiator, the absence of gears, and the high fragile-spoked wheels, Citroen blood had been crossed with that of the Model T. After that, any efforts to spot family traits would have brought confusion on the thought of the greatest living authorities. The thick slanting glass windscreen could have been wrenched from a limousine designed to divert bullets from Balkan princelings. The general colour-scheme, considerably chipped and cracked, was canary yellow. And there was Hookey at the wheel, then my brother and father, and Peter on the outside left where he could leap in and out to perform the menial duties of assistant engineer; and in the wide and windy acres of the back seat, my mother, myself and my three sisters.

High above the town the church bell rang. It was the bell to warn the worshippers still on their way that in ten minutes the vested priest would be on the altar but, as it coincided with our setting out, it could have been a quayside bell ringing farewell to a ship nosing out across the water towards the rim of vision.

Peter leaped to the ground, removed the two stones that, blocked before the front wheels, acted as auxiliaries for the hand brake. Hookey released the brake. The car was gathering speed when Peter scrambled aboard, settled himself and slammed the yellow door behind him. Sparing fuel, we glided down the slope, backfired twice loudly enough to drown the sound of the church bell, swung left along John Street and cleared the town without incident. Hands waved from watching groups of people but because this was no trivial event there were no laughs, no wanton cheers. The sound of the bell died away behind us. My mother expressed the hope that the priest would remember us at the offertory. Peter assured her that we were all as safe as if we were at home in bed. God's good green Sunday countryside was softly all around us.

Squat to the earth and travelling at seventy you see nothing from cars nowadays, but to go with Hookey was to be above all but the highest walls and hedges, to be among the morning birds.

—Twenty-seven em pee haitch, said Hookey.

—Four miles covered already, said Peter.

—The Gortin Mountains over there, said my father. And the two mountains to the north are Bessy Bell and Mary Grey, so

named by the Hamiltons of Baronscourt, the Duke of Aber-
corn's people, after fancied resemblance to two hills in
Stirlingshire, Scotland. The two hills in Stirlingshire are so
called after two ladies of the Scottish court who fled the plague
and built their hut in the wild wood and thatched it o'er with
rushes. They are mentioned by Thomas Carlyle in his book on
the French Revolution. The dark green on the hills by Gortin
Gap is the new government forestry. And in Gortin village
Paddy Ford the contractor hasn't gone to mass since, fifteen
years ago, the parish priest gave another man the job of
painting the inside of the sacristy.

—No paint no prayers, said the third sister.

—They're strange people in Gortin, my mother said.

—It's proverbial, said my father, that they're to be distinguished anywhere by the bigness of their backsides.

—Five miles, said Peter. They're spinning past.

—Running sweet as honey, said Hookey.

He adjusted his goggles and whistled back to the Sunday
birds.

—Jamie Magee's of the Flush, said my father.

He pointed to a long white house on a hill slope and close to a
waterfalling stream.

—Rich as Rockefeller and too damned mean to marry.

—Who in heaven would have him, said the third sister.

—Six miles, said Peter.

Then, with a blast of backfiring that rose my mother a foot in
the air, the wobbling yellow conveyance came to a coughing
miserable halt. The air was suddenly grey and poisoned with
fumes.

—It's her big end Hookey, said Peter.

—She's from Gortin so, said the third sister.

The other two sisters, tall and long-haired and normally quiet
girls, went off at the deep end into the giggles.

—Isn't it providential, said my mother, that the cowslips are a
glory this year. We'll have something to do, Henry, while you're
fixing it.

Hookey had been christened Henry, and my mother would
never descend to nicknames. She felt that to make use of a
nickname was to remind a deformed person of his deformity.

Nor would she say even of the town's chief inebriate that he was ever drunk: he was either under the influence or he had a drop too many taken. She was, my mother, the last great Victorian euphemiser.

—We won't be a jiffy, ma'am, said Hookey. It's nothing so serious as a big end.

The three sisters were convulsed.

The fields and the roadside margins were bright yellow with blossom.

—Gather ye cowslips while you may, said my father.

He handed the ladies down from the dizzy heights. Peter had already disembarked. Submitting to an impulse that had gnawed at me since we set sail I dived forwards, my head under Hookey's left elbow, and butted with both fists the black rubber punch-ball horn; and out over the fields to startle birds and grazing cattle went the dying groan of a pained diseased ox.

—Mother of God, said my father, that's a noise and no mistake. Here boy, go off and pick flowers.

He lifted me down to the ground.

—Screw off the radiator cap, Peter, said Hookey.

—It's scalding hot, Hookey.

—Take these gauntlet gloves, manalive. And stand clear when you screw it off.

A geyser of steam and dirty hot water went heavenwards as Peter and my brother, who was always curious about engines, leaped to safety.

—Wonderful, said my father to my brother, the age we live in. They say that over in England they're queued up steaming by the roadsides, like Iceland or the Yellowstone Park.

—Just a bit overheated, said Hookey. We won't be a jiffy.

—Does it happen often? said my father.

Ignoring the question, descending and opening the bonnet to peer and poke and tinker, Hookey said: Do you know a funny thing about this car?

—She's chuman, said Peter.

—You know the cross-roads at Clanaboagn churchyard gate, Hookey said. The story about it.

—It's haunted, said my father.

—Only at midnight, said Peter.

As was his right and custom, my father stepped into the role
of raconteur: Do you know that no horse ever passed there at
midnight that didn't stop—shivering with fear. The fact is well
attested. Something comes down that side road out of the heart
of the wood.

Hookey closed over the bonnet, screwed back the radiator cap
and climbed again to the throne. He wiped his hands on a
bunch of grass pulled for him and handed to him by Peter.
Slowly he drew on again his gauntlet gloves. Bedecked with
cowslips and dragging me along with them the ladies rejoined
the gentlemen.

—Well, would you credit this now, Hookey said. Peter and
myself were coming from Dromore one wet night last week.

—Pouring rain from the heavens, said Peter, and the hood
was leaking.

—A temporary defect, said Hookey. I mended it. Jack up the
back axle, Peter, and give her a swing. And would you credit it,
exactly at twelve o'clock midnight she stopped dead at the gate
of Clanabogan churchyard?

With an irony that was lost on Hookey, my mother said: I
could well believe it.

—She's chuman, said Peter.

—One good push now and we're away, said Hookey. The
slight gradient is in our favour.

—Maybe, he said to my father and brother, you'd lend Peter a
hand.

Twenty yards ahead he waited for the dusty pushers to climb
aboard, the engine chug-chugging, little puffs of steam escap-
ing like baby genii from the right-hand side of the bonnet. My
father was thoughtful. He could have been considering the
responsibilities of the machine age particularly because when it
came to team pushing Peter was more of a cheer leader, an
exhorter, a counter of one two three, than an actual motive
force.

—Contact, said Hookey.

—Dawn patrol away, said Peter. Squadron Leader Baxter at
the joystick.

He mimicked what he supposed to be the noises of an
aeroplane engine and, with every evidence of jubilation, we

were once again under way; and a day it was, made by the good
God for jubilation. The fields, all the colours of all the crops,
danced towards us and away from us and around us; and the
lambs on the green hills, my father sang, were gazing at me and
many a strawberry grows by the salt sea, and many a ship sails
the ocean. The roadside trees bowed down and then gracefully
swung their arms up and made music over our heads and there
were more birds and white cottages and fuchsia hedges in the
world than you would readily imagine.

—The bride and bride's party, sang my father, to church they
did go. The bride she goes foremost, she bears the best show...

—They're having sports today at Tattysallagh, said Hookey.

—But I followed after my heart full of woe, for to see my love
wed to another.

We swept by a cross-roads where people and horses and traps
were congregated after the last mass. In a field beside the road a
few tall ash plants bore fluttering pennants in token of the
sports to be.

—Proceed to Banteer, sang my father, to the athletic sporting
and hand in your name to the club comm-i-tee.

—That was a favourite song of Pat O'Leary the Corkman, he
said, who was killed at Spion Kop.

Small country boys in big boots, knickerbockers, stiff celluloid
collars that could be cleaned for Sunday by a rub of a wet cloth,
and close-cropped heads with fringes like scalping locks above
the foreheads, scattered before us to the hedges and the grass
margins, then closed again like water divided and rejoining, and
pursued us, cheering, for a hundred yards. One of them, frantic
with enthusiasm, sent sailing after us a half-grown turnip,
which bounced along the road for a bit, then sought rest in a
roadside drain. Looking backwards I pulled my best or worst
faces at the rustic throng of runners.

—In Tattysallagh, said my father, they were always an un-
civilised crowd of gulpins.

He had three terms of contempt: Gulpin, Yob and, when
things became very bad he became Swiftian, and described all
offenders as Yahoos.

—Cavanacaw, he said, and that lovely trout stream, the
Creevan Burn. It joins the big river at Blacksessiagh. That

there's the road up to Pigeon Top Mountain and the mass rock at Corraduine, but we'll come back that way when we've circumnavigated Dooish and Cornavara.

We came to Clanabogan.

—Clanabogan planting, he said.

The tall trees came around us and sunlight and shadow flickered so that you could feel them across eyes and hands and face.

—Martin Murphy the postman, he said, who was in the survey with me in Virginia, County Cavan, by Lough Ramor, and in the Glen of Aherlow, worked for a while at the building of Clanabogan Church. One day the vicar said to him: 'What height do you think the steeple should be?' 'The height of nonsense like your sermons,' said Martin, and got the sack for his wit. In frosty weather he used to seal the cracks in his boots with butter and although he was an abrupt man he seldom used an impolite word. Once when he was aggravated by the bad play of his wife who was partnering him at whist he said: 'Maria, dearly as I love you there are yet moments when you'd incline a man to kick his own posterior.'

—There's the church, my father said, and the churchyard and the haunted gate and the cross-roads.

We held our breath but, with honeyed summer all around us and bees in the tender limes, it was no day for ghosts, and in glory we sailed by.

—She didn't hesitate, said Peter.

—Wonderful, said the third sister.

It was more wonderful than she imagined for, as the Lord would have it, the haunted gate and the cross-roads of Clanabogan was one of the few places that day that Hookey's motor machine did not honour with at least some brief delay.

—I'd love to drive, said my brother. How did you learn to drive, Hookey?

—I never did. I just sat in and drove. I learned the basic principles on the county council steamroller in Watson's quarries. Forward and reverse.

—You have to have the natural knack, Peter explained.

—What's the cut potato for, Hookey? asked my brother.

—For the rainy day. Rub it on the windscreen and the water runs off the glass.

—It's oily you see, said Peter.

—Like a duck's back, said the third sister.

—Where, said my father, sniffing, do you keep the petrol?

—Reserve in the tins clipped on the running board. Current supply, six gallons. You're sitting on it. In a tank under the front seat.

—Twenty miles to the gallon, said Peter. We're good for more than a hundred miles.

—Godalmighty, said my father. Provided it isn't a hundred miles straight up. 'Twould be sad to survive a war that was the end of better men and to be blown up between Clanabogan and Cornavara. On a quiet Sunday morning.

—Never worry, said Hookey. It's outside the bounds of possibility.

—You reassure me, said my father. Twenty miles to the gallon in any direction. What care we? At least we'll all go up together. No survivors to mourn in misery.

—And turn right here, he said, for Cornavara. You'll soon see the hills and the high waterfalls.

We left the tarred road. White dust rose around us like smoke. We advanced half a mile on the flat, attempted the first steep hill and gently, wearily, without angry fumes or backfiring protests, the tremulous chuman car, lying down like a tired child, came to rest.

—We'll hold what we have, said Hookey. Peter... pronto. Get the stones behind the back wheels.

—Think of a new pastime, said the third sister. We have enough cowslips to decorate the town for a procession. With the sweet face of girlish simplicity she asked, Do you buy the stones with the car?

—We'd be worse off without them, Hookey muttered.

Disguised as he was in helmet and goggles it was impossible to tell exactly if his creative soul was or was not wounded by her hint of mockery, but my mother must have considered that his voice betrayed pain for she looked reprovingly at the third sister and at the other two who were again impaled by giggles, and withdrew them out of sight down a boreen towards the sound of a small stream, to—as she put it—freshen up.

—Without these stones, Peter panted, we could be as badly off as John MacKenna and look what happened to him.

—They're necessary precautions, said Hookey. Poor John would never use stones. He said the brakes on his car would hold a Zeppelin.

The bonnet was open again and the radiator cap unscrewed but there was no steam and no geyser, only a cold sad silence, and Hookey bending and peering and probing with pincers.

—She's a bit exhausted, Peter said.

—It's simple, Hookey said. She'll be right as rain in a jiffy. Going at the hill with a full load overstrained her.

—We should walk the bad hills, Peter explained.

—Poor John MacKenna, Hookey said, was making four fortunes drawing crowds to the Passionist monastery at Enniskillen to see the monk that cures the people. But he would never use the stones, and the only parking place at the monastery is on a sharp slope. And one evening when they were all at devotions doesn't she run backways and ruin all the flowerbeds in the place and knock down a statue of Our Lord.

—One of the monks attacked him, said Peter, as a heathen that would knock the Lord down.

—Ruined the trade for all, said Hookey. The monks now won't let a car within a mile of the place.

—Can't say as I blame them, said my father.

—Poor John took it bad, said Hookey. The lecture he got and all. He was always a religious man. They say he raises his hat now every time he passes any statute: even the Boer War one in front of the courthouse.

—So well he might, said my father.

Suddenly, mysteriously responding to Hookey's probing pincers, the very soul of the machine was again chug-chugging. But with or without cargo she could not or, being weary and chuman, would not assault even the first bastion of Cornavara.

—She won't take off, said Hookey. That run to Belfast and back took the wind out of her.

—You never made Belfast, said my father, in this.

—We did Tommy, said Peter apologetically.

—Seventy miles there and seventy miles back, said my father incredulously.

—Bringing a greyhound bitch to running trials for Tommy Mullan the postman, said Hookey.

—The man who fishes for pearls in the Drumragh river, said Peter.

They were talking hard to cover their humiliation.

—If she won't go at the hills, my father said, go back to the main road and we'll go on and picnic at the seven streams at the Minnieburns. It's mostly on the flat.

So we reversed slowly the dusty half-mile to the main road.

—One night in John Street, Peter said, she started going backways and wouldn't go forwards.

—A simple defect, Hookey said. I remedied it.

—Did you turn the other way? asked the third sister.

Artlessly, Peter confessed: She stopped when she knocked down the schoolchildren-crossing sign at the bottom of Church Hill. Nipped it off an inch from the ground, as neat as you ever saw. We hid it up a laneway and it was gone in the morning.

My father looked doubtfully at Peter. He said: One of those nice shiny enamelled pictures of two children crossing the road would go well as an overmantel. And the wood of the post would always make firewood.

Peter agreed: You can trust nobody.

Hurriedly trying to cut in on Peter's eloquence, Hookey said: In fact the name of Tommy Mullan's bitch was Drumragh Pearl. Not that that did her any good at the trials.

—She came a bad last, burst out the irrepressible Peter.

—And to make it worse we lost her on the way back from Belfast.

—You what? said my father.

—Lost her in the dark where the road twists around Bal-lymacilroy Mountain.

My mother was awed: You lost the man's greyhound. You're a right pair of boys to send on an errand.

—'Twas the way we stepped out of the car to take the air, said Hookey.

By the husky note in his voice you could guess how his soul suffered at Peter's shameless confessions.

—And Peter looked at the animal, ma'am, and said maybe she'd like a turn in the air too. So we took her out and tied her lead to the left front wheel. And while we were standing there talking didn't the biggest brute of a hare you ever saw set out as cool as sixpence in the light of the car. Off like a shot with the bitch.

—If the lead hadn't snapped, Peter said, she'd have taken the wheel off the car or the car off the road.

—That would have been no great exertion, said my father. We should have brought a greyhound along with us to pull.

—We whistled and called for hours but all in vain, said Peter.

—The hare ate her, said the third sister.

—Left up the slope there, said my father, is the belt of trees I planted in my spare time to act as a wind-breaker for Drumlish schoolhouse. Paddy Hamish, the labouring man, gave me a hand. He died last year in Canada.

—You'd have pitied the children on a winter's day, my mother said, standing in the playground at lunchtime taking the fresh air in a hilltop wind that would sift and clean corn. Eating soda bread and washing it down with buttermilk. On a rough day the wind from Lough Erne would break the panes of the windows.

—As a matter of curiosity, my father said, what did Tommy Mullan say?

—At two in the morning in Bridge Lane, said Peter, he was waiting for us. We weren't too happy about it. But when we told him she was last in the trials he said the bloody bitch could stay in Ballymacilroy.

—Hasn't he always the pearls in the river, my mother said.

So we came to have tea and sandwiches and lemonade in a meadow by the cross-roads in the exact centre of the wide saucer of land where seven streams from the surrounding hills came down to meet. The grass was polished with sunshine. The perfume of the meadowsweet is with me still. That plain seemed to me then as vast as the prairies, or Siberia. White cottages far away on the lower slopes of Dooish could have been in another country. The chief stream came for a long way through the soft deep meadowland. It was slow, quiet, unob- trusive, perturbed only by the movements of water fowl or trout. Two streams met, wonder of wonders, under the arch of a bridge and you could go out under the bridge along a sandy promontory to paddle in clear water on a bottom as smooth as Bundoran strand. Three streams came together in a magic hazel wood where the tiny green unripe nuts were already clustered on the branches. Then the seven made into one, went away from us with a shout and a song towards Shaneragh, Blacksessiagh, Drumragh and Crevenagh, under the humpy crooked King's Bridge where James Stuart had passed on his way from Derry to the fatal brackish Boyne, and on through the town we came from.

—All the things we could see, said my father, if this spavined brute of a so-called automobile could only be persuaded to climb the high hills. The deep lakes of Claramore. The far view of Mount Errigal, the Cock of the North, by the Donegal sea. If you were up on the top of Errigal you could damn' near see, on a clear day, the skyscrapers of New York.

In his poetic imagination the towers of Atlantis rose glimmering from the deep.

—What matter, said my mother. The peace of heaven is here.

For that day that was the last peace we were to experience. The energy the machine didn't have or wouldn't use to climb hills or to keep in motion for more than two miles at a stretch, she expended in thunderous staccato bursts of backfiring. In slanting evening sunlight people at the doors of distant farmhouses shaded their eyes to look towards the travelling commotion, or ran up whinny hills for a better view, and horses and cattle raced madly around pastures, and my mother said the country would never be the same again, that the shock of the noise would turn the milk in the udders of the cows. When we came again to the crossroads of Tattysallagh the majority of the spectators, standing on the road to look over the hedge and thus save the admission fee, lost all interest in the sports, such as they were, and came around us. To oblige them the right rear tyre went flat.

—Peter, said Hookey, jack it up and change it on.

We mingled unobtrusively with the gulpins.

—A neat round hole, said Peter.

—Paste a patch on it.

The patch was deftly pasted on.

—Take the foot pump and blow her up, said Hookey.

There was a long silence while Peter, lines of worry on his little puckered face, inspected the tube. Then he said: I can't find the valve.

—Show it to me, said Hookey.

He ungoggled himself, descended and surveyed the ailing member.

—Peter, he said, you're a prize. The valve's gone and you put a patch on the hole it left behind it.

The crowd around us was increasing and highly appreciative.

—Borrow a bicycle Peter, said Hookey, cycle to the town and ask John MacKenna for the loan of a tube.

—To pass the time, said my mother, we'll look at the sports.

So we left Hookey to mind his car and, being practically gentry as compared with the rustic throng around us, we walked to the gateway that led into the sportsfield where my mother civilly enquired of two men, who stood behind a wooden table, the price of admission.

—Five shillings a skull missus, barring the cub, said the younger of the two. And half a crown for the cub.

—For the what? said my mother.

—For the little boy ma'am, said the elder of the two.

—It seems expensive, said my mother.

—I'd see them all in hell first—let alone in Tattysallagh, my father said. One pound, twelve shillings and sixpence to look at six sally rods stuck in a field and four yahoos running round in rings in their sock soles.

We took our places on the roadside with the few who, faithful to athletics and undistracted by the novelty of the machine, were still looking over the hedge. Four lean youths and one stout one in Sunday shirts and long trousers with the ends tucked into their socks were pushing high framed bicycles round and round the field. My father recalled the occasion in Virginia, County Cavan, when Martin Murphy was to run at sports and his wife Maria stiffened his shirt so much with starch it wouldn't go inside his trousers, and when he protested she said: Martin, leave it outside and you will be able to fly.

We saw two bicycle races and a tug-of-war.

—Hallions and clifts, he said.

Those were two words he seldom used.

—Yobs and sons of yobs, he said.

He led us back to the car. Peter soaked in perspiration had the new tube on and the wheel ready.

—Leave the jack in and swing her, Hookey said. She's cold by now.

There was a series of explosions that sent gulpins, yobs and yahoos reeling backwards in alarm. Peter screwed out the jack. We scrambled aboard, a few of the braver among the decent people rushing into the line of fire to lend a hand to the ladies. Exploding, we departed, and when we were a safe distance away the watchers raised a dubious cheer.

—In God's name, Henry, said my father, get close to the town before you blow us all up. I wouldn't want our neighbours to have to travel as far as Tattysallagh to pick up the bits. And the yobs and yahoos here don't know us well enough to be able to piece us together.

Three miles further on Peter blushingly confessed that in the frantic haste of embarkation he had left the jack on the road.

—I'll buy you a new one, Henry, my father said. Or perhaps Peter here could procure one on the side. By now at any rate they're shoeing jackasses with it in Tattysallagh.

—A pity in a way, he said, we didn't make as far as the stone fiddle. We might have heard good music. It's a curious thing that in the townlands around that place the people have always been famed for music and singing. The Tunneys of Castle Caldwell now are noted. It could be that the magic of the stone fiddle has something to do with it.

—Some day, he said, we'll head for Donegal. When the cars, Henry, are a bit improved.

He told us about the long windings of Mulroy Bay. He explained exactly how and why and in what year the fourth Earl of Leitrim had been assassinated in Cratloe Wood. He spoke as rapidly and distinctly as he could in the lulls of the backfiring.

Then our town was below us in the hollow and the Gortin mountains, deep purple with evening, away behind it.

—Here we'll part company, Henry boy, said my father. 'Tisn't that I doubt the ability of Peter and yourself to navigate the iron horse down the hill. But I won't have the town blaming me and my family for having hand, act or part in the waking of the dead in Drumragh graveyard.

Sedately we walked down the slope into the town and talked with the neighbours we met and asked them had they heard Hookey and Peter passing and told them of the sports and of the heavenly day it had been out at the seven streams.

My father died in a seaside town in the County Donegal—forty miles from the town I was reared in. The road his funeral followed back to the home places led along the Erne shore by the stone fiddle and the glistening water, across the Boa Island where there are no longer cross-roads' dances. Every roadside house has a television aerial. It led by the meadowland saucer of the Minnieburns where the river still springs from seven magic sources. That brooding place is still much as it was but no longer did it seem to me to be as vast as Siberia. To the left was the low sullen outline of Cornavara and Pigeon Top, the hurdle that our Bucephalus refused to take. To the right was Drumlish. The old schoolhouse was gone and in its place a white building, ten times as large, with drying rooms for wet coats, fine warm lunches for children and even a gymnasium. But the belt of trees that he and Paddy Hamish planted to break the wind and shelter the children is still there.

Somebody tells me, too, that the engine of Hookey Baxter's car is still with us, turning a circular saw for a farmer in the vicinity of Clanabogan.

As the Irish proverb says: It's a little thing doesn't last longer than a man.

"They Also Serve..."

By Mervyn Wall

One afternoon a middle-aged man walked up to the gateway of Dublin Castle. He had such a smart way of walking and held himself so upright that the policeman on duty had touched his helmet respectfully before he noticed the little man's outmoded and shabby clothes. Mr. Carmody coughed nervously before he spoke.

"I beg your pardon. Is this Dublin Castle?"

The policeman stared down at him as if suspicious of a joke. "Yes," he admitted, "it is."

"I have an appointment with Mr. Watkins," Mr. Carmody explained. "Perhaps you would be so kind as to tell me where I would find him."

The policeman looked him up and down and replied sternly:

"There are seven departments of government in the Castle and a staff of over two thousand."

Mr. Carmody shifted nervously.

"He's in the Department of Fisheries."

The policeman moved two paces and stood with his arm stretched out like a signpost.

"Go down there," he said, "across the Lower Yard, round by the Chapel Royal, and when you come up against a blank wall, turn to the left."

Mr. Carmody began to thank him, but the policeman went on without heeding him.

"The Department of Fisheries is moving out today to another building, but you may get the man you're looking for if he hasn't left."

Mr. Carmody thanked him again, crooked his umbrella on his arm and walked through the gates. He crossed the Lower Castle Yard, glancing up at the black battlements of the Wardrobe

Tower. He turned the corner by the Chapel Royal, gazing with admiration at the Latin inscription over the doorway. He did exactly as the policeman had told him, and in a few minutes he came to a group standing round a door. Officials were hurrying in and out giving directions to some workmen who were loading filing boxes and bundles of papers on to a van. Mr. Carmody went up to some young men who stood with waterproof coats folded over their arms.

"I beg your pardon," he said, "could you tell me if this is the Department of Fisheries?"

"Yes," answered one, "but we're moving out today to make room for Internal Affairs. Were you looking for anyone in particular?"

"I have an appointment with Mr. Watkins," explained Mr. Carmody.

"I don't know that he hasn't left. Try the second floor, turn to the right, and when you come to a fire extinguisher it's the third door on the left."

Mr. Carmody thanked him and went in. He mounted two flights of stairs and, turning to the right, found himself on a landing from which he could see quite a number of fire extinguishers. He was standing in a narrow passage summoning up courage to enter one of the rooms when a door suddenly opened and out came a heavy table and pinned him to the opposite wall. From the other end of the table a workman's red face gazed across at him in astonishment. When Mr. Carmody was released he thanked the workman and knocked at the first door he came to. A voice said: "Come in," and Mr. Carmody hastily took off his bowler hat and entered. An elderly man was sitting at a table writing.

"Hello," he said, "have you come to move the safe?"

Mr. Carmody said he had come to see Mr. Watkins.

"I don't know that Watkins is in the building," replied the elderly man. "You see, we're vacating these offices. Is there anything I can do?"

Mr. Carmody coughed with some embarrassment. "Well, it was about a post," he said. "I have been looking for a job for some time past, and someone, a friend of mine, spoke to Mr. Watkins, who wrote to me to call and see him."

The elderly man looked at him severely.

"You can't get into the Civil Service that way," he said. "You must pass a qualifying examination and receive a certificate of appointment from the Minister. Besides, I doubt if Mr. Watkins—he holds a comparatively junior position."

"It wasn't a post in the Civil Service," Mr. Carmody put in hurriedly. "I thought he might know of something outside in the city. I thought he'd be able to give me some advice as to how I should proceed."

The elderly man looked at Mr. Carmody for a moment.

"How old are you?" he asked.

"Forty-two."

The elderly man seemed to become suddenly embarrassed.

"You'd better wait for Mr. Watkins," he said.

He led the way to the door. Mr. Carmody took his umbrella and followed. The elderly man tried to bring Mr. Carmody up another flight of stairs, but he was prevented by two diminutive workmen who had got into difficulties with a large filing press at a place where the banisters curved.

"They're moving furniture," said the elderly man. "It's hardly safe to be out in the corridors."

Mr. Carmody agreed with him.

"You'd better wait in here," the elderly man said, leading the way to a room at the end of the passage. "I'll send Watkins when he turns up."

Mr. Carmody thanked him and took the liberty of sitting down on the edge of a chair.

The room was small and ugly. There was a calendar on the wall with the day's date, 27th January 1922. The only furniture was the chair on which he was sitting, and a table littered with papers. Among them was a file of about forty typed pages of foolscap fixed together with a brass fastener. Mr. Carmody blew off the dust and read: "Suggested Scheme for the Industrial Development of the Ballinacorrig Oyster Beds." He turned the first page and began to read with mild interest.

An hour passed. He suddenly realized that everything was very quiet. He could no longer hear the workmen in the passages. He tiptoed to the door, opened it and put out his head. For some time he heard nothing, then he became aware of approaching footsteps, and a young man turned the corner and came down the passage reading a sheet of paper as he walked, so that he did not see Mr. Carmody until he was close by.

"Hello," he said in a surprised voice when he saw Mr. Carmody's head. "Are you waiting for someone?"

Mr. Carmody told him about his appointment.

"The Department of Fisheries has moved out," said the young man, "but, of course, if you have an appointment with someone, no doubt he'll turn up."

He was a friendly young fellow with ginger hair, and he seemed to have time on his hands for he offered Mr. Carmody a cigarette and loitered round the room talking for a bit.

"I'm from Internal Affairs," he explained. "We'll be moving in this evening, and they sent me on in advance with a list of the rooms we're to occupy. That's in case the Department of Arts and Crafts tries to grab any of our rooms. They're in the same building, you see. They're extending, too. They're getting some of these rooms Fisheries were in."

"I didn't know two Government departments were ever housed in the same building," said Mr. Carmody.

"Oh, Lord, yes," replied the young man, "often. Just according as there's accommodation. In this building Arts and Crafts were all mixed up with Fisheries, one room one department, the next room the other department. They'll be all mixed up with us now."

"A very remarkable system," said Mr. Carmody.

"Ah," declared the ginger-headed young man, "what does it matter? We get to know our own rooms quick enough, and a stranger has only to inquire."

"A country's Civil Service is a wonderful organization," said Mr. Carmody.

"Ay," grinned the young man. "You see, it's only a few weeks since the Irish Government took over from the British. That's why all this changing of buildings is going on. And there have been practically no hitches. The Civil Service isn't really such a funny institution as people make out. It's slow in its movements, but it's sure." He went to the window. "I think I hear the Board of Works men arriving with the furniture. I wonder is this room of yours on my list." He opened the door. "Number 107. No. Arts and Crafts must be coming in here."

"I hope Mr. Watkins hasn't forgotten that he made an appointment with me," said Mr. Carmody. "I'm sure I've been waiting over an hour."

The young man hesitated at the door. "He may have been delayed, there's so much confusion today on account of the staff moving out. Might be worth your while waiting for a bit, that's if you're not in a hurry anywhere."

Mr. Carmody assured him that he wasn't in a particular hurry anywhere and that he'd wait for another while.

"Goodbye now," said the ginger-headed young man, and he went out.

Mr. Carmody sat down again and, resting his head between his hands, went on with his reading. He was re-perusing Section 23, which was not at all clear, when the trampling of feet and an occasional crash informed him that Government furniture was once more being moved. He continued to read until the sounds of activity came to the corridor outside. He listened for a while, and then as he was getting anxious lest Mr. Watkins had indeed forgotten him, he went over again and opened the door. Workmen were moving tables into the room next to his. An official stood alongside with a piece of paper and a red pencil in his hand. A workman came down the passage carrying a pile of papers.

"Arts and Crafts stuff," he said.

"Right," said the official. "Bring them in."

"What about the end room?" asked another. "Is there anything to go in there?"

The official read the number over Mr. Carmody's head, 107, and he consulted his list. "No, we're not getting 107. Internal Affairs must be moving in there."

"That's all, then?" asked the first workman.

"That's all," said the official, and without as much as a glance at Mr. Carmody they all went down the corridor.

For a few minutes he stood in the doorway, then he stepped back into the room. "That's queer," he said to himself, "this room is not on the Internal Affairs list and not on the Arts and

Crafts list, and each of them thinks it belongs to the other department."

He sat thinking what a great organiztion the Civil Service of a country was, and yet how easily a mistake like that could be made. Then he sat for a long time watching the light fade out of the sky above the roof of a tenement house in Ship Street. It was growing late in the afternoon, the room was no longer light, soon it would be half dark. He knew suddenly that Mr. Watkins must have forgotten the appointment and that the right thing for him to do was to go away and call tomorrow at the new offices, wherever they were; but he found he was unwilling to go. His heart sickened when he thought of having to go out again into the chill fog of the city. He thought of the misery of his position, the heart-breaking search for a job, any job at all, and the interviews with successful patronizing men, which were such a hurt to his shyness and his pride.

Christ Church Cathedral bell sounded its warning notes, and then it slowly struck the hour. Four o'clock. He remembered his miserable lodgings where there was no fire and where the rent was not paid. He thought of the misery of having to go on living at all. "I'll stay till five when they all go," he said to himself; "at least there are hot pipes here and the room is warm." He got up and groped for the electric light switch. He took off his overcoat and hung it behind the door. Then he seated himself at the table again with his head in his hands and forced himself to go on with his reading.

Half past four had struck when he was surprised by a quick step in the passage and a knock at the door. A young man came in.

"Good evening," he said briskly, laying on the table what seemed to be a list of names. "I hardly know where I am with all this moving about of staff. What's your name, please?"

Mr. Carmody told him, and the young man added the name quickly to the list.

"I'll be round on the thirty-first about eleven," he said. "You'll be here about that time I suppose?"

"Here?" said Mr. Carmody.

"Yes, at eleven on Friday, the thirty-first. In this room."

"Oh, you're from Mr. Watkins?"

"No," replied the young man, looking puzzled, "from Mr. O'Brien."

"Oh," said Mr. Carmody, not understanding a word.

"I'll always be here at eleven," said the young man. "Good evening," and he went out briskly, leaving Mr. Carmody gaping after him in astonishment.

On Friday at eleven o'clock Mr. Carmody sat in the room at the end of the corridor waiting for the young man to arrive. He did not understand why he was to be there, but he believed it was all connected in some way with the original appointment made by Mr. Watkins. The room was unchanged, the table was still littered with abandoned papers. At five past eleven the young man came in, brisk as before, with a bundle of paper slips in his hand.

"Good morning," he said. "Awful work we have over in Finance, what with the change of Government and the staffs moving all round the city. Your name is—?"

"Carmody," said the other, wondering what was going to happen next.

"Benedict Carmody," said the young man selecting a slip of paper from his bundle and laying it on the table. "I'll be here at the same time on the last day of next month. Good morning."

When the door closed Mr. Carmody gazed with amazement at the slip of paper. It was headed "Department of Internal Affairs Vote" and it was a cheque for thirty pounds.

Mr. Carmody has now been in the occupation of the little room for seventeen years. He comes in every morning about a quarter to eleven and reads the newspaper, then he looks at the ceiling and smokes cigarettes through a long holder until lunchtime. He meditates at times on the vastness of a country's Civil Service and says to himself that it isn't such a funny institution as people make out. The "Suggested Scheme for the Industrial Development of the Ballinacorrig Oyster Beds" lies permanently on the table before him, lest by not appearing to be at work he should give scandal to anyone who may come into his room by mistake. He is very rarely disturbed, however, since in his second year he wrote "Private" on a sheet of paper and pasted it on the door.

He feels himself perfectly secure, as the officials of each department no doubt imagine he belongs to the other one whenever they chance to see him in the passages, that is if they think about him at all.

In the afternoons he usually goes for a stroll through the streets or sits in one of the city parks until the evening editions of the newspapers come out. Sometimes he takes a week's or a fortnight's holiday, but he is always careful to be back on the last day of the month to receive a brisk young man with a bundle of cheques.

He has six years to run before he reaches the retiring age. He is beginning to worry about whether they will give him a pension.

The Stolen Ass

By Liam O'Flaherty

The accused, Patrick Haughy, went into the witness-box and was duly sworn. Just as he was about to begin his statement, District Justice Murnihan interrupted him:

"What did you say your name was?" said the Justice.

The accused was a very disreputable young tinker with red hair and a pointed chin.

"Patrick Haughy, yer hounour," he said.

"Oh!" said the Justice. "What I mean is, how do you spell it?"

"Begob," said the tinker, shrugging his shoulders, "I never spelt it in me life."

There was laughter in court.

District Superintendent Clarke informed the Justice that the name was spelt H-A-U-G-H-Y.

"Oh!" said the Justice. In that case I should think the correct pronunciation is Aw-Hee."

"It's usually pronounced Haw-Hee," said Clarke.

"Or would it be Och-ee?" said the Justice. "There were Irish kings of that name."

"Yer hounour," said the accused, "I was arrested by the pronunciation Haw-Hee."

There was further laughter in court. The accused then began his statement.

"It was this way, yer honour," he said. "I started from Kilmacshanahan to go to Kilnamaramaragull with a black she-ass. The ass had cast one of her hind shoes, so she got lame in the way, an' begob I was afraid that I'd get taken for her if I carried her any farther, with the laws there be now about cruelty to animals. So I met another ass, he was a jackass with a great welt across his hind quarters, same as somebody struck him with a hot iron, maybe a blacksmith or some divil of a woman that found him atin' her cabbages; well, anyway, I said

204

to mesel" 'I'll borrow this fellah an' lave me own ass in his place.'
Ye see, yer honour, my ass was a lot better of an ass, an' I only
left her there so as I'd get her comin' back."

"Where was this?" said the Justice.

"At Ballyfarnagaoran, yer honour."

"I see," said the Justice. "So you stole a jackass at Bally-er-so-
and-so?"

"No, yer honour," said the accused. "I didn't steal him. I just
borrowed him."

There was loud laughter in court. The accused continued:

"Well, I wasn't far on the road when I met a man comin' along
an' he with another ass, a mangy-lookin' animal, that was
knockin' his hind legs together and his nose to the ground
blowin' up the dust with every step he took and coughin' his
insides out, savin' yer honour's presence. Me an' this man
started talkin', and after a while he offers to swap asses with me
an' five shillings into the bargain. Well, I thought to messel' that
I had left a better ass in the place o' the jackass I borrowed, an'
so I'd be the loser anyway in givin' the other fellah's ass to this
fellah—"

"What other fellow?" said the Justice.

"The fellah I took the jackass from," said the accused.

"But you said you found him on the road."

"Well, ye know, he must have belonged to somebody, so
supposin' he did...."

Here the tinker scratched his head, wrinkled up his face and
looked worried.

"What's the matter now?" said the Justice.

"Aw begob," said the accused, "ye got me all mixed up, yer
honour, what with this fellah an' the other fellah that weren't in
the story atall, only be way of comparison."

"What nonsense are you talking about?" said the Justice
angrily. "Now where were we?"

At this moment there was loud laughter in court. The Justice
completely lost his temper and threatened to clear the court.

"Where were we, I say?" he repeated to the accused. "I want
no further nonsense."

"It was at Ballymorguttery I met him, yer honour," said the
accused calmly.

"Whom did you meet at this village?" snorted the Justice.

"It wasn't exactly in the village but near it," said the accused. "The fellah that had the old crock of an ass, I mean."

"Goodness gracious!" said the Justice. "What an extraordinary story! Continue."

"Well," said the accused, wiping his mouth on his sleeve, "after I left that fellah I set off with the old ass I bought from him, or it would be more like it with the ass he bought from me. No, but after lavin' him my jackass that I borrowed instead of my own ass. Ye see, he gave me five bob, and anyway, I thought to mesel', five bob is five bob, an' if the ass didn't die on the way I could always get my own ass back on the return journey at Ballyfarnagaoran. But sure I might as well be lashin' a tin-can as that old ass for all the walkin' I could get out of him, an' after a couple o' miles he lay down in the road altogether. I got him up be pullin' at his tail and then I got him on another mile until we came to Kilnamaramaragull. An' there I saw an ass in a field an' I says to mesel': 'I'll take that ass an' lave this fellah in his place.' Ye see, be that means everybody ud have an ass, because I'd lave the old fellah in the field instead of the one I'd take, and then I'd bring back the one I'd take to Ballyfarnagaoran, where I'd find my own black she-ass, and then I'd leave the ass I took out of the field instead of her and go home to Kilmacshanahan with my own ass."

"Just a moment," said the Justice, "which ass do you mean?"

There was a titter in the court, but the Justice looked very stern. The tinker completely lost control of his memory. He just dropped his lower jaw and stared at the Justice.

"Now, better be clear about it," said the Justice. "Which ass did you...er...I mean what ass did you...er...look here, my man, what ass are you talking about?"

"There were several asses," said the tinker, waving his arms in despair, "but now I've no ass atall, an' is that fair, I ask yer honour? Mr. Clarke arrested me an' I takin' the ass out o' the field an' he put the old ass in the pound an' he died there the following day, so I got no ass to put instead of my own ass at Ballyfarnagaoran."

"But how do we know it was your own ass?" said the Justice, leaning back and looking very cunningly at the accused.

"The ass I bought is it, yer honour?" said the accused.

"Look here," said the Justice furiously, again losing his temper and turning to the District Superintendent of Police, "what do you make of this fellow?"

"I don't believe he had any ass in the first instance, sir," said Mr. Clarke.

"Ha!" said the Justice. "Is that true, Haughy?"

"Yer honour," said the accused, "if ye give me time to go to Ballyfarnagaoran an' look around for her, I'd bring her to yer house to-morrow mornin'."

There was loud laughter once more in court and this time the Justice was unable to stop it.

"Look here, my man," he said to the accused, "it's quite obvious you never had an ass and all these stories about asses are deliberately concocted to misdirect the court. I sentence you to fourteen days' hard labour without the option of a fine."

"Many thanks, yer honour," said the accused; "but about me own ass..."

The Fur Coat

By Sean O'Faolain

When Maguire became Parliamentary Secretary to the Minister for Roads and Railways, his wife wound her arms around his neck, lifted herself on her toes, gazed into his eyes, and said, adoringly:

"Now, Paddy, I must have a fur coat."

"Of course, of course, me dear," Maguire cried, holding her out from him admiringly, for she was a handsome little woman still, in spite of the graying hair and the first hint of a stoop. "Get two fur coats! Switzer's will give us any amount of tick from now on."

Molly sat back into the chair with her fingers clasped between her knees and said, chidingly:

"You think I'm extravagant!"

"Indeed, then, I do not. We've had some thin times together and it's about time we had a bit of comfort in our old age. I'd like to see my wife in a fur coat. I'd love to see my wife take a shine out of some of those straps in Grafton Street—painted jades that never lifted a finger for God or man, not to as much as mention the word Ireland. By all means get a fur coat. Go down to Switzer's tomorrow morning," he cried with all the innocence of a warmhearted, inexperienced man, "and order the best fur coat that money can buy."

Molly Maguire looked at him with affection and irritation. The years had polished her hard—politics, revolution, husband in and out of prison, children reared with the help of relatives and Prisoners' Dependents' funds. You could see the years on her fingertips, too pink, too coarse, and in her diamond-bright eyes.

"Paddy, you big fool, do you know what you'd pay for a mink coat? Not to mention a sable? And not as much as to whisper the word broadtail?"

"Say a hundred quid," said Paddy, manfully. "What's a hundred quid? I'll be handling millions of public money from now on. I have to think big."

She replied in her warm Limerick singsong; sedately and proudly as befitted a woman who had often, in her father's country store, handled thousands of pound notes.

"Do you know, Paddy Maguire, what a really bang-up fur coat could cost you? It could cost you a thousand guineas, and more."

"One thousand guineas? For a coat? Sure, that's a whole year's salary."

"It is."

Paddy drew into himself. "And," he said, in a cautious voice, "is that the kind of coat you had in mind?"

She laughed, satisfied at having taken him off his perch.

"Yerrah, not at all. I thought I might pick up a nice little coat for, maybe, thirty or forty or, at the outside, fifty quid. Would that be too much?"

"Go down to Switzer's in the morning and bring it home on your back."

But even there, she thought she detected a touch of the bravo, as if he was still feeling a great fellow. She let it pass. She said she might have a look around. There was no hurry. She did not bring up the matter again for quite fifteen minutes.

"Paddy! About that fur coat. I sincerely hope you don't think I'm being vulgar?"

"How could you be vulgar?"

"Oh, sort of nouveau riche. I don't want a fur coat for showoff." She leaned forward eagerly. "Do you know the reason why I want a fur coat?"

"To keep you warm. What else?"

"Oh, well, that too, I suppose, yes," she agreed shortly. "But you must realize that from this on we'll be getting asked out to parties and receptions and so forth. And—well—I haven't a rag to wear!"

"I see," Paddy agreed; but she knew that he did not see.

"Look," she explained, "what I want is something I can wear any old time. I don't want a fur coat for grandeur." (This very scornfully.) "I want to be able to throw it on and go off and be as well dressed as anybody. You see, you can wear any old thing under a fur coat."

"That sounds a good idea." He considered the matter as judiciously as if he were considering a memorandum for a projected bypass. She leaned back, contented, with the air of a woman who has successfully laid her conscience to rest.

Then he spoiled it all by asking, "But, tell me, what do all the women do who haven't fur coats?"

"They dress."

"Dress? Don't ye all dress?"

"Paddy, don't be silly. They think of nothing else but dress. I have no time for dressing. I'm a busy housewife and, anyway, dressing costs a lot of money." (Here she caught a flicker in his eye which obviously meant that forty quid isn't to be sniffed at either.) "I mean they have costumes that cost twenty-five pounds. Half a dozen of 'em. They spend a lot of time and thought over it. They live for it. If you were married to one of 'em, you'd soon know what it means to dress. The beauty of a fur coat is that you can just throw it on and you're as good as the best of them."

"Well, that's fine! Get the ould coat."

He was evidently no longer enthusiastic. A fur coat, he had learned, is not a grand thing—it is just a useful thing. He drew his briefcase towards him. There was that pier down in Kerry to be looked at. "Mind you," he added, "it'd be nice and warm, too. Keep you from getting a cold."

"Oh, grand, yes, naturally, cozy, yes, all that, yes, yes!"

And she crashed out and banged the door after her and put the children to bed as if she were throwing sacks of turf into a cellar. When she came back he was pouring over maps and specifications. She began to patch one of the boy's pajamas. After a while she held it up and looked at it in despair. She let it sink into her lap and looked at the pile of mending beside her.

"I suppose when I'm dead and gone, they'll invent plastic pajamas that you can wash with a dishcloth and mend with a lump of glue."

She looked into the heart of the turf fire. A dozen pajamas—underwear for the whole house—

"Paddy!"

"Huh?"

"The last thing that I want anybody to start thinking is that I, by any possible chance, could be getting grand notions."

She watched him hopefully. He was lost in his plans.

"I can assure you, Paddy, that I loathe—simply loathe all this modern show-off."

"That's right."

"Those wives that think they haven't climbed the social ladder until they've got a fur coat!"

He grunted at the map of the pier.

"Because I don't care what you or anybody else says, Paddy, there is something vulgar about a fur coat. There's no shape to them. Especially musquash. What I was thinking of was black Indian lamb. Of course, the real thing would be ocelot. But they're much too dear. The real ones. And I wouldn't be seen dead in an imitation ocelot."

He glanced sideways from the table. "You seem to know a lot about fur." He leaned back and smiled benevolently. "I never knew you were hankering all this time after a fur coat."

"Who said I'm hankering! I am not. What do you mean? Don't be silly. I just want something decent to wear when we go out to a show, or to wear over a dance frock, that's all. What do you mean—hankering?"

"Well, what's wrong with that thing you have with the fur on the sleeves? The shiny thing with the what-do-you-call-ems—sequins, is it?"

"That! Do you mean that? For heaven's sake, don't be talking about what you don't know anything about. I've had that for fourteen years. It's like something me grandmother wore at her own funeral."

He laughed. "You used to like it."

"Of course, I liked it when I got it. Honestly, Paddy Maguire, there are times when—"

"Sorry, sorry, sorry. I was only trying to be helpful. How much is an ocelot?"

"Eighty-five or ninety—at the least."

"Well, why not?"

"Paddy, tell me honestly. Honestly, now! Do you seriously think that I could put eighty-five pounds on my back?"

With his pencil Maguire frugally drew a line on the map, reducing the pier by five yards, and wondered would the county surveyor let him get away with it.

"Well, the question is: will you be satisfied with the Indian lamb? What color did you say it is? Black? That's a very queer lamb."

Irritably he rubbed out the line. The wretched thing would be too shallow at low water if he cut five yards off it.

"It's dyed. You could get it brown, too," she cried. "You could get all sorts of lamb. Broadtail is the fur of unborn Persian lambs."

That woke him up: the good farmer stock in him was shocked.

"Unborn lambs!" he cried. "Do you mean to say that they—"

"Yes, isn't it awful? Honest to Heavens, Paddy, anyone that'd wear broadtail ought to be put in prison. Paddy, I've made up my mind. I just couldn't buy a fur coat. I just won't buy it. That's the end of it."

She picked up the pajamas again and looked at them with moist eyes. He turned to devote his full attention to her problem.

"Molly, darling, I'm afraid I don't understand what you're after. I mean, do you or do you not want a fur coat? I mean, supposing you didn't buy a fur coat, what else could you do?"

"Just exactly what do you mean?"—very coldly.

"I mean, it isn't apparently necessary that you should buy a fur coat. I mean, not if you don't really want to. There must be some other way of dressing besides fur coats? If you have a scunner against fur coats, why not buy something else just as good? There's hundreds of millions of other women in the world and they all haven't fur coats."

"I've told you before that they dress! And I've no time to dress. I've explained all that to you."

Maguire got up. He put his back to the fire, his hands behind him, a judicial look on him. He addressed the room.

"All the other women in the world can't all have time to dress. There must be some way out of it. For example, next month there'll be a garden party up at the President's house. How many of all these women will be wearing fur coats?" He addressed the armchair. "Has Mrs. de Valera time to dress?" He turned and leaned over the turf basket. "Has Mrs. General Mulcahy time to dress? There's ways and means of doing everything." (He shot a quick glance at the map of the pier; you could always knock a couple of feet off the width of it.) "After all, you've told me yourself that you could purchase a black costume for twenty-five guineas. Is that or is that not a fact? Very well then," triumphantly, "why not buy a black costume for twenty-five guineas?"

"Because, you big fathead, I'd have to have shoes and a blouse and hat and gloves and a fur and a purse and everything to match it, and I'd spend far more in the heel of the hunt, and I haven't time for that sort of thing and I'd have to have two or three costumes—Heaven above. I can't appear day after day in the same old rig, can I?"

"Good! Good! That's settled. Now, the question is: shall we or shall we not purchase a fur coat? Now! What is to be said for a fur coat?" He marked off the points on his fingers. "Number one: it is warm. Number two: it will keep you from getting cold. Number three—"

Molly jumped up, let a scream out of her, and hurled the basket of mending at him.

"Stop it! I told you I don't want a fur coat! And you don't want me to get a fur coat! You're too mean, that's what it is! And like all the Irish, you have the peasant streak in you. You're all alike, every bloody wan of ye. Keep your rotten fur coat. I never wanted it—"

And she ran from the room sobbing with fury and disappointment.

"Mean?" gasped Maguire to himself. "To think that anybody could say that I—Mean!"

She burst open the door to sob:

"I'll go to the garden party in a mackintosh. And I hope that'll satisfy you!" and ran out again.

He sat miserably at his table, cold with anger. He murmured the hateful word over and over, and wondered could there be any truth in it. He added ten yards to the pier. He reduced the ten to five, and then, seeing what he had done, swept the whole thing off the table.

It took them three days to make it up. She had hit him below the belt and they both knew it. On the fourth morning she found a check for a hundred and fifty pounds on her dressing table. For a moment her heart leaped. The next moment it died in her. She went down and put her arms about his neck and laid the check, torn in four, into his hand.

"I'm sorry, Paddy," she begged, crying like a kid. "You're not mean. You never were. It's me that's mean."

"You! Mean?" he said, fondly holding her in his arms.

"No, I'm not mean. It's not that. I just haven't the heart, Paddy. It was knocked out of me donkeys' years ago." He looked at her sadly. "You know what I'm trying to say?"

He nodded. But she saw that he didn't She was not sure that she knew herself. He took a deep, resolving breath, held her out from him by the shoulders, and looked her straight in the eyes. "Molly, tell me the truth. You want this coat?"

"I do. O God, I do!"

"Then go out and buy it."

"I couldn't Paddy. I just couldn't."

He looked at her for a long time. Then he asked: "Why?"

She looked straight at him and, shaking her head sadly, she said in a little sobbing voice:

"I don't know."

The Last Of Mrs. Murphy

By Brendan Behan

Over Mrs. Murphy's bed hung a picture of a person wearing a red jacket and a white head. When I was small I thought it was a picture of herself, but she laughed one day and said no, that it was Pope Leo. Whether this was a man or a woman I was not sure, for his red cloak was like Mrs. Murphy's and so was his white head.

The day I was five, Mrs. Murphy said we must go over to Jimmy the Sports for a quick one, the day that was in it.

"While I'm putting on me clothes, you can be giving the cat her bit of burgoo."

I got up the saucerful of porridge and put the milk on it, and called under the bed, "Minne Murphy, come out from that old shoe-box at once, and eat your breakfast."

"Before *he* eats it," muttered Mrs. Murphy to herself putting a skirt on over her head.

I was caught once, sitting the far side of a plateful of lights with the cat, but that was a long time ago, when I was only three: we eating, share and share alike.

We got out of the parlour all right, and into the hall. Someone had left a pram in it and Mrs. Murphy gave it a blessing when she nearly fell over it. She supported herself going round it, and opened the hall-door. Going down the steps into the street, she rested her hand on my head. I didn't mind for she was very light, and it was easy for her to reach me, though I was not that tall, for she was bent nearly double since the winter.

Half-way up the street, she sat on the steps of 16 and said I was to run up to the corner for a quarter ounce of white snuff.

I had to wait my turn in the shop. There were women in front of me.

"I says to myself when I seen her," says one woman, "The dead arose and appeared to many."

"It's all very fine and large," says the other one, "but I've had her in the Society since before the war. If she dropped dead this minute, God between her and all harm, I'd still be losing money. When she got over the Spanish 'flu, and was missed be the Tans on Bloody Sunday, I said it was only throwing good money after bad, and I'd cut me losses and let the policy lapse, for nothing less than an Act of God or a hand grenade could make a dent in her."

"Ah sure, what nicer am I? And we're not the only ones. There's more money invested in old Murphy nor the GSR."

The shopman looked over the counter at me, "Well, me little man?"

"A quarter ounce of white snuff."

The women nudged each other, "And how's poor Mrs. Murphy today, *a mhic*?"

"She's powerful."

"God bless her and spare the poor old creature."

"Barring the humane-killer," muttered the other old one, and they went out.

In the pub she sat in the corner and ordered a bottle of stout for herself and a dandy glass of porter for me.

"An orange or something would be better for the child," said Jimmy the Sports.

"The drop of gargle will do him good," said Mrs. Murphy, "it's only a little birthday celebration."

"You must be the hundred," said Jimmy the Sports.

"I'm not," said old Murphy, "nor nothing like it. I was born in the year eighteen hundred and thirty seven."

"You'd remember the famine then," said Jimmy the Sports.

"We were respectable people round this street and didn't go in for famines. All shut hall-doors that time. Down in Monto they had the famine. They didn't do a stroke of work for months only unloading the stuff off of the boats. The people that brought it over didn't mind. It was for the hungry Irish, and it saved them the trouble of going any further with it. They had the life of Riley down on the quay, while it lasted."

Jimmy the Sports ground his teeth and looked as if he might cry. "God forgive you, and the you an old woman. My poor mother fell from her own dead mother's arms outside Loughrea workhouse."

Mrs. Murphy took a pinch of snuff. "Well, we all have our troubles. If it's not an ear, it's an elbow. What about the gargle?"

Jimmy the Sports put them up and paid him. "Sorrow sign of famine on you anyway, Jimmy. The land for the people," she muttered to herself, "will you ever forget that?"

We spent a bit of time in Jimmy the Sports and then went back down the street. I walked in front for her to lean on my head, slow and in time with her. The pram was still in the hall, and she muttered a few curses getting round it, but the baby from the back drawing-room was in it this time, and she leant a minute on the side looking in at him.

"What's this the name of that crowd that owns this child is?"

"It's Rochfords' baby," said I. "Out of upstairs. He's only new out of the Roto this week."

"How do you know he's out of the Roto?"

"I heard my mother and them saying it. That's where all the babies are from. They have pictures there too."

She waved her hand. "Shut up a minute, can't you?" She put her hand to her forehead. "That'd be Dan Rochford's son's child, or his child maybe." She fumbled in her handbag. "I've two thrupenny bits. Here, take one of these in your hand. It has to be silver. Put it in the baby's hand and say what I say: 'Hold your hansel, long life and the height of good luck to you.' Come on."

I tried to speak but the tears were choking me. I thought she would give me one of the thrupenny bits anyway. It was like a blow in the face to me, and I'd done nothing on her but walked nice and easy down the street when she leaned on my head, and went over and got the snuff.

She looked down at me, and I put the thrupenny bit into the pram, and turned my heart, and—cheeks and eyes all full of tears—ran through the hall and out into the street.

My mother only laughed and said she didn't mean that Mrs. Murphy fancied the baby more than she did me. It could have been any new baby. It was the thing to do, and I a big fellow that had run out of two schools to be jealous of a little baby that couldn't even talk.

She brought me into Mrs. Murphy, and the two of them talked and laughed about it while I didn't look at them but sat in the corner playing with Minnie Murphy who, if she was vicious enough to scrawb you if she thought she'd get away with it, didn't make me feel such a fool. When my mother went I wanted to go too but my mother said Mrs. Murphy was sick and I could mind her till she came back.

Mrs. Murphy called me to the bedside and gave me a pinch of snuff, and had one herself, and the new baby went out of our heads.

The doctor came and said she'd have to go to the Refuge of the Dying. He told her that years ago.

Mrs. Murphy didn't know whether she'd go or not. I hoped she would. I heard them talk about it before and knew you went in a cab, miles over the city and to the southside. I was always afraid that they might have got me into another school before she'd go for, no matter how well you run out of them or kick the legs of the teacher, you have to go sometime.

She said she'd go and my granny said that she'd order a cab from the Roto to be there in the morning.

We all got into the cab. Mrs. Murphy was all wrapped up in blankets. She didn't lean on my head, but was helped by the jarvey, and off we went.

Going past a pub on the corner of Eccles Street, she said she didn't like to pass it, for old times' sake. My granny and Long Byrne and Lizzie MacCann all said they'd be the better of a rozziner. And the jarvey came in with the rest of us. On the banks of the other canal we went in and had another couple. We stopped there for a long time and my granny told the jarvey she'd make it up to him.

Glasses of malt she ordered, and Mrs. Murphy called on Long Byrne for a bar of a song.

The man in the pub said that it wasn't a singing house, but Mrs. Murphy said that she was going into the Refuge and it was a kind of a wake.

So Long Byrne sang, 'When the Cock, Cock Robin, comes hop, hop, hoppin' along,' and 'On Mother Kelly's Doorstep,' and for an hour it was great and you'd wish it could go on forever, but we had to go or the Refuge would be shut.

We left Mrs. Murphy and waited in the hall. Long Byrne said you get the smell of death in it.

"It's the wax on the floors," said my granny.

"It's a very hard-featured class of a smell, whatever it is," said Lizzie MacCann.

"We'll never see her again now, till we come up to collect her in the box," said Long Byrne.

"For God's sake, whisht up out of that, you," said my granny, "people's not bad enough." She fumbled with her handkerchief.

"All the same, Christina," said Lizzie MacCann, "you feel bad about leaving the poor devil in a place like this."

The jarvey was trying to smoke without being caught. "It's a very holy place," he said, but not looking too sure about it.

"Maybe, it's that we're not that holy ourselves," said Lizzie MacCann. "We might sooner die medium holy, like."

"It's not the kind of place I'd like to leave a neighbour or a neighbour's child," said Long Byrne.

"Oh, whisht your mouth," said my granny, "you'd make me feel like an...an informer or something. We only do the best we can."

A very severe looking lady in a white coat came out and stood in front of us. The jarvey stuck the pipe in his pocket and straighened his cap.

"Whars in charge of the peeshent?" she says in a very severe tongue.

My granny stood up as well as she could. "I am, with these other women here. She's a neighbour of ours."

"There are no admissions here after five o'clock. The patient arrived here in an intoxicated condition."

"She means poor old Murphy was drunk," says Long Byrne.

"The poor old creature had only six halves, the couple of glasses of malt we had to finish up, and the few bottles we had over in Eccles Street," said Lizzie MacCann, counting on her fingers. "God forgive them that'd tell a lie of an old woman, that she was the worse for drink."

"And I get a distinct smell of whiskey here in this very hall," said the woman in the white coat.

"How well you'd know it from the smell of gin, rum or brandy," said Long Byrne, "Ah well, I suppose practice makes perfect."

The woman in the white coat's face got that severe that if she fell on it she'd have cut herself.

"Out." She put up her hand, pointing to the door. "Out, at once."

There was a shuffling in the back of the hall, and Mrs. Murphy came out, supported by two nurses.

"I wouldn't stop where my friends aren't welcome," said Mrs. Murphy.

"Come on so," says my granny.

When they got back to Jimmy the Sports, they had a few and brought some more over to Mrs. Murphy's while they put her to bed.

Long Byrne said herself and Lizzy MacCann would look after between them.

My granny liked laziness better than she did money and said she'd bunce in a half a bar towards their trouble.

"And it won't break you," says Long Byrne, "damn it all, she's not Methuselah."

Blarney, Bulls and Cracks

Celtic Comedians

By John McCarthy

The standard evening public concert in any village, town or city in Ireland is composed of performances by young, proficient Irish dancers, a few native, sad, sentimental songs by tenors of all ages usually emulating John McCormick, the famed Irish singer who, not too long ago, was one of the world's top entertainers. And then, of course, there are performances by the local Celtic comedians.

Normally, these confident comedians, seemingly endowed with the grand gifts of satire and mordant humor, will occupy the stage longer than any of the other performers and will garner the largest share of applause.

Interestingly, exactly the same type of concert program given in Ireland will usually be followed strictly among the Irish in America, Britain, Canada and Australia. Even though many of the Irish in these countries, are second and third generation and have never seen Ireland, they enjoy these Celtic concerts just as much as did their ancestors from the Emerald Isle.

Like their progenitors, their popular preference is for the Celtic comedians. A possible explanation for this is rendered by the ancient proverb: "Love of laughter is an Irish heritage."

To insure in advance high glee and an appreciative audience, the Celtic comedians and their associates will often include in their repertoires excerpts from the classic comedies by such great Irish playwrights as Dion Boucicault, Bernard Shaw, Lady Gregory, Oscar Wilde, and John Millington Synge.

Actually, a few Irish concert groups devote their entire evening programs not only to the works of these playwrights but also the witty works of leading Irish playwrights of the 1700s, especially those of the celebrated Richard Brinsley Sheridan, born in Dublin in 1751. His trio of famous plays are

The Rivals, The School for Scandal, and *The Critic,* all of which, still centuries later, rate production today not only by Irish concert groups but by producers for theaters worldwide. For thirty years, Sheridan was a distinguished member of the British Parliament, holding many cabinet posts.

An accomplished actor, the dashing Dion Boucicault, as a prolific and powerful playwright, was the creator in his many plays of what is known as "The Stage Irishman," a merry, whiskey-drinking rogue, a loving personality who ignored the accepted Victorian respectability of his period, defied the Anglo-Saxon landlords in Ireland, and frequently bested their laws and ordinances. Always the adventurous chap, the Boucicault-built lead character, usually played by himself, was not only the darling of his village and popular with the locals but also was a big favorite with Irish, English, and American audiences.

Born in Dublin in 1820, Boucicault as a young man acted with the famed British star, Macready, in London. His first play, *London Assurance,* was a terrific success and he committed himself to writing and stage management, usually adapting plays from books and other sources. Before his death in 1890 in America, he had scripted and produced some 140 plays. *London Assurance* has been revived in London repeatedly since his death while his three most famous Irish plays, *The Colleen Bawn* (1859), *Arrah-na-Pogue* (1864) and *The Shaughraun* (1875) are still staged in Ireland by enthusiastic amateur thespians. Boucicault also composed more than three hundred songs including such well-remembered ones as "The Wearing of the Green" and "The Sidewalks of New York."

In the early part of the present century, Jimmy O'Dea was the premier Celtic comedian. He had his own company, wrote his own shows and the material for his monologues which, as his legions of fans would say, "rolled them in the aisles."

Intriguingly, O'Dea was just as big a draw in Belfast as he was in Dublin. Unlike most other Irish performers, O'Dea mastered the distinctly different Northern accent and could deliver local Belfast jokes with the expertise of a native. Even today, the mere mention of Jimmy O'Dea's name will bring a smile of happy memory to the most sullen oldster in either Northern Ireland or the Irish Republic.

Currently in Dublin, Morine Potter and Eamon Kelly are the chief comics in productions respectively written and produced by themselves. For nearly two decades, Potter has been Ireland's most resourceful, versatile, and leading commedienne providing her loyal legions of followers with a new and different show annually—a farce one year, a musical comedy the next, or a rousing revue. No matter what the show's form takes, the multitalented Potter, who can sing, dance, and act, will be its leading performer. As the saying in show biz goes, "Dubliners start laughing at the box office when they buy their tickets for a Morine Potter show!"

Incidentally, though Potter has had a number of offers to play abroad, particularly in London's West End and on Broadway in New York, she has spurned them, preferring to perform for her own loyal Dublin audiences. Besides, Morine likes her happy home life in Ireland too much to put up with the travails of travelling.

For his hit comic shows, which have been sellouts for several seasons at the Peacock Theatre in Dublin, Eamon Kelly has resurrected the role of *the shanachie*, the old time local village storyteller in Ireland who reported and commented on his neighbors and events in his own inimitable and oft sardonic style.

The single scene of his show has Kelly sitting in the front room of an Irish cottage alone and delighting his avid audiences the entire evening with town tales, descriptions of odd folks, family feuds, *et al.* The only action is when Kelly gets up to make himself a cup of tea or take a more comfortable chair. His consistently amusing script, which he writes, along with his natural, realistic, amusing delivery of same is an exclusively fashioned comic achievement.

Apropos of the shanachies, once we had an engaging afternoon encounter with one in an Irish village pub. One of the local shanachie's alleged true tales was a whopper about the trouble that a farmer down the road was having with crows resting on the backs of his cattle. A neighbor advised him that since crows avoid the smell of black tar, he should rub a supply of same on his cows' backs. Shortly after he had done this, the farmer spotted a group of crows settled blissfully on the broad back of one of his prized heifers and promptly shooed them away. As the crows flew off, they carried with them the prized heifer, who has never been seen since.

Before he starred on Broadway and later in Hollywood in the late 1930s, Barry Fitzgerald worked days in the General Post Office in Dublin and essayed key comic roles nights at the famous Abbey Theatre. He had major comedy parts in plays by Bernard Shaw, Sean O'Casey, Brinsley McNamara, Paul Vincent Carroll and other eminent Abbey dramatists. After his Abbey performances, Barry would quickly buy a couple bottles of Guinness at a nearby pub and grab the last bus to his seaside suburban home.

Arriving home around midnight, Fitzgerald would start enjoying his Guinness while playing the piano till the wee hours when he would finally retire. None of his Irish neighbors ever complained. "Ach, shure," reasoned they, "the man works both day and night. He has earned and deserves some diversion and pleasure."

When Fitzgerald went to Hollywood, he once again got himself a seaside house and a piano. After a long, long day at the movie studio, Barry bought his Guinness and looked forward to a long night's enjoyment. No sooner had he struck the piano keys than his phone began ringing. After he had ignored it for a quarter hour, the police arrived and threatened to put him in jail if he tried the piano any more that evening or anytime after dark.

In one of his earlier pictures in Hollywood, *The Quiet Man*, Fitzgerald, in the role of an Irish cab-driver and village marriage broker, became the leading figure even though the cast included such vaunted film stars as John Wayne, Maureen O'Hara and Victor McLaglen. The film was made in the tiny town of two hundred souls called Cong in County Galway, Ireland, where the elderly locals have never forgotten Fitzgerald and his Hollywood star pals. A memorable line from this film was a marriage proposal from a young Irisher to his prospective bride: "How would you like to be buried with my people?"

For generations, an imposing array of Americans of Irish ancestry have brought comic artistry to stage roles in the U.S.A. and overseas. Among the first of these were Ned Harrigan and Tony Hart in the 1880s and 1890s whose talented theatrical team of Harrigan and Hart, with their Celtic comical revues, were acclaimed from the Atlantic to the Pacific.

A first-rate musician, Harrigan wrote both the lyrics and music for all the many songs in their revues, which satirized the national antics of their period. For instance in the 1880s, as a likely holdover from the Civil War times, uniformed marching clubs were the rage and taken very seriously. However, Harrigan and Hart's hilarious *The Mulligan Guards* so burlesqued the marching clubs to the delight of huge audiences across the nation that the marching club craze soon faded.

The charming, personable Tony Hart, who had a touching tenor voice, played the female character parts in all their shows. In those far-off times, there were not very many comediennes in comical revues; the female roles were usually played by men in drag. Among the early comediennes was the American-Irish Maggie Cline, rather sharp and funny, whose song, "Throw him down, McCloskey!" became a national hit.

Other starring American colleens included the beautiful, superb Ina Claire, born Ina Fagan, whose amusing, winning, whimsical ways brought her the limelight and raves from critics for over forty years for comedy performances on Broadway and throughout the States and in the U.K.; Helen Broderick, the droll, deadpan comic for years in Ziegfeld's Follies; and the prankish Patsy Kelly, longtime favorite stage and screen comedienne.

The lengthy list of Yank Irish male performers enacting outstanding comic roles has such major names as Chauncey Olcott, George M. Cohan, Eddie Foy and the Little Foys, Pat Rooney, Sr. and Jr., Bobby Clark and Frank McCullough, John Coll, Frank Tinney, Bert Fitzgibbon, Dancing Dooleys, James Cagney, Fred Allen, whose real name was John Florence Sullivan, Pat O'Brien, Jim McCool, and many, many more.

Irish Bulls

The Republican political party once held a huge rally in Newark, New Jersey, to help its candidate, Ray Bateman, against Governor Byrne, the incumbent Deomcrat. The principal speaker was former U.S. President Gerald Ford whose ancestry is Irish.

After giving the qualities of Bateman a rousing half hour endorsement, Ford concluded dramatically with "Here's to Ray Bateman, the next Governor of Michigan!"

This was not the first public blooper for the former President. Intriguingly, several political commentators described these Ford howlers as "Irish bulls." And that they truly were. According to the Random House Dictionary of the English Language, an Irish Bull is "a paradoxical statement that appears to make sense." Today, the expression is rarely used or applied.

However, for decades beginning in the Civil War days up until the end of World War I in 1918, Irish bulls and many another derisive term were applied gleefully to the Irish. Those were the times of the great Irish immigration into America and their coming was somewhat resented by the native U.S. population whose major complaint was that they took away employment from Americans.

As a youngster growing up in Philadelphia, which had a large Irish Catholic immigrant community around the turn of the century, I remember quite a few "Irishisms," besides Irish bulls, which our Philly playmates used to poke fun at us of Irish ancestry. Among them were Irish confetti—a brick; Irish wedding—two black eyes; Irish raise—a reduction in pay or position; and Irish battleship—a barge.

During the half century before World War I, Irish bulls were the favorite fodder for columnists, comedians, cartoonists and public speakers, and the daily conversations of many Americans. The U.S. laboring elements were openly hostile to the Irish, made them the butt of many jokes and to a degree persecuted them.

The Irish met the challenge by playing it safe, as they had done at home under English persecution but in a way which would not give offense to anyone. In short, the Irish were not as dumb as their critics would make them out to be.

Basically, they possessed an earthy shrewdness and showed it repeatedly. Being uneducated, untrained and new to America, naturally, they made mistakes—plenty. However, the Irish were able with innate charm and cheerfulness to laugh along with those who found them inexperienced and amusing.

For example, I remember well my Donegal grandfather, himself an immigrant, laughingly reading to our family an editorial from the Irish-American newspaper he subscribed to in which the editor congratulated himself that "half the lies told about him are not true." Or another notice in the same paper: "Whereas, Patrick O'Connor lately left his lodging, this is to give notice that if he does not return immediately and pay for same, he will be advertised."

And my Irish grandmother, a kindly and well-being soul, amusingly telling of stopping and having a conversation with Mike Haggerty, a neighbor, who was planting shade trees in front of his home.

"You're digging out the holes, are you, Mr. Haggerty?" asked grandma.

"No, mum, Oi'm digging out the dirt an' lavin' the holes."

The leader of our Philadelphia political ward was Bill Carey, a man from Mayo. In his speeches, his record for Irish bulls far outpaced President Ford's. In fact, almost every statement Bill made had one or more. Here are a few:

"I know every cranny and crook in Philly"; "I've been keeping my ear to the grindstone"; "That kind of business gets my dandruff up"; "He got to do something to get a toehold in the public eye."

When I was in the U.S. Navy during World War I, we had a tough Corkian as bosun. One of his tasks was to distribute rifles to us for drilling. One day to make sure we were all supplied, he called out: "All of ye that are without arms, hold up your hands."

Sir Boyle Roche is claimed by Irishmen as father of the bulls, though one Aladich Bull, an Irish lawyer in London, is said to have made his name famous by his blundering. Sir Boyle was the son of a Limerick gentleman, served with the British army against the French in Canada, was later in the Irish Revenue Department and represented various boroughs in Parliament. He died in Dublin in 1807.

Perhaps Sir Boyle's most celebrated bull is: "Why should we beggar ourselves to benefit posterity? What has posterity done for us?" Inviting a friend to visit him, he wrote: "If you ever come within a mile of our house, will you stop there all night?" One of his most cherished bulls was: "Along the untrodden paths of the future, I can see the footprints of an unknown hand." In a message to a friend he declared: "While I write this letter, I have a pistol in one hand and a sword in the other."

The following gems are connected by long usage with Sir Boyle's name:

"I smell a rat. I see him floating in the air but mark me, I shall nip him in the bud."

"Many thousands of them were destitute of even the goods they possessed."

To guard the Shannon he proposed: "Sir, I would anchor a frigate off each bank of this river, with strict orders not to stir, and so, by cruising up and down, put a stop to smuggling." But not all the bulls are Sir Boyle's.

Sir John Parnell, in a debate in the Irish House of Commons in 1795, advised that "in the prosecution of the present war every man ought to be ready to give his last guinea to protect the remainder."

R. J. Mercredy in *Irish Cyclist* advised that "the best way to pass a cow on the road when cycling is to keep behind it," and an anonymous do—gooder has suggested that "there is nothing keeps the feet warm like an empty petrol tin full of hot water."

The classic description of an Irish Bull was provided by Sir John Pentland Mahaffy, noted Dublin wit and scholar, when asked by a lady to define it. Said he: "An Irish Bull, Madam, is always pregnant." A formidable figure for decades on the

Dublin scene, Mahaffy was a popular professor at Trinity College for fifty-five years and numbered among his students were Oscar Wilde and Oliver Gogarty.

Once on the campus, Mahaffy was stopped by a young co-ed and asked to explain the difference between a man and a woman. "I can't conceive," he replied. Mahaffy was also responsible for commenting, "Ireland is the place where the inevitable never happens and the unexpected oft occurs."

Cute Cracks

In Ireland, the teller of an amusing story or a tall tale usually is rewarded by his listeners with a hearty laugh or a broad smile and invariably the comment, "Ach, now that was a cute crack!"

One afternoon in Letterkenny, Donegal, I had an hour or so to kill before the bus left for Dublin, so I stopped into a pub not far from the bus station. It was one of the most depressing, dirty pubs that I had ever been into. It looked as though it had not been cleaned in years. However, the young barmaid was very well dressed with a lovely hairdo and politely asked for my order, which was a bottle of Guinness.

When she brought the Guinness, she said pleasantly, "That, sir, will be 27 pence." A little later, to make conversation, I inquired of the charming colleen, "You know the normal pub price of a bottle of Guinness anywhere in Ireland is 25 p., so why do you charge the extra two pence?"

Promptly responded she: "Sir, to keep the riff-raff out."

According to Milt Wyatt in the New York *Daily News,* it happened on a New York City bus on a rainy afternoon. An elderly man entered the bus holding aloft a very wet umbrella. The driver, speaking with a pronounced Irish brogue, asked the passenger to put his umbrella down and move to the back of the bus.

The old man glowered at the driver and didn't move.

The driver, now in a louder and angrier brogue, repeated his demand. The passenger reluctantly put the umbrella down and moved to the rear of the bus.

Then the passenger turned and glared at the driver with a look of burning anger and shouted—in a brogue as thick as the driver's, "Why don't you go back to where you came from!"

Charged with reckless driving in a County Mayo court, the defendant refuted with: "But, shure, I ran into that tree to avoid an accident."

Three neighboring Irish farmers in the late afternoon used to adjourn to the village pub for refreshments before returning to their homes for their evening tea. Once after repeated rounds, Declain, standing at the bar in the middle of the trio, suddenly slided to the floor and passed out. Brendan, on his left, looked down at him admiringly and commented, "Well, Declain is truly a man who knows when he has had enough!"

Two young Irishers, known to some of their fellow countrymen as "patriots" and by others as "terrorists," were driving along one of the Republic's really rocky roads on a mission near the Ulster border when they hit a hefty pothole.

"Careful now, Michael" warned passenger Packey. "Another deep dip like that last one and that bomb we have in the boot will go off."

"Stop worrying, Packey," replied driver Michael. "Just before we left, I hid an extra bomb under the back seat."

Journalist Murray Walter Illson, a retired staffer of *The New York Times,* recalls a Sunday in April 1942, when several hundred yardbirds (raw Army recruits) who were standing on the parade ground in Aberdeen, Maryland, had their chatter interrupted by a piercing whistle. Looking around they saw standing at the edge of the parade ground a burly–looking soldier with Master Sergeant's stripes on his sleeves. In complete silence the new yardbirds heard this Hibernian formidable-looking individual announce in a stentorian voice.

"I want to introduce myself. I am Master Sergeant Chauncey McManus and I'm from Pittsburgh, Pee A. And this being Sunday, I want you all to attend religious services of your choice. I want all the Protestants in that corner of the field, all the Jews in the other corner, and all the Mackeral Snappers over here." Everybody but one man went to their respective places. Sergeant Chauncey McManus of Pittsburgh, Pee A, stared at the lone yardbird standing in the middle of the parade ground and said:

"And you—what's the matter with you?"

The loner replied firmly: "I'm an atheist."

"You're a what?" exclaimed Master Sergeant McManus incredulously.

"I'm an atheist," repeated the loner as all the other yardbirds watched breathlessly.

Sergeant McManus stared hard at the man for several seconds and then rendered his verdict: "Okay," he boomed out, "you go with the Protestants!"

James Joyce's famed Dublin novel, *Ulysses*, which appeared in 1922, has long been recognized by the literary world as a classic. But one reader of same on its first day of publication never thought it was, and held that opinion until his death in 1957, even though in his youth, he had been a close friend of Joyce and had roomed with him in Dublin.

That was Oliver St. John Gogarty, eminent surgeon, poet and author, and one of the first Senators chosen when Ireland formed its own government. In *Ulysses*, Joyce had depicted Gogarty as one of the book's prominent Dublin characters under the name of *Buck Mulligan*. Gogarty was indignant and felt it a betrayal that his old friend, Joyce, should have written about him as he did. Said Gogarty vehemently:

"That bloody Joyce whom I kept in my youth has written a book you can read on all the lavatory walls of Dublin."

Ironically, on the strength of his reputation of having been *Buck Mulligan* in Joyce's *Ulysses*, Dr. Gogarty, in his later years, received and accepted a contract for a very lucrative lecture tour of the United States.

Overheard in the Dublin bus terminal. Traveller: "I want a return ticket." Ticket seller: "Where to?" Traveller: "Back here, of course."

Speaking of travellers, many hotels in the United Kingdom and on the Continent have a nice traditional custom for their guests to leave their shoes outside their door for the hotel porter to clean and shine during th night.It has been my experience of years of travel in Ireland, that this custom has never been accepted there.

For instance, one afternoon in Cavan, I dropped in to a local hotel for tea served at tables in the hotel's spacious lobby. After the waitress had taken my order and was enroute to the kitchen, she was stopped by an English commercial traveller just entering the lobby, who commanded her in a loud, irritated voice to get the proprietor.

When the proprietor appeared, the Englishman, again in a loud voice, said:

"Sir, when I picked up my shoes outside my door this morning, they were just as I had left them there last night— untouched entirely."

"Ach, now sir, I'm not surprised," reassured the hotel owner. "If you've forgotten to take them in and came back here three months or even a year later, they still would be there untouched. I'm proud to say my hotel is the most honest in all Ireland."

In front of hundreds of startled tourists on the eighty-sixth floor observation deck of the Empire State Building in New York on a lovely morning in April 1986, a happy Hibernian from London, Michael McCarthy, twenty-five, and his British pal, Alisdair Boyd, twenty-seven, took a laughing leap from the deck's eighteen-inch-wide concrete ledge into the *Guinness Book of Records* as the first ever to parachute safely from the top of that skyscraper.

Some sixty seconds, and 1,050 feet later, the two amateur parachuters landed nicely two blocks down from the Empire State Building on Fifth Avenue. It was the first time anyone had tried to make a parachute jump from the landmark building since it was built fifty-six years ago.

Another Hibernian, Manhattan Police Officer William J. O'Brien, and his partner, strolling their Fifth Avenue beat, were astounded to see the two Londoners dropping from the sky. "My partner and I looked at each other and then looked back— we couldn't believe it at first." Seeing the police, Alisdair quickly folded his parachute, grabbed a taxicab and got away. But

McCarthy was still fumbling with his parachute when Officer O'Brien and partner arrived. They cordially congratulated him before handcuffing and arresting him.

Feigning indignation, McCarthy explained, "Ah, come on, officers, when the guard up there on the observation deck told us to get off the ledge, we quickly obeyed and did."

Notice in a Galway pub: "Credit might be considered for ONLY those over 85 accompanied by both their parents and a grandparent."

Driving in the Rosses section of Donegal, a Yank tourist noted an imposing black grayish peak looming up ahead. Stopping his car, he hailed a local and inquired; "What's that mountain in the distance?"

"That's Errigal, the world's largest mountain," came the quick reply.

"But what about Everest?" followed up the American.

"Oh," responded the local, "excepting those in foreign parts."

Having taught theology for years at the famed Maynooth Seminary, outside of Dublin, Canon Cathal O'Callaghan was transferred to a remote town in Northwest Ireland where he was to be the parish priest. Worried whether his sermons might be over the heads of his new parishioners, the Canon, after a few weeks of residence, stationed himself after his late Sunday Mass outside his church to get a firsthand reaction.

A friendly, elderly lady immediately approached him, shook his hand and congratulated him on his sermons. "You know, Canon," said she, "I'm going to like your sermons even better when I can understand them."

On a Saturday Afternoon in Dungloe, a lovely, tidy town in Donegal, Mickey Anthony, the town toper, making his daily round of the pubs, was haltingly wending his way through the throngs of shoppers down from the top of Main Street. Coming up the street was Dungloe's popular parish priest, Canon John Mulloy.

A former chaplain of the famed Irish Guards in World War II,

Canon Malloy saw his parishioners plain and had not the slightest hesitancy of telling them off. However, when, without exception, any one of them had troubles, the Canon was always in their corner. The parishioners appreciated that and accorded him their highest respect. Hence, when he spotted the Canon, the swaying Mickey Anthony did his best to straighten up and give the Canon the traditional friendly Donegal salute of a nod of the head and quickly get by his parish priest.

But, when they met, the Canon stopped him with "Mickey Anthony, you're on the road to Hell!"

After respectfully pausing and listening, Mickey Anthony replied, "Shure, Canon, if I'm on the road to Hell, I never expected to meet yourself there."

Here is another Canon Malloy story told by Canon Eugene McDermott, D.D. One Sunday morning, his curate, Doctor Eugene McDermott, who had said an early Mass in the adjoining village of Meenacross, arrived in Dungloe rather late for the last Mass of the day at noon. Furious, Canon Malloy was waiting for him in the sacristy when he arrived and lashed into him. "But Canon," explained Doctor McDermott, "the thick ice on the Meenacross road was terrible, and my car kept sliding from one side of the road to the other. I was very lucky not to wind up in those deep ditches alongside."

"Well, then Doctor," responded the Canon, as he departed the sacristy "in that case, only a damn fool would be out today driving on that Meenacross road."

In America, only 20 percent of alcoholic beverages are consumed on-premises, such as bars, grills, etc.; in Ireland, 80 percent of alcoholic consumption is carried on in the pubs. Hence, when the Irish government, faced with an enormous budget deficit, slapped heavy extra duties on all alcoholic beverages the Irish publicans were up in arms. Thousands of them gathered in Dublin from all parts of Ireland and marched in a huge demonstration to present a petition of protest to the government. Their customers protested loudly, too, and joined the publicans in their Dublin march.

The Irish Times carried this news on its front page coyly headlined: "Drinkers Find Duty A Sobering Prospect."

One Irishman, unanimously popular and acclaimed both in Northern Ireland as well as in the South in the Irish Republic, is Barry McGuigan, the world's featherweight boxing champion. Even though champion McGuigan could likely garner far larger purses meeting challengers in London, New York, and elsewhere, Barry insists his bouts be held in Belfast or Dublin where his family, friends, and local adherents can witness them firsthand. His Irish fans appreciate that no end.

When McGuigan visited New York, Cardinal John O'Connor at St. Patrick's Cathedral autographed Barry's boxing glove, then quipped: "Don't hit anyone with it. It has power!"

Agnes K. Bantle, Charlotte, North Carolina, told us about a neighbor of hers. He is Patrick Loftus whose relatives all came from County Sligo. Recently, Patrick took a trip to Ireland to see how many of his father's people were still there. Renting a car in Dublin, he made the long drive north to his dad's native town. Getting there, Patrick went into a local pub and asked if there were any families named Loftus still around.

"Indade there are," said the publican. "As a matter of fact, they buried one of them this morning from that wide gray house at the top of the hill out there." Patrick went up the hill and knocked on the door. It was opened by a solemn oldster in a black suit and tie. Patrick said, "I'm Patrick Loftus from the USA and I'm looking up my family."

"Be japers," replied the oldster, breaking into a wide smile, "we no sooner put one down when another walks in the door!"

The Clan Loftus treated their visiting Yank member royally. His long drive from Sligo back to Dublin was pleasanter by far than the one coming up. For Patrick had a delightful companion, Cousin Finbar Loftus of Dublin, who cued Patrick in on the wake and the various relatives in attendance, besides pointing out scenic places of interest enroute.

When we retired, we settled in an old house in the remote but lovely Donegal seaside village of Maghery where my wife's family came from and where she had gone to school as a youngster. One day, while my wife was driving into the nearest town, Dungloe, she gave a lift to a lady neighbor. After thanking her, the Irish lady asked what I did, meaning in the local sense whether I was engaged in farming, fishing, or working on the roads. Proudly, my wife stated that I write.

A pause in the conversation ensued. Finally, the Irish lady spoke up with: "Ach, shure that passes the time."

After we had been in Maghery, Donegal, for several months, I was having a drink alone one evening in the village's Packey's Pink Pub when I was joined by a native neighbor from up the road who had spent some twenty years working in America. After sitting down, he took a long pull on his pint, looked around to make sure none of Packey's other patrons were tuned in and then whispered, "I hear you are staying. Well, let me tell you. Ireland is a paradise if you can take it."

In an Irish court action for damages for personal injuries and the loss of a cow, as *The Donegal Democrat* reported, the defendant began his cross-examination of the plaintiff:

Counsel:	You have now informed us in reply to your counsel that you were seriously injured in the accident.
Plaintiff:	I was so, and so was my heifer.
Counsel:	Never mind your heifer. How do you reconcile your story now with your statement to my client immediately after the accident that there was nothing the matter with you?
Plaintiff:	Well that's not the whole of the story.
Counsel:	Did you say that or not?
(The Judge to Counsel):	You have re-opened the question. The witness is entitled to explain his answer.
Plaintiff:	Thank you sir. Well, the truth of it is that I was driving the heifer along the road minding our own business when that man over there came whipping around the corner at ninety miles an hour, and the next thing me and the heifer is lying in the ditch, and the pair of us pumping blood. With that your man got out of the car, and sez to me: "That beast is badly injured," so he took a gun out and shot her there and then in the ditch.

Then he turns around and sez he: "Tell me, my man, would there be anything wrong with you?" and I sez to him 'Begod sir, I never felt better in my life!'

Tom Ronan, a retired foreign correspondent for *The New York Times*, admits that he was an easy touch for a gent, exiting from an Irish bar on Third Avenue, New York City, who put the arm on him for a grub stake by pleading: "If I don't eat a good meal soon, I'm gonna be too thin to bless myself."

According to Don Nelson, the popular Broadway columnist for the New York *Daily News*, there was not a New York saloon, no matter how remote, that Brendan Behan had not sampled.

"One night some years ago" recalls Nelson, "I and two other night rascals were driving Behan and his wife to their hotel. It was around midnight. The car stopped for a light in Little Italy. Suddenly, Behan bolted from the car and ran to an ill-lit bar with no discernible name on its windows or doorway. All gave pursuit and we reached Behan just as he opened the door to find a burly gent barring his entry. Said the gent to Behan: "I know you. You're not coming in here again.""

In his remarks recently before the New York Society of Security Analysts, Irish born and reared Dr. Anthony J. F. O'Reilly, the prominent, popular president and chief executive officer of the international food firm H.J. Heinz Company, related how the need for keeping in shape was sharply brought home to himself via that mordant witty fashion of which the Hibernians are the past masters.

"Two weeks ago," said O'Reilly, once one of Ireland's foremost rugby players, "I went to watch Ireland play England. As I was coming out of the grounds afterwards, two Irish rugby supporters looked at me with a sort of distant recollection and one said to the other: 'Hey, look at that man there!' The other fellow asked: 'Who is he?' The first chap replied: 'He used to be Tony O'Reilly.'"

Interesting Characters

Born Politicians and Statesmen

From that small Emerald Isle, Ireland, nations the world over have benefited from talented, outstanding, Irish political practitioners. After emigrating from Ireland, a number of them also proficiently served as well in their adopted countries' military ranks in wars and been honored as national heroes.

In fact, wherever the Irish have settled after leaving their native heath, they and their descendants, politics and governmental services evidently have had a basic natural lifetime appeal to them. Consequently, many native Irish and those of Irish ancestry figure prominently in national historical records of Britain, Europe, Latin America, Australia, Canada and the United States. Having the inherited Irish sense of humor, gift of gab and shrewd practicality were likely assets for these Celtic emigres.

In England's long history of parliamentary activities, the names of Burke, Swift, Sheridan, Wellington, O'Connell, and Parnell loom large and favorable. A number of Ireland's famous so-called "Wild Geese," Irish Army officers and soldiers who flew to France in the late eighteenth century, namely, MacMahon, Lacy, O'Reilly, Dillion, Cusack and Clarke, became French Marshalls for their distinguished service in the Napoleonic wars. Later, nearly all of them held high governmental posts. General De Gaulle's great grandfather was a MacCartan from Cork. Briand, eleven times elected premier of France, was the great grandson of Conal O'Brien, one of the Wild Geese.

O'Donnell, from the Irish county of Roscommon, and Wall, from Waterford, served Spain as prime ministers. Another Irisher, Lawless, was the Spanish Ambassador to England. An

O'Farrel, who had been a Spanish Army General, was Spain's Ambassador to Berlin. O'Daley served as the Spanish Governor of Rosas while General O'Donahue, who had been Spanish chief of staff in the Peninsular war, became the viceroy of Mexico. Taaffe, also from Roscommon, was twice premier of the Austro-Hungarian Empire.

Irish born Ambrosio O'Higgins, the eighteenth century Spanish Viceroy of Peru, conquered Chile for his adopted country. After his death, his son, Bernardo O'Higgins, undid much of papa's achievements by leading successfully the struggle for independence. In history, he is known as "The Liberator of Chile." Alvaro Obregon, popular president of Mexico in the 1920s, belonged to the Clan O'Brien.

Gavan Duffy, a political exile from Ireland, became prime minister of Australia and was knighted by Queen Victoria. Another Irish political activist who had to flee from Ireland, Thomas D'Arcy McGee, became the highly respected head of the Canadian Parliament. Currently, another charming, capable Celt, Brian Mulrooney, is Canada's premier.

Out of the forty presidents of the United States, ten have had Irish blood in their veins. All, presidents Jackson, Grant, Arthur, McKinley, Wilson, Kennedy, Nixon, Ford, Carter and Reagan, have been proud of every drop of it. Away back on July 4, 1776, when a group of American Colonial leaders met in Philadelphia and signed the Declaration of Independence, three were Irish born. They were James Smith, a lawyer, and George Taylor, an ironmaster, both from Pennsylvania along with Matthew Thornton, a physician from New Hampshire.

Regarding this great, historic document, Abraham Lincoln, stopping in Philadelphia, February 23, 1861, enroute to his presidential inauguration, had this to say about it:

"I have never had a feeling, politically, that did not spring from the sentiments embodied in the Declaration of Independence....I have often inquired of myself what great principle or idea it was that kept this Confederacy so long together. It was not the mere matter of separation of the colonies from the motherland, but that sentiment in the Declaration of Independence which gave liberty not alone to the people of the country, but hope to all the world for all future time. It was that which gave promise that in due time the weights would be lifted from the shoulders of all men, and that all should have an equal chance. This is the sentiment embodied in the Declaration of Independence....I would rather be assassinated on this spot than surrender it."

Ronald Reagan is the first professional actor and movie star ever to be elected President of the United States. Being sixty-nine years of age in 1981, he was the oldest president at his inauguration; hitherto, the record had been held by William Henry Harrison who was sixty-eight at his inauguration in 1841. President Theodore Roosevelt, at forty-two, was the youngest at his inauguration in 1901; the second youngest was President John F. Kennedy who was forty-three when inaugurated in 1961.

Another rare record, considered somewhat of a high honor in rural Ireland, is that Ronald Reagan is the first and only U.S. president ever to have an Irish pub named after him. It is located in Ballyporeen, a two-street town in County Tipperary where the president's great grandfather, Michael Reagan, was born in 1829. The Ronald Reagan pub beams the president's name in green Gaelic lettering from a sixteen-foot electric sign.

The Reagan's publican is John O'Farrell, who was first informed of the Reagan link to Ballyporeen in 1980, when Hugh Peskett, a genealogist with Debrett's Peerage Ltd., London, dropped by his pub and over a pint told him the news. "We immediately saw the potential in it," said O'Farrell. "Two days later the illuminated Reagan sign was ordered and was erected within a matter of weeks." Incidentally, a few years later, President Reagan on an official visit to Ireland also dropped by and had a wee drink in the pub named after himself.

True to his Irish ancestry, President Reagan is a prolific story teller and a collector of jokes. As James Reston, the eminent political writer of *The New York Times,* aptly points out, being a superb story teller with smart timing has enabled the President to do so well as a political stump speaker. Reston says, "The President is like Vice President Barkley of Kentucky who, when confronted with a hard question, always remembered a funny story that diverted the questioner from the facts. The President's humor is usually directed at the Democrats, but it's gentle. He mocks but never wounds, and increasingly, he pokes fun at himself, particularly at his age."

Addressing the Conservative Political Action Conference, Reagan conceded his Administration had a serious trade deficit. "The United States," he said, "had a merchandise trade deficit in almost all the years between 1790 and 1875." Then he added, deadpan: "I remember them well. Of course, I was only a boy at the time."

About Congress the President said, "I know there was one young person with his parents who was up in the gallery one day at the Congress and asked who the chaplain was. And his father said, 'Well, that's the chaplain. He prays.' And the child said, 'For the Congress?' And he said, 'No; for the country.'"

During his official visit to Ireland, President Reagan was confronted with a couple of demonstrations against his policies. When he got back to Washington, he was asked about them in a press conference.

Q. "Sir, are you disturbed about the Irish demonstrations?"

A. "Oh, the Irish demonstrations! I think that's just Irish hospitality. They know that I haven't gone any place in years that there hasn't been a demonstration, and they don't want me to feel as if I'm not at home!"

During a speech at the National Press Club, that great dancer and actor, Gene Kelly, replied to a question as to whether actors should be so active in politics with: "Try telling that to President Reagan!"

One January, after both sides of the House of Representatives sang "Happy Birthday" on the occasion of his seventieth birthday, House Speaker Democrat Thomas Patrick "Tip" O'Neill responded with, "That action is against the House, and you are all out of order!"

In Buffalo, William F. Buckley, the conservative commentator, was addressing a dinner of 300 of the more generous contributors to the political campaigns of Representative Jack F. Kemp, Republican of New York. In the question period, one member of the audience asked Buckley what White House position he would seek if Kemp should be elected President in 1988. Without a flicker, he replied, "Ventriloquist."

Former Governor of New York, Alfred E. Smith, and an associate were walking through the library of the New York Law School enroute to an appointment when they passed a student diligently making notes out of one huge law book with another pile of big law books on the table beside him. "There," commented the governor, "is an ambitious, young potential lawyer trying to find out how to make a bribe into a fee."

When asked why he ran for Congress, the Republican representative from Florida, Connie Mack, III, grandson of the famed owner of the Philadelphia Athletics and whose right name was Cornelius McGillicuddy, answered: "I found out I couldn't hit a curve ball."

In 1932, Mayor James J. Walker of New York resigned and sailed to Europe. He left behind an investigation by the Seabury Commission, which elicited testimony from Sheriff Thomas A. Farley that he had found $100,000 in a "wonderful tin box."

There also was James A. McQuade, a minor official from Queens, New York, who said he borrowed $510,597—he couldn't remember from whom— since he was the sole support of himself and thirty-three relatives. They were dubbed "the thirty-four starving McQuades."

Back in the 1890s, a lively lad, Michael Patrick Walsh, from County Mayo settled in Manhattan and became an ardent Tammany Hall supporter. Before long, Michael Patrick was in Congress. His trouble was that he was a continuous complainer, criticising everybody, including members of his own Demorcratic Party. Result. He was not even renominated when his term ended. After Michael Patrick's death, some years later, it was discovered that he never had found the time to become a citizen.

On the after-dinner circuit, Bill Bradley, the serious Senior U.S. Senator from New Jersey, and former noted professional basketball star, is not an outstanding performer. He is aware of same, albeit being of the Celtic Clan Bradley, the Senator has a sense of humor, which he displayed at a roast of Governor Mario Cuomo of New York.

"I, Bill Bradley, taught Mario Cuomo how to make a political speech," the New Jersey Deomcrat said. "I said, 'Mario, just watch me and then do the opposite.'

"Yes, you know I have this reputation of being a wooden speaker. Besides speaking ability, Governor Cuomo and I have something else in common. We were both athletes. Not being a great natural athlete myself, I struggled along on the basketball court while Mario excelled in many sports. He was a promising quarterback on the high school varsity football team, but because of his small, pudgy hands, he couldn't play when they blew up the football. His mother says even as a child, when he'd leave a ring around the bathtub, he'd throw his hat into it.

"Our states are rivals," Bradley continued, adding that Cuomo "is trying to bring our states together—that's why he's trying to pave over half the Hudson River."

The suave Senior U.S. Senator from New York, Daniel Patrick Moynihan, who has been active and successful in politics for decades, observes, "The professional life expectancy in our business is about that of a second lieutenant on the Somme."

A Man Like Grady, You Got to Know Him First

By John McNulty

Some of the people that inhabits this saloon on Third Avenue requires explanation. Grady the Cabman is one of them, and the other night, for want of anything better to do, Paddy Ferrarty was trying to explain him the best he could and make talk anyway for a while while there was hardly anybody in the place.

"A man like Grady, you got to know him first," Paddy said, "Else you won't make any headway at all understanding a man like that. Grady befuggles even me sometimes, and I know him since they said then he was only about seventy. Some around here says he's around a hundred, putting it on a little perhaps, but he's anyway old. Maybe he's sixty-eight, but God knows. And God'll tell you sooner than Grady.

"The thing about Grady is he seems to be always doing two things that works opposite each other and spending all his time doing it. Like he takes a cab out of the garage every night and then he spends half the night trying to keep people from getting into it and making him take them someplace. If he don't want to have people in the cab, and God knows he don't most of the time unless he can pick out who gets in his cab, well then why does he take out the cab in the first place? That's the part about Grady, you got to know him first. And even then it ain't any too clear what Grady's all about. Maybe it ain't important.

"He only wears a wig when he goes to court, or did you know he's as bald as a banana? Well he is, but how hardly anybody knows that is he wears that cabby cap night and day, wouldn't take it off for anybody. You'd get him raving mad if you yanked it off his head. Never takes the cap off even if he goes into somebody's house—I mean into a friend of his's that's drunk and got to be carried in and help the wife get him into bed and his collar unbuttoned and his shoes off so he won't choke and can sleep easy.

"One day Grady come in here in the middle of the afternoon, which was surprising to see Grady in daylight ever. I happened to be here on account a cousin of mine was with me at a funeral and I had to get up in the daytime, and after the funeral I brought my cousin in here to show him where I work because he beeslong in Brooklyn and don't get around much. Anyway, there was Grady wearing the wig and his cap off sitting at the end of the bar. He claim he found the wig one time in the back of the cab off a customer and it fit him, but so help me God I think he bought the thing. He explained why he had it on after he had to admit it was a wig, couldn't fool anybody any more than a wax apple. He got into some kind of traffic trouble, which don't happen often, I'll say that for him, and he had to go into court. He knew there's no getting away with keeping your hat on in court. Grady or no Grady, lifelong custom or no lifelong custom, take off your hat and no goddam arguments. So he wore the wig. The wig's unimportant anyway, but it's one of the things you got to understand about Grady and I'm only starting with the wig. It's hardly anything at all.

"The funny part is Grady got his own way making about three bucks a night with the cab. Even if he don't, he don't worry. You take the start of a nice summer night for instance here around Third Avenue, say take six blocks up here and say five blocks down from here. Well, that makes eleven blocks in all and in eleven Third Avenue blocks it stands to reason they got a slather of saloons.

"Well, we'll say it's the start of a fine summer night around here. Maybe seven o'clock and the 'L' is roaring down from time to time and some kids standing in a bunch on a stoop on the side street and singing 'Don't Sit Under the Apple Tree with Anybody Else but Me Till I Come Marching Home,' and the little guy, they call him Shorty, smoking a cigar on the corner, God knows where he gets all the cigars, and everything like normal for the start of a fine summer night and along comes Grady.

"He starts sizing up the terrain as they say. He puts the cab at the corner, facing the wrong way chances are, and he walks a ways smoking that dudeen of his.

"Calm enough, he goes into this saloon and he goes into that saloon along the line. Maybe he'll see Junior Connors lined up at the bar in the first saloon. He's a big fat guy with a fine rum blossom for a nose and looks nothing at all like a junior so they call him that. He's a regular customer or ward, or whatever it is, of Grady's. Wards is better. They're more like wards than customers. Grady chooses them, they don't have hardly any hand in picking Grady for a cabman, he takes care of them year after year. Anyway, Junior is like most of the guys Grady'll allow in the cab, you might say. They're nearly all fellahs that have good enough jobs to keep them in liquor money, works regular but mostly devotes themselves to drinking and singing and arguing. Not rum-dumbs but warmin' up to be rum-dumbs.

"Anyway, to get back to Junior, Grady takes a look at him beginning to drape over the bar. Grady got little squint eyes and some says he doesn't see good, but I think he can. He can spot Junior and the rest of them. A man that claims Grady can't see good any more claimed to me one time Grady drives up and down Third Avenue by memory and don't see much ahead of him. This man claim that's why Grady don't like to drive on the West Side, because he can't remember it and don't see it, and the same guy claim it's a terrible thing for Grady they're tearing down the Elevateds because the way Grady drives he counts on the 'L' being there and it'll ball up his driving if the 'L' ain't. I think the man was exaggerating about Grady. He sees well enough I believe.

"When Grady takes a look at Junior, Grady says nothing, don't even say hello, but in his own mind Grady says to himself, 'Connors'll be ready by ten o'clock.' In other words he kind of make a mental note of Connors and the shape he's in figuring like an estimate the shape he'll be in by ten o'clock probably ready to be taken home. Then Grady leaves that saloon for the next saloon that's only no distance at all.

"In the next saloon we'll say Grady spots another regular of his, maybe Shauno Haggerty that already, and it's only ha-past seven, is standing there reciting 'Dawn on the Coast of Ireland'—I'm so gaddam sick of hearing about dawn on the coast of Ireland from Shauno. 'Oh-oh' says Grady to himself, making a mental note of Shauno, 'he'll be the first, he's almost ready already. I'll get him home first, soon as I take a look around the other places.' Out goes Grady and to the next adjoining gin mill.

"That's the way Grady does. In a half-hour after he gets the cab parked on the corner, and a trip made into the saloons, he's kind of got himself booked for the night. You know how I mean—he's got to take Shauno at eight o'clock and steer him into the cab and home, then Junior at ten o'clock, and some other guy he's spotted will be drunk and ready at one o'clock, and so on.

"When these times come it sometimes gives me the shudders to see Grady circlin' around the guy he got picked to take home soon. He looks like a buzzard closing in on the guy sagging over the bar, but when all is said and done it's a good thing. Somebody got to take them home or God knows where they'd wind up and Grady takes care of them like a mother you might say. But a pretty tough mother it'd be running up nickels on a taxi clock taking care of her son, now wouldn't it?

"You can see in the meantime between these guys to be taken home at certain times Grady got fixed in his mind why he don't want a lot of strangers climbing in the cab. Grady gets into the euchre game, and the hack out at the curb bold as you please. I seen guys, strangers, push the horn and push the horn, trying to find the driver, and finely come in and say, 'Where's the guy drives this cab out here?' and all the while Grady'll be whispering loud out of the corner of the mouth, 'For God's sake don't tell him. Don't tell him for God's sake.' That's what he'd be saying to me, in deadly fear he'd be cornered into carrying a stranger around in the cab. You got to know Grady first to understand a man'd act like that.

"It ain't that he's surly. I seen him kindhearted often. One time I had to climb in the hack, run an errand around Fifty-ninth. It was about seven P.M. and when I got into the cab what was in the seat but a scooter, two dolls, and three tops. 'What the hell is this?' I says to Grady. 'Oh, never mind them,' he says, 'the

McNally kids were playing house in the cab, leave the kids' things alone.' Grady wouldn't stop kids playing house in the cab. He's kindhearted.

"But Grady's even worse than I told you about regarding the cab as a private affair of his own and not something for every Tom, Dick, and Harry to get into that's got a couple of bucks and wants to be taken someplace. I've seen guys get into the cab while Grady was sitting in it, dopey, and not seeing them get in, and you ought to see Grady then. He steps on the starter without turning on the switch and it make a discouraging noise, whirrrrrrr, and of course the engine don't start. Grady looks around his shoulder at the stranger while he does this a few times and the stranger finely gets out and looks for another cab. Grady's tickled to death and turns back to reading the intelligence test in the *News*. The intelligence test is a favorite of his, especially if it's got geography in it.

"Grady claim he been everywhere but you can't tell where lies start in and the truth leaves off but you can be sure it's early in what Grady is saying because he's an awful liar. He claim he worked in shipyards everywhere. Whenever there's a war comes up, Grady's bragging about how he makes ships in the old days. Nobody knows, but this I do know. He disappeared one time four years. Four solid years. The way it happened Grady thinks nothing of it, but some would think it was mystifying. He sometimes takes little rides for himself to look at things, the way an old gentleman might take a ride for a whim to look at something. This day, it was years and years ago, Grady druv himself down to the Battery, he wanted to look at some ships going by, he thought at the moment he needed to see some ships for a chnage.

"Well, he went down there and four years later he came into the house up in the Bronx where he lives, and his wife and his kids were still there. One of the kids had growed up, you might say, in the meanwhile because this kid was fourteen when Grady took the ride to the Battery and he was naturally eighteen when Grady come back. That's the growing-up time, between fourteen and eighteen.

"Grady's wife seem a little surprise to see him, he told me later on, but no great fuss made. She must be quite a woman, or at least she know Grady. He said it was just dinnertime and one more for dinner in a house like that makes no difference so he pull up a chair. He told her he was working those four years in a shipyard in Clyde that's in Scotland, and that's all there was to it, those whole four years.

"I remember asking him what the hell he thought the wife and kids would do when he just plain left the cab at the Battery, abandoned it, and saunters over, maneuvers himself onto a ship and to the Clyde. 'Aw,' says Grady, 'the wife have a rich aunt. They was nothing to worry about with the rich aunt sure to take care of them all soon as it dawn on them I'm gone for a while.' A guy like that Grady, how you going to understand him without knowing him first?"

Help for the Hay

By Cormac MacConnell

It was the lone and lonesome look of the old man alone in the middle of the five-acre meadow which made me stop last Wednesday in Mayo and jump the ditch and go across the felled sways of crackling hay to him. I'd give him a half-hour, I thought and maybe get some story or other out of him, or the skeleton of a story and at the worst of times, a mug of tea out of the bottle.

Nothing tastes as good as meadow tea, ten minutes away from the kitchen, one minute from Heaven. I felt like a very good Samaritan approaching an old haymaker in such obvious need of assistance.

"You could do with a hand," says I, heading towards a pile of pitchforks and rakes lying beside him. "Are you by yourself?" says he. "Who in the name of God are you?"

I told him.

"Then," says he, "for the love of God hide over there behind the ditch or you'll ruin me altogether."

"That's no way to treat a good Samaritan," says I hiding nevertheless under a sally bush and raising the voice so that he could still hear me. "I often worked in a meadow and any help is better than none."

"No offence, and I'm thankful to you for stopping," says he. "But you'd have blistered hands and you'd be gone out of here in an hour at most, one crooked cock of hay only, and the sight of anyone with me in the meadow will chase away the men I'm after."

"Oh fair enough," says I, still a bit offended.

"You're too wise a man to be annoyed," says he. "Do you think I'm standing here by accident, just in this spot in the red shirt. Did you see me the minute you came over the hill?"

"Yes."

"That's my plan," says he, feebly shaking out a fork of hay so that it wisped around his legs. "You have to use the head these days."

"Yes?"

"If you saw me, the postman Masterson will see me coming over the hill finishing his rounds and he'll half brake the bicycle and he'll say to himself 'poor Martin is by himself, I can't pass him.' And he'll stop the bike and come in the gate and pick up a handful of hay and he'll say 'it's in great form for going up Martin' and he'll pick up a fork and get stuck in.

"As good as three men and he won't leave until the field is finished. He's due in five minutes, ten if he takes two pints, but he won't because it's only Wednesday."

"Where did you park the car?"

"Round the bend."

"All right, he won't see it. Stay well-hidden now."

"Is he the only one you'll catch?"

"Not at all."

"About 4 o'clock young Master Toole will be coming home and since I'll have Masterson down in the corner, he won't see him until its' too late and he'll stop the Volkswagen and say to himself, 'poor Martin, no help' and come in the gate intending to stay an hour only and then I'll get him talking about the big win last Sunday and he'll be, here to finish in time as well—two bad blisters tomorrow, for him, but he's not a bad lad."

"Will that be enough?"

"It would be in a pinch. But about half six the two Lallys will get off the bus at the cross, coming out from town—they work in the factory, you know—and by that time we'll be having the tea sitting up beside where you are now, maybe eight or nine cocks made, and one will say to the other 'we'll hear a couple of ould Martin's yarns, there's great sport in him,' and I'll have them too and the best of workers they are, hardy young lads, until I need them no more, and every cock of hay is up clean and decent as you like."

"You are a smart man," I said.

"You have to be these days," says he. "Stay well hid now, well hid, for the postman is due."

He worked the fork feebly again, the red shirt sleeve making a pathetic enough show in the middle of all the whitening swathes of labour and, together, we watched the top of the hill.

The postman Masterson had only the one pint, for he was dead on time. I saw him braking the bike on the top of the hill. He disappeared into the dip and then after a half-minute or so, the bike clanged against the gate and this fine, strong-looking man walked into the field.

I saw him take up a handful of hay and he came up the field and he said: "It's in good form for making up Martin."

I slipped the back way over the ditch and they never saw me go.

Toasts & Songs

Irish Toasts

Toasting began in Ireland in the seventeenth century. Then, Irish revelers dropped a piece of warm bread or toast into their glasses either to add flavor to their drink or to pick up the flavor from the drink. Soon, from the bread ritual, another early Celtic custom evolved. Irishmen started adding verbal flavor to their drinking sessions and naturally called it "Toasting." With the Irish proverbial proclivity for talk, toasts in abundance for any and all social occasions eventually came about.

However, Irish toasts, many of which are generations old, are always gracious and still apropos. Two of the oldest, most popular and shortest of Irish toasts, usually rendered in the Irish language, are "Sláinte!," the Irish word for "Health!," pronounced *Slawn-che,* while the other is "Erin Go Bragh!" meaning "Ireland Forever!"

The Irish originated three of today's oldest and leading worldwide alcoholic beverages—Irish Whiskey, Guinness Stout and Hennessy Cognac, known in earlier years as brandy. Most likely, these were among the first beverages to inspire ambitious authors to compose classic toasts. In fact, an ancient Hibernian legend has it that "Unless the glass you lift contains gentle Irish Whiskey, your toast won't work."

Irish whiskey was the first to be distilled—probably in the sixth century and almost certainly by Irish monks. The earliest Irish whiskey was known as "Uisce Beatha," meaning in Irish, "the water of life." Today in the pubs of Ireland, admiring patrons oft reverently refer to it as "pure holy water."

It was the Irish word *uisce* that evolved into the English word whiskey. From its start, mellow Irish has been the favorite of many distinguished people. Among them: Queen Elizabeth I, Sir Walter Raleigh, Dr. Samuel Johnson, Peter the Great, Oliver Goldsmith and James Joyce.

Irish, like Scotch, begins with barley and crystal-clear water, but there the similarity ends. The distilling techniques of Ireland and Scotland are different, so the great whiskeys are subtly different as well. Irish is a smooth spirit with a clear barley-malt taste and without the smokey note that gives Scotch its particular character. All Irish brands are distilled by the Irish Distillers Group in two distilleries in Ireland. One is located in County Antrim in the North. It's the world's oldest distillery, with a license dated 1608. The other distillery, one of the newest, most modern in the universe, is in County Cork in the South.

Many, especially Americans, enjoy Irish via a unique after dinner drink known as Irish Coffee. According to Jack McGowan, former Official Toastmaster for the Irish Whiskey Industry, the first Irish Coffee was served right after World War II by one Joe Sheridan, a kindly, creative chef at Shannon Airport. "Feeling sorry for a group of cold, tired, impatient Americans awaiting their homeward flight, Sheridan wanted to warm them up, to send them off comfortable and sated," said McGowan. "Joe knew Yanks are addicted to their coffee. So he decided to add a bit of Irishness to the coffee."

As to Guinness Stout, an epochal story has it that back in the Eighteenth Century, an Irish gentleman farmer named Arthur Guinness was brewing beer for his own estate's consumption when, by mistake, he burned his hops. This lapse resulted in the birth of Ireland's famed black beverage.

Actually, the first Guinness brewery opened in 1759. Since then, Guinness has grown to be one of Ireland's largest and popular employers. Consumer acceptance of its Stout has so expanded that it is now produced in twenty-seven different locations around the world.

The founder of Hennessy Cognac, Richard Hennessy, was born the third son of an eighteenth century Irish squire in Ballymaccoy, County Cork, Ireland. Since, according to the local laws then, the first son always inherited the family property at the father's passing, Richard Hennessy decided to seek his fortune abroad.

Settling in Cognac, France, in 1740, Hennessy joined the

French armed forces and arose to the rank of captain before retiring. He started his own Cognac firm in 1765 and prospered. Today, Hennessy Cognac, all of which is still produced in Cognac, France, is one of France's best-known exports.

Over the centuries, the French branch of the Clan Hennessy has kept up a close relationship with Ireland. A number of the Hennessy males have been educated there and some have married Irish women. For decades, Hennessy have sponsored Irish sporting events; perennially it has been the number one Cognac seller there as it has been in the United States where there are forty million of Irish ancestry.

There are some millions more of Irish exiles in the United Kingdom, Canada, Australia, and elsewhere. This has not exactly hindered the sales of Hennessy Cognac. Many Irish natives and exiles consider Hennessy Cognac to be as Irish as Guiness Stout and Irish whiskey.

Certainly, the millions of Irish exiles have also contributed to the origin and popularity of Irish Toasts.

GENERAL

May the grass grow long on the road to Hell for want of use.

Here's a health to your enemies' enemies!

May we be alive at the same time next year
In Irish, it's:
Go mbeirimíd beo ar an am seo arís

May you have the hindsight to know where you've been
the foresight to know where you're going
and the insight to know when you're going too far.

Here's to you, as good as you are.
Here's to me as bad as I am.
As good as you are and as bad as I am,
I'm as good as you are, as bad as I am.

To our good qualities—and they are not a few.

May you have warm words on a cold evening,
a full moon on a dark night,
and a smooth road all the way to your door.

May the road rise to meet you.
May the wind be always at your back,
the sun shine warm upon your face,
the rain fall soft upon your fields,
and until we meet again
may God hold you in the hollow of His hand.

GOOD WISHES

Health and long life to you.
The wife (or husband) of your choice to you.
A child every year to you.
Land without rent to you.
And may you be half-an-hour in heaven
before the devil knows you're dead.
Sláinte!

May the frost never afflict your spuds.
May the outside leaves of your cabbage
always be free from worms.
May the crows never pick your haystack,
and may your donkey always be in foal.

(For the Bachelor)

May you have nicer legs than your own under the table before
the new spuds are up.

May you be poor in misfortune,
rich in blessings,
slow to make enemies,
quick to make friends.
But rich or poor, quick or slow,
may you know nothing but happiness
from this day forward.

May your doctor never earn a dollar out of you
and may your heart never give out.
May the ten toes of your feet steer you
clear of all misfortune, and, before you're much older,
May you hear much better toasts than this.

WEDDING

A generation of children
on the children of your children.
(In Irish, it's:
Sliocht sleachta ar shliocht bhur sleachta.)

May you have many children
and may they grow as mature in taste
and healthy in color
and as sought after
as the contents of this glass.

BIRTHDAY

May you live as long as you want
and never want as long as you live!

May you die in bed at ninety-five years,
shot by a jealous husband (or wife).

May you live to be a hundred years—
with one extra year to repent.

HEALTH

The health of the salmon to you:
a long life,
a full heart
and a wet mouth!

TO IRISH WHISKEY

Here is to Irish, a whiskey with heart,
that's smooth as a Leprechaun's touch,
yet as soft in its taste as a mother's embrace
and a gentleness saying as much.

ANNIVERSARY

Here is to loving, to romance, to us.
May we travel togther through time.
We alone count as none, but together we're one;
for our partnership puts love to rhyme.

I have known many,
liked not a few,
loved only one.
I drink to you.

DINNER PARTY

May the roof above us never fall in,
and may we friends gathered below never fall out.

(A Thank-you Toast for Couples)

Here's a health to thine and thee,
not forgetting mine and me.
When thine and thee again meet mine and me,
may mine and me have as much welcome
for thine and thee
as thine and thee have had for mine and me tonight.

WAKE

May every hair on your head turn into a candle
to light your way to heaven,
and may God and His Holy Mother
take the harm of the years away from you.

TO ST. PATRICK ON HIS ANNUAL
FEAST DAY, MARCH 17

St. Patrick was a gentlemen
who through strategy and stealth
drove all the snakes from Ireland.

Here's a toasting to his health—
but not to many toastings
lest you lose yourself and then
forget the good St. Patrick
and see all those snakes again.

Old Irish Comic Songs
Still Popular Today

Contrary to a widespread opinion, the native Irish songs are not all sad. Far from it. Actually, the favorites most frequently rendered today both in the Irish Republic in the South and in Northern Ireland at concerts, in the pubs and at social gatherings in the home are the old Irish comical ones.

The best and most popular of these Celtic classic comic songs are those of Percy French who composed a vast array of amusing Irish songs back in the nineteenth century. These have charmed generations of his fellow Irish and still are sung. Despite keen competition in Ireland from pop music and American country music, the present younger Irish generation know the Percy French songs, like them and enjoy singing them just as their parents and grandparents did.

Today, at any Irish social gathering when either young Michael or Molly are called upon "to give us a wee song," it's likely to be the rousing "Phil The Fluter's Ball," "Mrs. Brady" or any other one of Percy French's perennial popular songs that are certain to bring instant audience participation in the choruses.

Percy French was a multi-talented personage. Born in 1854 into wealthy landed gentry in Roscommon County, French was educated at Dublin's Trinity College where he got his degree in engineering. At Trinity, French gained a reputation more as banjo player and entertainer than as a scholar. Actually, he spent some eight years there before being awarded his degree. French claimed the Trinity Board gave it to him to prevent his applying for a pension.

During his extended leisurely collegiate career, French had his first song hit, "Abdul Abulbul Amcer," which was widely hailed not only in Ireland but also in Britain and abroad.

However, the song was pirated by unscrupulous publishers, who ruthlessly garnered the fortune that was rightly French's.

After Trinity, French went to work as an engineer in County Cavan. This brought him into close contact with farmers and laborers as well as construction crews, road-builders and the railway people. The personable and proficient French mixed well with them; he caught their penchant for laughter and easy joking as they went about their daily tasks and translated some into songs. During his Cavan period, French wrote some of his better lyrics.

Later, French gave up engineering and became a full time showman. He wrote two musicals, *The Irish Girl* and *Dublin-up-to-Date,* which played to capacity audiences both in Dublin and London. Recent revivals of these musicals in Dublin attracted packed houses. In 1892, in collaboration with Dr. Houston Collisson, French produced an Irish comic opera called *Strongbow, or the Bride of the Battlefield.* It was not a great success, although the London critics praised the French offering as having the definite quality of a vaunted Gilbert and Sullivan production.

At the turn of the century, French had his own one-man show and successfully toured Europe, the United States and Canada. Besides being a composer, playwright and performer, he was also a painter. Some of his paintings were bought by King Edward VII of England. French died in 1920.

Herewith is a selection of French's funny folk songs, which, over sixty years after his death, are as popular as ever in Ireland.

PHIL THE FLUTER'S BALL

Have you heard of Phil the Fluter, of the town of Ballymuck?
The times were going hard with him, in fact, the man was bruk',
So he just sent out a notice to his neighbours, one and all,
As how he'd like their company that ev'ning at a ball.
And when writin' out he was careful to suggest to them,
That if they found a hat of his convaniant to the dure,
The more they put in, whenever he requested them,
"The better would the music be for battherin' the flure."

Chorus

With the toot of the flute,
And the twiddle of the fiddle, O'
Hopping in the middle, like a herrin' on a griddle. O'
Up, down, hands a-rown'
Crossin' to the wall,
Oh! hadn't we the gaiety at Phil the Fluter's Ball!

There was Misther Denis Dogherty, who kep' "The Runnin'
Dog";
There was little crooked Paddy from the Tiraloughett bog:
There were boys from every Barony, and girls from every "art,"
And the beautiful Miss Bradys, in a private ass an' cart.
And along with them came bouncing Mrs. Cafferty,
Little Micky Mulligan was also to the fore;
Rose, Suzanne, and Margaret O'Rafferty,
The flower of Ardmagullion, and the Pride of Pethravore.

Chorus

First little Micky Mulligan got up to show them how,
And then the widda' Cafferty steps out and makes her bow.
"I could dance you off your legs," sez she, "as sure as you are
born,
If ye'll only make the piper play 'the hare was in the corn'."
So, Phil plays up to the best of his ability,
The lady and the gentleman begin to do their share;
Faith, then Mick, it's you that has agility!
Begorra! Mrs. Cafferty, yer leppin' like a hare!

Chorus

Then Phil the Fluter tipped a wink to little crooked Pat,
"I think it's nearly time," sez he, "for passin' round the hat."
So Paddy passed the caubeen round, and looking mighty cute,
Sez, "Ye've got to pay the piper when he toothers on the flute."
Then all joined in wid the greatest joviality,
Covering the buckle and the shuffle, and the cut;

Jigs were danced, of the very finest quality,
But the Widda bet the company at "handeling the fut."

Chorus

MRS. BRADY

Ould Brady's gone to glory, and the widda has the land,
And as she's good to look at, you can easy understand
That eligible suitors from the town of Athenry
Put on their best embellishments, and thought they'd have a try.
Jim Flynn, the stationmaster's son, though not in Brady's set,
Was kind enough to say to her, one evening when they met:

Chorus

"Mrs. Brady, just a whisper!
To your mouring bid adieu!
I know a fine young gentleman
Who'd not object to you.
My family may cut me,
But you've brass enough for two."
"I know who has the brass," says Mrs. Brady.
"Brass enough for three," says Mrs. Brady.

Pat Dempsey heard that Jimmy had been sent against the wall,
Says Pat, "It's not gentility the widda wants at all.
But 'pity is akin to love,' as everybody knows,
I'll tell her how I've got no girl to wash or mend my clothes."
When Flynn, who keeps the grocer's shop, and owns a bit o'
land,
Came home and heard how Pat had got the back of Mary's
hand,

Says he, "Myself and Mary has been friends through thick and
thin,"
So he put on all his Sunday clothes, and barbarised his chin.
He called on her that morning, she was very sweet and kind.
And this was how he hinted at the thoughts were in his mind:

Chorus

"Mrs. Brady, just a whisper!
Sure I don't know how to woo;
But I've got a growin' business,
And I've love enough for two;
So name the happy day,
And would to-morrow mornin' do?"
"Why not this afternoon?" says Mrs. Brady.
"There's danger in delay!" says Mrs. Brady.

"ARE YE RIGHT THERE, MICHAEL?"

A Lay of the Wild West Clare.

You may talk of Columbus's sailing
Across the Atlantical sea
But he never tried to go railing
From Ennis as far as Kilkee.
You run for the train in the mornin',
The excursion train starting at eight,
You're there when the clock gives the warnin',
And there for an hour you'll wait.

(Spoken)

And as you're waiting in the train,
You'll hear the guard sing this refrain:—

"Are ye right there, Michael? are ye right?
Do you think that we'll be there before the night?
Ye've been so long in startin',
That ye couldn't say for sartin'—
Still ye might now, Michael, so ye might!"

They find out where the engine's been hiding,
And it drags you to sweet Corofin;
Says the guard, "Back her down on the siding,
There's the goods from Kilrush comin' in."
Perhaps it comes in in two hours,
Perhaps it breaks down on the way;
"If it does," says the guard, "be the powers,
We're here for the rest of the day!"

Uphill the ould engin' is climbin',
While the passengers push with a will;
You're in luck when you reach Ennistymon
For all the way home is down-hill.

(Spoken)

And as you're wobbling through the dark,
You hear the guard make this remark:—

"Are ye right there, Michael? are ye right?
Do you think that ye'll be home before it's light?"
"'Tis all dependin' whether
The ould engin' howlds together—"
"And it might now, Michael, so it might!"

Wilde and Shaw: Two of the Greats

Oscar Wilde's Wit

By Hesketh Pearson

Several writers of reminiscences dealing with the eighties and nineties suddenly come to life when Oscar Wilde enters their pages, and coin neat repartees at his expense; which suggests that he, like Falstaff, was not only witty himself but the cause of wit in others. There is no doubt that he did inspire many succeeding novelists, dramatists and talkers, whose epigrams may be described as Wilde and water. But memory is so treacherous, and we shall not be far out if we assume that in real life he won all his contests with wit, the memory of which rankled until the losers could pay him back in fiction. The enduring animosity of Whistler, due entirely to Wilde's superiority as a man, a talker and a wit, is sufficient proof that no one else had a dog's chance against Oscar when he cared to exert himself. We have already seen him winning Henley's reluctant praise; we have heard that Shaw was content to play second fiddle to him; we know that Carson, the cleverest cross-examiner of his day, was hopelessly outclassed by him on the intellectual plane; and all these, Whistler, Henley, Shaw and Carson, were born fighters, loving combat, while Wilde hated friction, loathed argument ("It is only the intellectually lost who ever argue," he said), and would head any list of famous Men of Inaction.

C. J. Holmes gives us a tantalizing glimpse of one witty interchange between Wilde and Charles Ricketts at the latter's studio: "Ricketts, perched on the edge of the table, engaged Wilde in a long verbal combat. So swiftly came parry and *riposte*, that my slow brain could only follow the tongueplay several sentences behind, and cannot remember a word of what passed, except 'Oh, nonsense, Oscar!' from Ricketts, although it lives in memory as the most dazzling dialogue which I was ever privileged to hear." But the most satisfactory evidence of Wilde's superiority as a wit over all his contemporaries comes from Wilfred Scawen Blunt, who had met pretty well every famous artistic, social and political figure between 1870 and 1920. He was present on July 17th, 1894, at "a brilliant luncheon" given by Margo Asquith and her husband some two months after their marriage. Wilde was then at the height of his social glory, says Blunt. "Of all those present, and they were most of them brilliant talkers, he was without comparison the most brilliant, and in a perverse mood he chose to cross swords with one after the other of them, overpowering each in turn with his wit, and making special fun of Asquith, his host that day, who only a few months later, as Home Secretary, was prosecuting him…" Another passage in Blunt's diary, written on hearing of Wilde's death, runs: "He was without exception the most brilliant talker I have every come across, the most ready, the most witty, the most audacious…Nobody could pretend to outshine him, or even to shine at all in his company. Something of his wit is reflected in his plays, but very little. The fine society of London and especially the 'souls' ran after him because they knew he could always amuse them, and the pretty women allowed him great familiarities, though there was no question of love-making."

Wilde's wit was entirely effortless and spontaneous. He never influenced the conversation in any direction, and never attempted to dominate it: he just slipped into it, became a part of the general give-and-take. Whatever the theme, his wit was as ready as it was kindly. His heavy features became sensitive and alert, his face alive with gaiety; good-nature seemed to exude from him, pleasure to radiate from him, happiness to enfold him. Frivolity was the keynote to his wit. What other people took seriously he dealt with humorously; what they dismissed as trivial he treated with great solemnity. His favourite method of ridiculing conventional standards was to change a word or two in a proverb or cliché, and so add an aspect to truth. Here are some good examples of his conversational flings:

"Work is the curse of the drinking classes."

"One of those characteristic British faces that, once seen, are never remembered."

"Everyone should keep someone else's diary."

"It is always a silly thing to give advice, but to give good advice is absolutely fatal."

"I can resist everything except temptation."

"Duty is what one expects from others; it is not what one does oneself."

"Don't be led astray into the paths of virtue."

"You can't make people good by Act of Parliament—that is something."

"She has the remains of really remarkable ugliness."

"The English have a miraculous power of turning wine into water."

"Genius is born, not paid."

"Ouida loved Lord Lytton with a love that made his life a burden."

"I rely on you to misrepresent me."

"Whenever I think of my bad qualities at night, I go to sleep at once."

"He is old enough to know worse."

"Never buy a thing you don't want merely because it is dear."

"Consistency is the last refuge of the unimaginative."

"Whenever a man does a thoroughly stupid thing, it is always from the noblest motives."

"I am due at the club. It is the hour when we sleep there."

"Nothing is so dangerous as being too modern. One is apt to grow old-fashioned quite suddenly."

"He hasn't a single redeeming vice."

"Morality is simply the attitude we adopt towards people whom we personally dislike."

"I usually say what I really think. A great mistake nowadays. It makes one so liable to be misunderstood."

"It is only by not paying one's bills that one can hope to live in the memory of the commercial classes."

"For an artist to marry his model is as fatal as for a *gourmet* to marry his cook: the one gets no sittings, and the other no dinners."

"Her capacity for family affection is extraordinary. When her third husband died, her hair turned quite gold from grief."

"Nowadays most people die of a sort of creeping common sense, and discover when it is too late that the only things one never regrets are one's mistakes."

"I choose my friends for their good looks, my acquaintances for their good characters, and my enemies for their good intellects. A man cannot be too careful in the choice of his enemies."

Most of Wilde's best sayings were a mixture of fun and profundity, and when the fun predominated he would often preface the remark with a laugh or dismiss it with a gesture to suggest the degree of significance which he attached to it. Wit is the salt of wisdom, humour the preservative of thought, and the reason Wilde is still read with delight, while his masters in philosophy, Ruskin and Pater, are mainly studied in the places where dead languages are cherished, is due to his temperamental levity, which helped to make him, with the sole exception of Sydney Smith, the wittiest of humorists and the most humorous of wits. It was his opinion that "Seriousness is the only refuge of the shallow"; and he was undoubtedly right when he said: "Humanity takes itself too seriously. It is the world's original sin. If the caveman had known how to laugh, History would have been different." The great humorist raises common sense to poetry, lifts the burden of life, releases the spirit, imparts happiness, creates brotherhood, and cleanses the mind of cant, pretentiousness and conceit. He is the chief civilising force in humanity, the real democrat and egalitarian, detested and dreaded by tyrants and humbugs. "That idiot laughter!" cries Shakespeare's King John: "a passion hateful to my purposes." The great humourist is also the true seer, but as human beings have only listened to the saint or the charlatan they have not profited in a practical way by the vision of their jesters. We know what serious people have made of the world, but we shall never know what humorous people would make of it, because the world will never be intelligent enough to give them a chance, and they would be too intelligent to take it: which is just as it should be, for the holy spirit of Humour is partly dependent on the unholy stupidity of man.

Wilde's humour, which glistened with wit, played around every subject so happily and continuously that people would sit listening to him, spellbound, oblivious of time, for four or five hours, and then beg him not to stop. Unfortunately for us, it was all so enjoyable that no one was capable of recording what Nellie Melba called "that brilliant fiery-coloured chain of words." And so we must content ourselves with occasional links detached from the chain and preserved by some of his listeners as feeble specimens of the fascinating whole. His manner of speech heightened the comedy of the matter. Sometimes he would start speaking with the utmost solemnity, as though giving the whole of his mind to an important theme which required the gravest deliberation; then there would be a pause, as if he were searching for the exact words to do justice to the occasion; then would come the flash of phrase and the explosion of mirth. The following incidents illustrate this side of his humour.

After Coulson Kernahan had given an honest summary of his religious beliefs, Wilde said: "You are so evidently, so unmistakably sincere, and most of all so truthful, that...I can't believe a single word you say."

"It is a kind of genius to be twenty-one," he informed a youthful writer; and having delivered a eulogy on the glories of adolescence, he concluded with: "To win back my youth, there is nothing I would not do—nothing...except take exercise, get up early, or be a useful member of the community."

Hearing of the malicious attacks on his character made by an acquaintance, he began what he had to say in a tone of mingled grief and indignation: "It is perfectly monstrous, and quite heartless, the way people go about nowadays saying things against one behind one's back that are absolutely and entirely...true."

While waiting for the arrival of a cable which was to tell him of the success or otherwise of the New York production of *Lady Windermere's Fan,* a look of painful apprehension crossed his face as he said, "This suspense is unbearable...I hope it will last." Which, together with several other remarks that were received with a roar of laughter, found its way into one of his plays.

One saying of his went so well that he repeated it on several subsequent occasions, and Mark Twain either heard it or heard of it, appropriated it, and spoilt it. This is the original version: "I never put off till to-morrow what I can possibly do...the day after."

It was related in an English paper that during his lecture tour in America he had been seen in Boston on an exceptionally fine day wearing a mackintosh and carrying an umbrella, and had given as a reason "I hear that it is raining in London this morning." Hoping that he had not been guilty of such an absurdity, Sherard asked him whether there was any truth in the story. Shaking his head mournfully, Wilde replied, "A false report." "Ah, I thought so," said Sherard, much relieved. "Yes," Wilde continued in a distressed tone of voice, "I discovered later, and the discovery upset me a good deal, that the weather had been perfect in London that day...so my mackintosh and umbrella were really quite unnecessary." For some reason best known to himself Sherard never published this.

In the latter part of last century the scholarly critics of Shakespeare spent much time and wrote many articles on the question of whether Hamlet was really mad or only pretending to be. Wilde listened carefully to a lunchtime discussion, in which the case for and against Hamlet's lunacy was judiciously put, and his interruptions showed that he was genuinely interested. At last, with a burst of enthusiasm, he announced that he would write a book on this absorbing topic. Everyone was thrilled. "Yes," he said, his eyes gleaming with the fanaticism of a scholar on the brink of some momentous discovery, "and I have already found a title for my book." A Chorus of "Tell us: what is it?" Back came the answer: *Are the Commentators on Hamlet Really Mad or Only Pretending to Be?*"

One day in Paris the talk centered upon the leading figures of the French Revolution, and the character of Marat was debated. One Frenchman said he was a genius, another that he was a gamin, a third that he was the spirit of the Revolution, a fourth that he was the spirit of evil, and so on. Someone turned to Wilde and asked for his opinion. "Poor fellow," he said dolefully: "What bad luck...for taking a bath just once in a way." He spoke of course in French, and this is the nearest English equivalent I can give.

His appearance could be as unexpected as his repartees. William Heinemann, the publisher, once asked him to lunch with Gérard Harry, in the hope that he would write an introduction to Harry's translation of Maeterlinck's first play *Princesse Maleine*. He arrived with a gloomy expression on his face, dressed in deep mourning, and Harry tactfully hinted that he did not wish to bother Wilde at a period of bereavement. Wilde explained the cause of his desolation: "This day happens to be my birthday, and I am mourning, as I shall henceforth do on each of my anniversaries, the flight of one year of my youth into nothingness, the growing blight upon my summer." As for the introduction, he said that he must wait for the necessary inspiration. He waited patiently, but it never came.

In quickness of repartee Wilde can have had few equals, in amiability of exchange none. Some examples have been preserved.

It was the fashion in his time for women to leave the dining-table before the men, who could then light their cigarettes. At one party, captivated by his talk, the women stayed too long, and it happened that a table-lamp began to smoulder. "Please put it out, Mr. Wilde: it's smoking," said the hostess. "Happy lamp," murmured Wilde.

Lord Avebury had published his list of the Hundred Best Books, and at a function where the views of celebrities were being canvassed Wilde was asked to compile a list of his hundred favourites. "I fear that would be impossible," said he. "But why?" "Because I have only written five."

A man who was present on the occasion told the following to Sir Bernard Partridge, who passed it on to me. Wilde was holding forth on the great suicides of history and claiming that all of them had committed their *felo de se* in the grand manner. "What about Judas Iscariot, Oscar?" asked someone. "Oh, Judas! I don't count him. After all he was merely a *nouveau riche*."

A youth was being informed that he, like everyone else, must begin at the bottom of the ladder, when Wilde cut in "No, begin at the top and sit upon it." On hearing that the lad was just going to Sandhurst, Wilde urged him to go to Oxford instead. "But I am going to be a soldier." "If you took a degree at Oxford, they would make you a colonel at once...at any rate in a West Indian regiment."

"Surely you remember knowing me in Manchester," said a man whom Wilde had failed to recognise. "Very possibly in Manchester I may know you again," was the reply. Another fellow, who greeted him with "Hullo, Oscar!" and a dig in the ribs, got this: "I don't know you by sight, but your manner is familiar." His apology for having apparently cut an old acquaintance was: "I didn't recognize you—I've changed a lot."

Puns were popular in the nineteenth century. Wilde was not addicted to them; but he made a good one at a wedding-party, when Lord Morris, who had a very strong Irish accent, was looking in vain for a shoe to throw after the young couple. "Why not throw your own brogue after them?" was Oscar's helpful suggestion.

Wilde was a master of satirical nonsense, the gravity of his measured utterance making his best efforts inexpressibly comical, though perhaps he never reached the sublime heights of Sydney Smith's imaginative outbursts, which actually prostrated people, making them ill with laughter. Fortunately we have something better than an echo of Wilde's nonsense in *The Importance of Being Earnest;* and here a few airy trifles from his table-talk must suffice:

"A well-tied is the first serious step in life."

"More women grow old nowadays through the faithfulness of their admirers than through anything else."

"When she is in a very smart gown, she looks like an *édition de luxe* of a wicked French novel meant specially for the English market."

"There is no secret of life. Life's aim, if it has one, is simply to be always looking for temptations. There are not nearly enough of them. I sometimes pass a whole day without coming across a single one. It is quite dreadful. It makes one so nervous about the future."

"Nothing is more painful to me than to come across virtue in a person in whom I have never expected its existence. It is like finding a needle in a bundle of hay. It pricks you. If we have virtue we should warn people of it."

"I know so many men in London whose only talent is for washing. I suppose that is why men of genius so seldom wash; they are afraid of being mistaken for men of talent only."

"Twenty years of romance make a woman look like a ruin; but twenty years of marriage make her something like a public building."

"It is sad. One half of the world does not believe in God, and the other half does not believe in me."

"No modern literary work of any worth has been produced in the English language by an English writer...except of course Bradshaw."

"I would sooner lose a train by the ABC than catch it by Bradshaw."

"West Kensington is a district to which you drive until the horse drops dead, when the cabman gets down to make enquiries."

"Bayswater is a place where people always get lost, and where there are no guides."

"Robert gave Harry a terrible black eye, or Harry gave him one; I forget which, but I know they were great friends."

"She is without one good quality, she lacks the tiniest spark of decency, and she is quite the wickedest woman in London. I haven't a word to say in her favour...and she is one of my greatest friends."

Speaking of a wealthy foreigner, who welcomed to his house every artist with the least claim to notoriety, Wilde said: "He came to London with the intention of opening a *salon,* and he has succeeded in opening a saloon."

When in the early nineties England was on the verge of war with France, Wilde was asked what he thought about it. "We will not go to war with France," he replied, "because her prose is perfect."

Lord Alfred Douglas and Wilde were sitting one day in the study of Dr. Warren, President of Magdalen College, Oxford. "I am thinking of presenting a statue of myself to the College," said Wilde. The consternation on Warren's face changed to relief when he added "Yes, to stand in the 'quad' here...a colossal equestrian statue."

He greeted a new arrival at a reception by the Countess de Grey with the words "Oh, I'm so glad you've come! There are a hundred things I want not to say to you."

"What terrible weather we are having," said a highly intellectual and very solemn woman he was taking in to dinner. "Yes, but if it wasn't for the snow, how could we believe in the immortality of the soul?" he rejoined. "What an interesting question, Mr. Wilde! But tell me exactly what you mean." "I haven't the slightest idea."

"Pray come to this symposium," said Wilde to E. F. Benson. "Everything nowadays is settled by symposiums, and this one is to deal finally with the subject of bimetallism...of bimetallism between men and women."

Wilde, however, could be as profound as he pretended to be superficial, and his genius enabled him to compress into a sentence what another would extend to a book. "Experience," he said, "is a question of instinct about life," and he was born with this instinct. No one ever said so many acute things in the guise of paradox. By shifting the viewpoint, he forced his listeners to look at life from unaccustomed angles and enlarged the boundaries of Truth. Though he owed something to La Rochefoucauld, he went deeper. His remark "We think that we are generous because we credit our neighbour with the posses- sion of those virtues that are likely to be a benefit to us" is more complete than La Rochefoucauld's "The gratitude of most men is but a secret desire of receiving greater benefits." And although it is generally true to say that every intelligent maxim- maker since his time has been indebted to La Rochefoucauld for his observation "Our virtues are most frequently but vices disguised," we may claim that Wilde was wittier, more penetrat- ing and more comprehensive than the Frenchman. Desmond MacCarthy has picked out four of Wilde's sayings and noted that they contain the pith of other men's theories and teachings. These are the four:

"As one reads history...one is absolutely sickened, not by the crimes that the wicked have committed, but by the punishments that the good have inflicted; and a community is infinitely more brutalised by the habitual employment of punishment, than it is by the occasional occurrence of crime."

"Man is least himself when he talks in his own person. Give him a mask and he will tell you the truth."

"Conscience must be merged in instinct before we become fine."

"Nothing can cure the soul but the senses, just as nothing can cure the senses but the soul."

Half of Tolstoy's message is in the last part of the first quotation, says Desmond MacCarthy; Yeats's theory of artistic composition is in the second; the essence of Samuel Butler's ethics is in the third; and the upshot of Meredith's philosophy in his novels, as it concerns love, is in the fourth. We may add that the core of Freud's doctrine is in Wilde's statement: "Every impulse that we strive to strangle broods in the mind and poisons us...The only way to get rid of a temptation is to yield to it." What follows, then, taken with what has already been quoted, would have made Wilde memorable as an aphorist if he had said and written nothing else:

"A cynic is a man who knows the price of everything and the value of nothing."

"The sentimentalist is always a cynic at heart. Indeed sentimentality is merely the Bank-holiday of cyncism."

"Conscience and cowardice are really the same things. Conscience is the trade-name of the firm."

"Each class preaches the importance of those virtues it need not exercise. The rich harp on the value of thrift, the idle grow eloquent over the dignity of labour."

"Young men want to be faithful, and are not; old men want to be faithless, and cannot."

"The tragedy of old age is not that one is old, but that one is young."

"There is a luxury in self-reproach. When we blame ourselves we feel that no one else has a right to blame us. It is the confession, not the priest, that gives us absolution."

"Nothing makes one so vain as being told that one is a sinner. Conscience makes egoists of us all."

"When a woman marries again it is because she detested her first husband. When a man marries again it is because he adored his first wife. Women try their luck; men risk theirs."

"Don't tell me that you have exhausted life. When a man says that one knows that Life has exhausted him."

"Science can never grapple with the irrational. That is why it has no future before it in this world."

"The reason that we like to think so well of others is that we are all afraid for ourselves. The basis of our optimism is sheer terror."

"The soul is born old, but grows young. That is the comedy of life. The body is born young, and grows old. That is life's tragedy."

"Each time one loves is the only time that one has ever loved. Difference of object does not alter singleness of passion. It merely intensifies it."

"Good resolutions are simply cheques that men draw on a bank where they have no account."

Most of the records of the childish controversies in the Victorian age can be boiled down to this passage by Wilde: "The English mind is always in a rage. The intellect of the race is wasted in the sordid and stupid quarrels of second-rate politicians or third-rate theologians...We are dominated by the fanatic, whose worst vice is his sincerity...There is no sin except stupidity." Another of his sayings should be remembered by the British people, for it warns them against a repetition of their behavior between the years 1919 and 1939: "There is only one thing worse than injustice, and that is justice without her sword in her hand. When right is not might it is evil."

Wilde was called upon to defend some of his aphorisms from the witnessbox. In September '94 Frank Harris took over the editorship of *The Saturday Review* and asked Wilde for something that would give the paper a fillip. With his usual good nature, Wilde jotted down a list of *Phrases and Philosophies for the Use of the Young*, and was about to despatch it when another friend begged him for something to give a new magazine for Oxford undergraduates called *The Chameleon* an auspicious start-off. With his usual good nature, he handed the *Phrases and Philosophies* to his friend, not troubling to make any enquiry about the publication; after which he forgot all about it. But his memory received a severe jolt when Jerome K. Jerome in *To-day* drew attention to the objectionable character of certain contributions in the first number of *The Chameleon* (December 1894), especially a story called "The Priest and the Acolyte." Wilde, who no doubt sympathised with the subject of the story, thought the treatment deplorable, and protested against it, with the result that the magazine was withdrawn, the first number being also the last. But a few months later Carson did his best to

identify Wilde with the publication of *The Chameleon;* and then
it was made clear that he had had nothing whatever to do with
it, but indeed had been instrumental in suppressing it, Carson
shifted the attack to Wilde's own contribution, trying hard, and
failing completely, to turn the *Phrases* into an indictment of
their coiner:

Carson: "Religions die when they are proved to be true." Is
that true? (Carson did not complete the quotation: "Science is
the record of dead religions.")

Wilde: Yes, I hold that. It is a suggestion towards a philosophy
of the absorption of religions by science, but it is too big a
question to go into now.

Carson: Do you think that was a safe axiom to put forward for
the philosophy of the young?

Wilde: Most stimulating.

Carson: "If one tells the truth one is sure, sooner or later, to be
found out?"

Wilde: That is a pleasing paradox, but I do not set very high
store on it as an axiom.

Carson: Is it good for the young?

Wilde: Anything is good for the young that stimulates
thought, in whatever age.

Carson: Whether moral or immoral?

Wilde: There is no such thing as morality or immorality in
thought. There is immoral emotion.

Carson: "Pleasure is the only thing one should live for?"

Wilde: I think that the realisation of oneself is the prime aim
of life, and to realise oneself through pleasure is finer than to
do so through pain. I am, on that point, entirely on the side of
the ancients—the Greeks. It is a pagan idea.

Carson: "A truth ceases to be true when more than one person
believes in it?"

Wilde: Perfectly. That would be my metaphysical definition of
truth; something so personal that the same truth could never be
appreciated by two minds.

Carson: "The condition of perfection is idleness?"

Wilde: Oh, yes, I think so. Half of it is true. The life of
contemplation is the highest life.

Carson: "There is something tragic about the enormous number of young men there are in England at the present moment who start life with perfect profiles, and end by adopting some useful profession?"

Wilde: I should think that the young have enough sense of humour.

Strangely enough Carson did not question Wilde about another of his axioms: "Any preoccupation with ideas of what is right or wrong in conduct shows an arrested intellectual development." Or not strangely. Under the circumstances Carson may have felt that it applied to himself.

The Man Who Knew It All

BY HUGH KENNER

"In the right key one can say anything," George Bernard Shaw wrote, "in the wrong key, nothing: the only delicate part of the job is the establishment of the key." Like all great comedians, Shaw had a principal key he'd spent much of a lifetime establishing. It permitted him to say perhaps not anything, but surely any number of outrageous things, composed in his own tonality of bright percussive knowingness.

War has just deprived the playwright St. John Ervine of a leg and Shaw offers consolation: "For a man of your profession two legs are an extravagance....The more the case is gone into the more it appears that you are an exceptionally happy and fortunate man, relieved of a limb to which you owed none of your fame, and which indeed was the cause of your conscription; for without it you would not have been accepted for service." It is hard to imagine who else could have carried that off. Or this, to H. G. Wells: "My dear H. G., I am all right about Russia. The longer I live the more I see that I am never wrong about anything, and that all the pains I have so humbly taken to verify my notions have only wasted my time." Or this, to a journalist he had never met: "Dear Sir, Your profession has, as usual, destroyed your brain."

A few more samples like that—more are easy to find in this third volume of the collected Shaw correspondence edited by the actor, critic and Shaw scholar Dan H. Laurence—and you would feel justified in agreeing with all the people who during eighty years have been dismissing G.B.S. as a heartless egotist. But brief excerpts can mislead. Any smarty might have contrived to insult a stranger, a journalist at that, by imputing brain damage, but what would any smarty have found to say next? Such an insult he might scribble across a letter he had no intention of answering. Shaw used it, though, to launch a detailed answer—one thousand words in pungent explication of what it was the journalist hadn't been noticing. Sheer expository energy redeems the opening sally, which comes to mean, "Why must I always explain the world to people whose alleged job is keeping an eye on it?" It does for the explanation what pepper can do for soup—prevents it from seeming an academic exercise.

As one grows saturated in his correspondence, Shaw's insults, like his boasts, turn transparently genial. And saturated one cannot but become: this book of nine hundred-odd pages is impossible to put down. Within a few pages G.B.S. is off to a strong start, responding to news that Gilbert Murray had translated *Oedipus Rex* with a brief outline to expose the defects of Sophocles:

"Edipus—(rushing in and scattering rose pink from his eyes all over the orchestra) Woe, woe! Pain! Ah me! Ai! ai! ai! Me miserable!

"Stupendous applause. The Messenger & Edipus take six calls and finally reappear with Sophocles between them. Immense enthusiasm.

"Chorus—Talk of bliss
            After this!"

Murray replied that he and his colleagues found it difficult to read without tears, and he seems not to have commented on Shaw's assertion that Sophocles was the sort of man the English like— "the brains of a ram, the theatrical technique of an agricultural laborer, the reverence for tradition of a bee."

"The sort of man the English like"—that's a useful clue. An Irish playwright in exile among the slow-witted English, whose idea of a playwright was the amiably incompetent Sophocles— such is one description of the role Shaw had to play. And the first mistake they make about this Irishman is expecting senti- ment and blarney. But no, he glitters with competence and logic; that underplublicized Irish trait he even exaggerates, in a way that alarmed his most famous Irish contemporary, W. B. Yeats. Yeats once had a dream of a sewing machine, a sewing machine that clicked and perpetually smiled, and he realized it was Bernard Shaw.

Another thing Shaw claimed to notice about the people around him is that not one of them had the least idea how to go about doing anything, so that he had to be always telling them. His machinelike reserves of energy were fortunate; you could select a thick how-to manual from these letters. For a random sampling, you'd have Shaw explaining punctuation, to Lawrence of Arabia ("no more to be trusted with a pen than a child with a torpedo"); articulation, to the actress Molly Tompkins ("Get out the words from which the audience can guess the rest;...the others...are useful only for rhythm"); the production of vocal tone, to the musician Arnold Dolmetsch ("You round the back of your throat and throw the column of air into vibration without forcing it out; and when you want to make a crescendo...you pull down your diaphragm, arch your soft palate, and enlarge the instrument generally, but you dont blow"); the whole art of rehearsing plays, to the producer Augustin Hamon (invaluable, and too long to sample; get the book).

It is easy to impute a passion for interfering to what was frequently a passion for teasing. On the scaffold, had it come to that, you'd have heard Shaw coaching the hangman. Late in 1915 "his attitude regarding the war" caused several members of the Dramatists' Club to want him expelled, and they didn't even know how to go about that. So he had to outline in full to the secretary a proper procedure for expelling a member, and then sit watching leaves fall from the calendar while they tried to follow it. (After a week, he tired of the game, and resigned.)

Which brings us to "his attitude regarding the war," which was outrageous to patriots who thought he was teasing when he wasn't. "England's difficulty," runs a well-known Irish maxim, "is Ireland's opportunity." So in August 1914 an Irishman whose gaze toward Germany trembled with anything more complex than lust for blood might well seem treasonable to Londoners. Shaw thought the Allied ruling classes had bungled the war into being. He also thought that, once engaged in, it must be won.

How those two propositions could be combined was more than the press or even associates could grasp, and Mr. Laurence is right in calling his thirty thousand words of "Common Sense

About the War" "the most audacious and courageous action of his life." "Former friends cut him dead.... Booksellers and librarians removed his works from their shelves." One socialist colleague (Robert Blatchford, editor of *The Clarion*) even described "Common Sense" as "insensate malice and dirty innuendo," and its authorship as "the meanest act of treachery ever perpetrated by an alien enemy residing in generous and long-suffering England."

"An alien enemy"—that phrase betrays the deep feeling that, however disguised, defined Shaw's lifelong plight. In 1914 an Irishman was a citizen of the United Kingdom and subject of the Crown, as much as any Welshman. It would be like Jimmy Breslin calling Tom Wolfe "an alien enemy" for his Old Dominion roots. Rage had stripped Blatchford of caution and made him expose the deepest English prejudice, one that exceeded genteel anti-Semitism. The Irish were treacherous animals indeed, most dangerous when (occasionally) they were clever. They might smoke clay pipes upside down, which was all right, or amusingly ornament hearth rugs and croon lyrics like "Innisfree." But let one of them venture an independent thought and instantly he became what at bottom he was, an alien enemy.

So Shaw was a man on guard. Nothing is more impressive than the good humor with which he repelled all attackers, even blind sharks out for the taste of his blood. By sheer force of character he sustained his role as the one sane man in a land of sentimentalists. He relished his own rationality. He spelled matters out—A, B, C. He claimed that he was never wrong about anything, and sometimes came to believe it.

In the process he became "G.B.S." someone he often thought of as a millstone tied to his neck. "G.B.S." naturally attracted biographers; one of these, with the improbably romantic name of Thomas Demetrius O'Bolger, surfaced about 1913 in Pennsylvania, where among other peccadillos he professed English. O'Bolger (1871-1923) spent the last ten years of his life trying to make something publishable of his Ph.D. thesis, "The Real Shaw," and took up unconscionable hours of the real Shaw's time. He'd surmised that there was something less than normative about Shaw's mother and father; that mother in particular had taken up with a figure named Vandeleur Lee, even moved herself and the children in with Lee, thus massaging the psyche of young G.B.S. toward all manner of cynical irregularity.

Enough of an Irish gentleman to defend his mother's honor, Shaw sent O'Bolger lengthy accounts of his childhood in which Vandeleur Lee (whose name he consistently misspelled) figured as a neglected genius into whose London house Mrs. Shaw had moved with her brood for the most rational of reasons—as rational as the reasons G.B.S. also set forth later when he married a woman of means, and quite honorably.

Readers of the letters can have fun with Vandeleur Lee. He was a how-to man like G.B.S.; his specialty was voice production, which he taught Mrs. Shaw. Shaw's father certainly didn't like him, but Mrs. Shaw "went her own way, which happened to be the musical way of Lee, just as Lee went his; and my father could only look on helplessly, just like Mr. Jellyby in Bleak House." Lee turned into "an amusing humbug" (not unlike G.B.S.?). O'Bolger (whose thesis I've not read; it's preserved at Harvard) may have been on to something. But he never got to publish it. Shaw's way was, at any rate, "the musical way." We've heard his words on getting the right key, in which you can say anything. More arresting, though, is a paragraph in a letter to O'Bolger which describes an essentially eighteenth-century musical upbringing: "Beethoven was modern and disturbing to us." "The modern realistic expression of erotic emotion was [to Shaw's mother]...unladylike and indecent," as it surely was to G.B.S.

More: "My deliberate rhetoric, and my reversion to the Shakespearean feature of long set solos for my characters, are pure Italian opera. My rejection of plot and *dénouement*, and my adoption of a free development of themes, are German symphony. My clown and ringmaster technique of discussion cannot be referred to French music: it is plain Molière; but I daresay I learned something from Gounod as well as from Fra Angelico as to the ease with which religious emotion and refined sexual emotion can be combined."

I dare say he did; and that was his ultimate evasion of the England where he spent nearly all his life. A literary people, for whom literature marches step after step like the alphabet, won't feel prepared for such irrational nonsense. They didn't stomach it when T. S. Eliot (following Wagner) did it in "The Waste Land." They stomached it from G.B.S. because his lines were so funny ("If you cannot think," wrote Wyndham Lewis, "you can always *laugh*," and they stomached G.B.S. himself because in his gallant energy he was always three skips ahead of where the flyswatter had landed.

STRANGERS IN
IRELAND

Language That the Strangers Never Knew

By Hugh A. Mulligan

"Is the salmon poached?" I asked the busboy at our seaside hotel in wild and wonderful West Cork.

"It is not," he replied with shocked indignation. "Sure the governor bought it down at the market this morning."

I should have known from the song and from my own heritage that in Ireland they speak a language that the strangers never knew. Full of flights of fancy that language is, and it falls on the ear like the melodious music of heavenly heart strings, which sometimes get entangled with the logic.

Others, like the Americans and the Australians, may be guilty of reginicide of the Queen's English, but in Ireland the old girl is simply deposed and sent into exile. The language of the people reigns instead, lovely and lilting and full of surprises.

"Are the oysters fresh?" I heard an English tourist ask the waiter at a golfing hotel in County Mayo.

"Indeed they are, sir," he answered in tones of truth varnished only by the twinkle in his dark eyes. "They came down on the bus this afternoon."

The hotel's venerable caddy master, they tell me, once had this advice for an American lady who had hooked a half dozen golf balls in the Clew Bay and left another dozen scattered about the benches on the first tee:

"I think you'd do a wee bit better, madam, if you didn't lift your hind leg so much."

Paddy, of course, was his name and after three days of going about the links with this particular specimen of Divota Americana he was heard to remark:

"Only I'm paid for doing this, I wouldn't have this job if you paid me."

Paddy took me out on the course to show me the general direction of the first hole, which was a dog's leg to the right across a brook hidden by a line of trees.

"Now take your lie on that big tree there," he said, pointing to an ancient oak that immediately put him in mind of an anecdote. "Do you know I had three Yanks playing here last week, and I told them to take aim on that tree there. And bejabers, all three of them hit it."

One of them, he told me, had a very important job in Hollywood. "He's a fil-lum maggot, like John Ford," Paddy said in tones of wondrous admiration.

Someone asked him if the caddy business slacked off a bit when the summer tourist season came to a close.

"Well, we get some Japanese in the off season," he said, pondering the question through knitted brows. "But you know at times it's that quiet you can hear the bees belch."

That evening around the polished brass stout knobs in the hotel bar one of the English visitors belched forth a solution to the Ulster problem that entailed replacing the British army with Commonwealth troops from Nigeria, Fiji and Malawi "to defuse the religious aspect."

"Now there an interesting bit of utter nonsense," said the publican in one of those scatback Irish sentences that can reverse their field and score in any direction.

Your London man, as they say here, tried to nod knowingly, but he couldn't. He was already decapitated. King James II was similarly scalped on the razor's edge of Irish wit after losing his throne at the Battle of the Boyne.

Fleeing from the scene, he managed to get to Dublin and burst in on his friend, Lady Tyrconnell, complaining about the conduct of the Irish troops on his side.

"The cowards ran," cried the king.

"Indeed, your Majesty," said Lady Tyrconnell with a smile thinner than a rapier. "I see you won the race."

A British judge presiding over the trial of an I.R.A. man on terrorist charges at the Old Bailey was likewise dewigged when he interrupted an Irish lawyer's flow of native oratory on a point of law.

"Surely," suggested His Worship, "your client is aware of the doctrine of de minimis non curat lex?"

"I can assure you, my Lord"—the Blarney Stone was rolled back with ease—"that in the remote and inhospitable hamlet where the defendant has his humble thatched cottage, it forms the sole topic of conversation."

Or as Senator Boyle Roche once told the Irish Parliament: "The cup of Ireland's troubles has been overflowing for years and it's not full yet."

The Only Way to Go in Ireland

By Eugene J. McCarthy

I know Americans who have driven cars in Ireland without mishap for days, even months, apparently having mastered the art of driving, on the left-hand side of the road, a car with its steering wheel on the right. I know others who blanch and tremble on recalling their experiences as riders or drivers on Irish roads. As for myself, until last August, I had never driven in Ireland. It was not that I was afraid to, just that I had never found it necessary.

My first extended experience with Irish roads and driving came in the summer of 1980 at a festival honoring Brian Meriman, an 18th-century Irish poet. Each day I was driven from Lisdoonvarna, where we stayed, across the Burren Plateau to Ballyvaughn, some eight miles away on Galway Bay, where the activities were held. The driver, Mary Caulfield of the United Arts Club of Dublin, did well. She seemed to know where the ancient sheep crossings were. She slowed for the narrowest bridges and lanes. She seemed to have the central part of the road well under control, or so I judged from the front seat to her left, the seat in which one's nerve and trust in the driver are tested.

The country roads of Ireland, although hard surfaced, offer nothing reassuring to the side, nothing that could be called a shoulder. By week's end I had cramps in my left arm and shoulder, left hip and leg from shrinking away from stone walls, hazel and thornbushes that had passed by my window. In the middle of the week, surreptitiously, I examined the sides of the car. The right, facing the center of the road, was unblemished; the left was scratched and lined, like the back of an Irish monk beaten with branches of hazel or thorn.

Last August I returned to Ireland with two daughters to attend a Yeats poetry festival at Sligo on the west coast. We took the train from Dublin to Sligo, where we had, we thought, reserved a car so that my daughters might drive or be driven through Donegal. Neither car nor driver was available when we arrived. But on the third day of our stay the rental company called to say that a car was available, without driver, for about $40 a day. I was not overjoyed, but on the urging of my daughters accepted the rental.

I was taken aback slightly when the young man who delivered the small Fiat said the insurance would not cover any damage to tires or wheels, as the roads were sometimes very rocky. I was ready to give up the project, only to be assured by my daughters that I could surely overcome dangerous roads, left-hand driving, and a foreign car with controls on the right side and a stick shift I would have to operate with my left hand.

The next morning we took off, not for nearby Donegal, but for Galway by the coast road. The first complication we discovered was in "The Blue Guide to Ireland" (available in paperback with maps for $19.95 through Rand McNally). Anyone planning to drive in Ireland should look to the order of directions given in that book. As a rough rule the driver should plan to go clockwise if driving in the Irish Republic and counterclockwise in the Northern counties. We were running counterclockwise in the south, which required reading the book from the bottom up.

Then there is the traffic: on main roads, a variety of cars and trucks, or lorries, and the fastest tractors, or tractor drivers, in the West; on supplementary roads—often called "picturesque" in the guides—cars, trucks and fast tractors. Also: bicyclists, most of them, in Sligo at least, men of decent age and dignity, never turning their "stately heads"; troops of hikers from the Continent; rough carts drawn by donkeys or ponies that give no ground; a few cattle feeding unattended, like Patrick Kavanaugh's soul, on the side of ditches; sheep and cows being driven to pasture or to market. There is the occasional distracting sign: a large square of white with a black center dot, like a bull's-eye, and the words "Black Spot Ahead." I thought it meant "new paving" or "hidden entrance," but learned from one Irish source that the signs warn motorists they are approaching the site of a previous highway death.

Whether the road be wide or narrow the tendency of Irish drivers is to stay in the middle. The sheep and the cattle have the same tendency. I sought in vain to find an explanation for this. With no better theory given me, I concluded that persistence in using the middle of the road until seriously challenged was a sign of resistance to British ways.

It is in passage through the towns that one's skill is most thoroughly tested. Streets barely wide enough for one vehicle carry traffic in two directions. My first attempt was marginally successful. After being forced onto the sidewalk to let an approaching car pass, I pulled back into the road, believing that the next car would permit me to proceed through an open space of approximately 50 feet to another space on the left where I was prepared to give way. Regrettably, the car forced me back to the left, where I grazed a parked car.

Stopping, I saw little evidence that my car had touched the other, except for a line or two in the dust on its side. But beyond, and predating my arrival, was much injury: a headlight gone on the road side, a smashed left fender, dented left-hand door and deep rusted scratches along the length of the body. The car, I was told, belonged to the man who owned the adjacent "pumps." I gave him a pound to settle for my scratch and left, convinced his car was parked where it was to accumulate bumps, dents and scratches—and settlement in pounds.

We went on, turning back to the main road as soon as we could, proceeding with care and continual warnings from the daughter who sat on my left to keep away from the side of the road. At Castlebar—exhausted, she said—she gave up the navigator's seat to her sister. All went well until Westport, in the shadow of Croagh Patrick, at about the point where the "toads, serpents, and other repellent beasts" fled toward the sea under force of Patrick's curse. Forced to the left by an oncoming truck, we struck a limestone curbing concealed by grass and blew out two tires. The wheels were not seriously damaged, but our spirits were. After flagging down a passing motorist and getting a mechanic to replace the tires, we returned to Westport, halfway to our destination, abandoned the car after a 64-mile trip and returned to Dublin by train.

My conclusion is that it is best to travel by train or bus or hire a driver in Ireland. If you drive there yourself, follow blindly the advice of your fellow travelers, especially the person in the front left seat. If you think you are a good driver let someone of lesser reputation take over; if possible, follow the practice suggested by Ian Robertson, the editor of *The Blue Guide to Ireland*.

After stating in the preface to the book that Ireland has "good roads, uncluttered by heavy traffic for the most part, and running through delightful country," and after thanking all who had helped him in compiling the book, he concludes with these words: "And to my wife, constantly at the wheel, my renewed thanks also due."

A final cautionary note: Go slowly through the herds of cattle, stop and let the sheep flow by.

A Visit to Paddy Joe's Pub

By John McCarthy

"What in the name of the All-Mighty has happened to you Yanks?" surily demanded Paddy Joe when I recently entered his snug, seaside pub in remote Donegal on a windy Saturday night. Before I could reply, he reached under the bar, pulled out a batch of letters and began waving them in my face.

As usual in an Irish country pub, a goodly crowd of regular patrons was there and broqued away over their pints of Guinness stout without evidently paying the slightest attention to Paddy Joe's blasting greeting to me, although every single one of them had automatically tuned in a greedy ear.

Otherwise tomorrow morning, after Mass in the village, when they picked up their Sunday papers at Nosey Johnny Frank's candy store, they'd be out of conversation always expected by its properietor. Nosey Johnny Frank is the permanent president of the local Pioneers, the famous Irish total-abstinence movement founded in 1838 by the crusading Capuchin Father Theobald Matthew. Naturally, in his presidential Pioneer position, Nosey Johnny Frank shuns Paddy Joe's and the other dozen village pubs, but that does not deter him from always inquiring of the regulars of these respective pubs, "Now what happen *there* last night?"

"It used to be that you Yanks," continued Paddy Joe loudly, "would try and impress us stay-at-homers Irish, how you came up in the world in America because your ancestors were poor but proud peasants.

"Now since those meddling Brits who publish the world's recognized ancestry book—Debrett's—discovered that your Irish President Ron Reagan was related to the Tipperary King Brian Boru, all of you Yanks are claiming that you are direct descendants of Irish kings. Look at these letters, Yank. They asking meself, Paddy Joe, to look up their ancestors' baptismal and marriage certificates proving that they are of royal Irish stock.

"Imagine, some of these Yanks in writing me have the gall to infer that all American-Irish were from royal roots because the Irish peasants didn't emigrate. The very nerve of those letter writers. Insulting, I say."

Why would Americans write him to trace their ancestry when the Irish government already has such a service in Dublin Castle for them to contact? I asked.

"Why not?" tartly asked Paddy Joe, true to the Irish tradition of answering the question with a question.

"Over the years, haven't I been most responsive to the many Yank tourists who have meandered in here, answering, patiently and intelligently, their many queer questions, most of which show their vast ignorance of Ireland's great men and history? Those Yanks who really listened to me now know that the Donegal Kings—the O'Donnells, the MacSweeneys, the O'Dohertys and the O'Neills—were the greatest. For centuries, they held off the broad British empire and were the very last to be conquered by the barbarian Cromwell.

"What's more, practically all the famed stronghold castles of the Irish Kings, Brian Boru's included, have crumbled and faded into forgotten glory. But not Doe Castle, built by *my* people, the capable MacSweeneys. Despite the savage sieges for hundreds of years by such yahoo invaders as the Vikings, the Normans and the Brits, there down the road in Creeslough stands Doe Castle, still intact and proud to this very day."

To further his eloquent arguing, Paddy Joe began reading, not just for my benefit but the entire pub, some excerpts from his Yank letters such as:

"Dear Sir: In Philly, there are many other Irish with my Dougherty name. But my boss who was in your saloon last summer says you claim there are no Doughertys in Ireland, only Dohertys, all descended from King O'Doherty. My dear departed mother always said we came from Irish royalty via my great grandfather who left Donegal sometime back in the nineteenth century. Please get his baptismal record and forward with it our family's royal Irish crest for our parlor."

Or this one: "Dear P.J.: Since our Uncle Mike visited Doe Castle on your advice, he has been struttering around like a king and says we would all be a wealthy noble Irish family today if our ancestor, Neal MacSweeney, hadn't dropped the "Mac" into the ocean when he came here during the Irish famine in 1843. Please check and send Donegal's legal records about his birth and antecedents, so we can put back the "Mac" in our name and claim our family's rights to Doe Castle."

With his ironical vocal twists and arch facial frowns accompanying Paddy Joe's reading the Yanks' letters, guffaws from all sides of the pub sounded. When he was finished, I asked him if he were going to answer them. "That will be the day!" retorted himself as he tossed the Yanks' missives under the bar and further laughter followed from his now captive audience.

"Ach, speaking of letters, I spotted a good apropos item in the *Irish Times* today," remarked Paddy Joe, fishing out a clipping from his vest pocket and proceeded to read it aloud for his patrons' benefit:

"The Ulster leader, Reverend Ian Paisley, purchased a stamp showing a picture of the Pope issued in Britain to commenurate the papal visit. Two minutes later he was back at the post office counter.

" 'This stamp will not stick,'" he roared.

" 'For goodness sake, Mr. Paisley'" said the weary post office clerk, " 'sure you're spitting on the wrong side.'"

The immediate jovial appreciative reception of the Paisley story from the entire pub caused Paddy Joe to beam and make a funny formal stage bow of acknowledgment. Seizing this moment of unusual exuberance in Paddy Joe, an elderly privileged patron called out "Aye, come on Paddy Joe, tis time to give us a song." "Yes, Yes, Paddy Joe" chorused a large group present.

The crowd's request was genuine. Actually, Paddy Joe has a fairly good tenor voice and really likes to sing and perform. Of course, as he says himself, "Shure, I'm no John McCormack by far but then I'm not so bad either." His singing repertoire consists mostly of dear, dour Donegal's many sad saga songs. His great favorite is *Mulroy Bay*, and he began rendering it pronto.

As Paddy Joe's voice lifted in song, his patrons stopped their whispering and rustling of glasses and listened in total silence as he sang verse after verse. And as they say in show business, there wasn't a dry eye in the house.

To Ireland for Talk

By David Dempsey

I visit France for good food, Italy for its pretty girls, Switzerland to buy my cuckoo clocks, and England to soak my bones in history. But I go to Ireland to talk. In public restaurants, dining alone, you will often be joined by a local inhabitant who cannot bear the thought of a meal without conversation; what is more, he assumes that you can't either. And since the food in Ireland is not very good, this turns out to be an excellent arrangement.

I have had seatmates on a Dublin bus miss their stop because they had involved themselves too deeply in talk; it was more important to finish the joke—no such thing as a brief one, either—than to get off the bus. On streetcorners, a casual inquiry of a stranger will result in the directions asked for, and possibly an invitation to dinner.

Actually, for an American, there are no strangers in Ireland. In the countryside, you will be routed to hotels and eating places not on the strength of the accommodations so much as the properietor's ability to entertain you. Aran Islanders volley stories at each other with the rapidity of tennis players, until the onlooker gets a crick in the neck trying to keep up with the wordplay. Linguistically refined, this is the basis of Joyce's wit, verbal *touchés* made for their own sake, malicious, slightly cutting, frequently pointless in the aggregate because they are so pointed in isolation.

There is not much else to do in Ireland but talk; and because the sun shines seldom and the rain falls often, most of the talk is indoors, which is to say, over a glass of stout. The daily weather forecasts in *The Irish Times,* contending with the monotonous climate, sound like something out of the *Celtic Twilight*—not always accurate, but invariably poetic. Sean O'Faolain's statement that "in Ireland, it is considered bad taste to be serious" explains this compulsion to be entertaining; in Brendan Behan's case, the combination—drink and performance—was lethal. (Behan was the comic Irishman *in extremis*—talkative for our good, too talkative for his own.)

In a sense, however, O'Faolain is misleading. The Irish are serious about their humor, their eternal wordsmithing. And yet something is missing, the element, for example, that is usually present among the French, whose cafe conversationalists deal with larger questions of philosophy and literature, so that we come away from these sessions instructed. But the pub talkers of Dublin, although they may recite poetry, are not likely to discuss it, and in the end one comes away with the sense that he has been entertained, but that all the fine talk has not added up to very much.

This was certainly Joyce's message, and it is also the problem in translating Irish humor onto the printed page, which is like trying to take home a handful of mist. So much of charm is in the ambience. Thinking it over later, we even wonder if we have not been had.

The Willing Heart

By Leonard Wibberly

I had hired a little Ford Anglia which we had named Peanut, upon arrival in Ireland, and it proved to be the most expensive automobile ever to come into my possession. It was not the gasoline consumption that put it in the luxury bracket. It did an honest thirty-five miles to the gallon, and driving it was somewhat like driving a roller skate down the road.

No, the car was economical on fuel. But the hire charge was a murderous fifty-one dollars a week. This is the minimum price for which the smallest of cars may be hired in Ireland in midsummer, and I suppose the price must be based on the rooted Irish belief that the sidewalks of New York are paved with gold. This is largely the fault of returning Irish-Americans, who act as though they are.

I decided at the end of two weeks to turn in Peanut, and out of the money budgeted for automobile expenses buy a second-hand car in Dublin. I have a fair amount of experience in the purchase of second-hand cars, but my experience is American. The man who deals in second-hand cars in Ireland, I thought, was very likely a horse dealer in his youth and served an apprenticeship in filling teeth and polishing hooves to make a broken-down dray horse look like a hunter. Suspecting this, whether rightly or not, I decided I'd best take Michael John along with me.

Michael John I had met the year before in Ireland. He runs a butcher's shop in the village of Kinvara and also a radio shop, a bicycle store, possesses the only cold storage facilities in the village, builds houses, helps organize the annual carnival and is very fond of my children. Michael John drives the sick to the hospital, the groom to the church and the intoxicated to their homes.

311

Anyway, I called in at Kinvara with Kevin and Patricia to see Michael John, and told him I was going to Dublin to turn in Peanut and buy another car. He looked at me with compassion and shook his head.

"They'll take the gold out of your teeth," he said, "and sell you a wheelbarrow."

"Pity you can't come," said I.

"A pity indeed."

"You have, I know, a new house to build."

"I have."

"And you must start on it immediately."

"I must."

"Well," I said, "I'll let you know how I get on."

"Wait a minute," said Michael John. "I'd never rest easy if I let you go alone. I'll get my pajamas and a toothbrush and go with you."

"What about the house?" I asked.

"I'll start tomorrow," said Michael John.

It takes about three and a half hours for a man of my age to drive from Galway to Dublin. The distance is only one hundred thirty miles and the road is excellent. But I am no hand at driving through flocks of sheep, herds of cattle and clutches of ducks and geese, all of which frequent the roads of Ireland. Some are being driven to or from the market. Some are being driven to or from the pasture. Others are there, in my view, because there is a sporting chance they'll get hit by a car and return a quick profit to the owner. We went through perhaps five or six times that many sheep, and at the other end of these flocks, there was Dublin, dirty and cheerful as ever, with the lovely white swans gliding among the shiploads of Guinness on the river. I proposed that we stay at the Gresham, but Michael John was horrified.

"Sure, nobody but rich people stay there," he said. "We wouldn't want to be seen mixing with them. We'll stay at the Belvedere."

We went round to the Belvedere, but the Belvedere was full. So was Grant's and so were the next six hotels we tried. I asked the clerk at one hotel why the city was so crowded.

"'Tis the Battle of the Boyne," he replied.

"The Battle of the Boyne?" I repeated.

"Yes. All the Orangemen are down here from Belfast, celebrating the great and glorious day when they licked the tar out of us Irish a couple of hundred years ago. And they've a great thirst on them, thanks be to God."

Without going too deeply into Irish history, the situation was roughly the equivalent of the Daughters of the American Revolution booking every hotel in London solid to celebrate the surrender of Cornwallis at Yorktown.

Eventually we stayed in a boarding house, where I believe we got the last room available in Dublin.

The next morning, after an abundant breakfast of bacon, and eggs, and sausages, and orange juice, and soda bread and tea, we went out to buy a car. I presumed that we would go to a second-hand car dealer or at least to an automobile agency. We went to a garage.

Before we went in, Michael John looked at my shirt and his own and shook his head. "They're too clean," he said. "They'll double the price on us."

Inside the garage a mechanic in clothes obtained from a ragbag was leaning, as in prayer, over a Chevrolet which had obviously run its last mile.

"Have you an old car for sale?" asked Michael John.

"I have," said the mechanic, eyeing the Chevrolet, and mildly surprised. I surmised that prayer should be answered so soon.

"Would you like my opinion on that car?" asked Michael John.

"I would," said the mechanic.

"Twould be wonderful for keeping the rain off the hens," answered Michael John.

"Oh, this isn't the car I had in mind at all," said the mechanic, "though you misjudge her. She looks bad, I know, but she has a engine that would surprise you. Tis that Hudson over there. She was running around the city as a hackney until three weeks ago."

"Was it the police that made you take her off the road?" asked Michael John, and walked thoughtfully over to the Hudson.

The car had the appearance of a wreck which had been straightened by an unskilled man using a sledge hammer. It was covered with a black substance which was sticky and smelled of tar. I opened the front door and inspected the speedometer. It gave the mileage as 98,000, which was probably the second time around for the gauge—so the true mileage was at least 198,000. I developed an immediate and idiotic affection for the car.

"How much," I asked.

"Twenty pounds," said the mechanic. He seemed to be holding his breath.

"Will it run?" I asked.

"Run?" said he. "Why, we'd enter it in the Galway Plate if it wasn't for the water jump."

"I suppose it will do all of five miles to the gallon," I said.

"Five miles to the gallon?" echoed the mechanic to Dublin at large. "Lord save us, how do you suppose we could use it as a hackney around the city at a profit at five miles to the gallon?"

Michael John detached one of the parking lights with a gentle blow of his hand and threw it into a box of junk on the floor.

"The upholstery is fit for a Lord Mayor," said the mechanic, retrieving the parking light and putting it back in place without a blush. "And if you had her out on the highway and gave her her head, she'd do twenty-eight."

"If ye got her out on the highway at all, it would be a miracle," said Michael John.

"Will she start?" I asked.

"She's no battery in her," said the mechanic. "I'll get one and start her and he'll be delighted with the sound of the engine. Are those your two little children now?"

"They are," I replied, looking at Kevin and Patricia, who had wandered into the garage.

"Aren't they the grandest little children I ever saw," he said, clucking like an overfond matron.

"Is this the car you're going to buy, Daddy?" asked Kevin, who is achingly devoid of any subtlety.

"No," said Michael John grimly, "Not if I have to strangle him."

The mechanic went off and returned with a battery. He also had with him the proprietor of the garage, who was doing his best to conceal his incredulity.

"I'll be sorry to part with her," said the proprietor. "She's a grand old car to this day."

"Yes," said Michael John, "tis like burying your grandmother. You know she'd go someday but tis always a surprise." He turned to the mechanic. "Never mind with the battery," he said, "we'll look somewhere else."

"I don't mind cutting the price a little," said the proprietor. "I need the floor space."

"You do that," said Michael John, looking around at the undergrowth of oil-smeared second-hand automobile parts that littered the floor. "You do that, indeed." He led me firmly outside and back to Peanut.

We now drove around through back streets where soot, damp, wind, dust, tattered papers, broken cardboard boxes, tottering houses, railroad tracks, cobblestones and noisome refuse made as wretched a slum area as I have ever seen. In this jungle of shattering poverty, only the children were cheerful. Underpriviledged, undernourished and underclothed they might be. But they were as merry as sparrows in a field of wheat, and played with balls made of brown paper rolled up and tied with string and wet with gutter water.

Through these crumbling streets lined by crumbling houses we drove until we came to an alley, and down the bottom of the alley found a building which was a surprise in that it was standing up when it should be falling down. The interior was dark and the greasy ganglia of automobiles were strewn about, like offal in a shambles. A man was lying under the chassis of a car, cutting it in half with an acetylene torch. Michael John summoned him upright by kicking the sole of his foot. The man came out and looked us over in wonderment.

"I'm looking for a car—cheap," said Michael John.

"How cheap?" asked the man.

"Twenty pounds," said Michael John.

The man shook his head. "When they get down to twenty pounds," he said, "they're more valuable as scrap,"

"Cash," said Michael John. The man shook his head in deep sorrow.

"I just cut one up that might have done you," he said. "Haven't a thing. You wouldn't go for an old motorbike now? There's a twin-port Norton over there—1925. Very good. Little hard to start, but a good runner."

I had visions of the four of us on the motorcycle braving the ocean of sheep and cattle, ducks, geese and donkeys which separates Dublin from Galway.

"No," said Michael John, "I'll try somewhere else."

"I'll give you a friendly word," said the man, relighting his electric torch. "When they see you coming they'll charge you double."

"That's the truth of it," said Michael John, eyeing his clean shirt again.

"Well, good luck," said the man, and returned to the task of cutting the car in two. We tried several more junk yards, but the best offer was a five-ton truck. The door fell off when I opened it. I had now come to the conclusion that Dublin is the final resting place of all the beaten-up, exhausted and dead automobiles in the world. Michael John finally agreed with some reluctance that we should try a used-car dealer. He was unwilling to do so as it seemed to be against both his principles and his best instincts.

We found one, again in a grimier part of Dublin. There was a fish barrow outside surrounded by tattered women. On the barrow were the remains of a small ray, butchered, bloodied and far from fresh. We found a salesman and he smiled brightly at us.

"I have just what you want," he said. "Nice little Morris 10. Runs very well. Good upholstery..."

"And you'll be sorry to part with it," said Michael John.

"Divil a bit of it," said the salesman. "I've been trying to get rid of it for weeks."

This astounding honesty produced a rapport between the two immediately. We went to look at the car. It was carefully placed in the gloomier part of the garage, so all I could see immediately was that there was something resembling a small automobile there. It had a heavy list to starboard forward, accounted for by the fact that the right front tire was flat.

"Will it start?" asked Michael John.

"I'll put it this way," said the salesman. "Sometimes it will and sometimes it won't. Tis like the rocket program at Cape Canaveral. Even the experts don't know."

"It will start," said a mechanic, emerging from the gloom.

He turned on the ignition and pulled a piece of baling wire

that protruded from the dashboard. The little Morris shuddered and roared into life. Kevin had been standing behind the car with Tricia, and they disappeared in a bank of dense blue smoke coming from the exhaust.

"She'll do thirty to the gallon," said the salesman.

"Of what—oil?" asked Michael John, eyeing the smoke cloud from which Kevin was beginning to emerge.

"I see that you're a cynic," said the salesman. "She has had a ring job—within living memory," he added, looking towards Heaven for forgiveness.

The mechanic switched off the engine and we all coughed a little. The salesman suggested with great daring that we drive her around the block. The flat tire was replaced, and we climbed in and trickled out of the garage. It soon developed that she was slow on her helm. A turn of the steering wheel to the right or the left produced no immediate effect. Several seconds later, however, the car would swerve abruptly in the direction desired like a sheep with the staggers.

The brakes worked but jerked the car crazily to the left or right—it was impossible to anticipate which. The clutch seemed good—I fancied she had no clutch lining but was operating on the rivets. The gearbox was sound and I could detect no knock from the crankshaft bearings. The oil pressure was nil, but that might have been because the gauge wasn't working.

We drove back to the garage and climbed out. "How much?" asked Michael John.

"Sixty pounds," said the salesman.

"I'll give you forty," I said, in spite of myself.

The salesman and Michael John exchanged looks of astonishment. The salesman looked a little disappointed, as if he had achieved a victory so easy that it was without savor. Michael John excused himself, led me out of the garage, and stood me by the barrow on which reposed the frightful remains of the ray.

"This gentleman," he said to the fishmonger, "is writing a book about Ireland, God help him, and would be interested in anything you can tell him about the fish business."

"Fivepence," said the fishmonger, wrapping up the ray's remnants and handing them to me. I paid him and returned to the garage, chastened.

Michael John and the salesman were in a huddle. I stood back and explained to Tricia that we were not going to have fish for dinner but I had been tricked into buying a piece of fish I didn't want and I had no means of disposing of it.

"Give it to me," said Tricia and I did so. She went away and returned without the fish but with two ice creams, one of which she gave to Kevin.

"What did you do with the fish?" I asked.

"I traded it to a man for two ice creams," she said. I thought this over and sent her down to help Michael John.

There now followed a great deal of bargaining between him and the salesman. Since I had been expelled to the edges of the arena as unworthy of the conflict, I caught but a snatch of what was going on. I pieced together the following:

"Will you put four new tires on her?"

"I will not. I have a large family and have to limit my public charities."

"She'll never get out of Dublin with the tires she has."

"I can see you're a pessimist. She would make Maynooth easy."

"That's a hundred and twenty miles from Galway."

"I can give you a retread on the one with the blister on it."

"Will you look at those two rear tires for the love of God. They'd wring tears from a heathen."

"It was my wife who told me not to come to work this morning," said the salesman. "She had a dream last night that I'd fall in with thieves and they'd take my last copper."

"I suppose that you'll buy her a nice bit of jewelry with the profit you're making out of the old car," said Michael John. "Or perhaps you'll treat her to a weekend in London."

So it went on while I stood fretfully in the background and Kevin and Tricia ate their ice cream and managed somehow to get a considerable amount of gearbox oil on themselves. Finally Michael John came to me gloomily.

"We can have her for forty-five pounds," he said. "He'll put two new tires on the rear and two retreads on the front." I made a quick calculation and discovered that discounting the tires we were getting the car for twenty-seven pounds. I was delighted, but Michael John was determined to pay no more than forty.

He made a last valiant effort, when it came to paying.

"Give him forty pounds," he hissed to me. "Count them out in fives, one by one. The sight of the money may soften his heart."

I did so, counting out the five-pound notes until I came to forty, and then I stopped.

"Forty-five," said the salesman.

"Forty," said Michael John.

"Forty-five."

I added the additional five-pound note, but Michael John had not done yet. We climbed into the car and he backed her up to the gas pump. "Fill her up," he said.

The salesman looked at him in pure admiration. "By God, you're a man after my own heart," he said, and the two of them shook hands.

With a tankful of free gasoline, which brought the price of the car down to forty pounds, we took off for Galway.

Just past Maynooth one of the tires blew out.

"They're all sharks in Dublin," said Michael John as we mounted the spare.

But the little Morris performed so well on the long haul from Dublin to Galway that we decided we should call her The Willing Heart.

About The Authors

BRENDAN BEHAN (1923–1964).
A Dublin playwright, short story writer and novelist who gained fame for his plays and stories and notoriety as a character.

DAVID DEMPSEY.
An American novelist and short story writer.

PETER FALLON.
Poet and publisher, Fallon founded the Gallery Press in Dublin in 1970, which specializes in Irish poetry and literature.

BRIAN FRIEL.
Playwright and short story writer, Friel was born in County Tyrone and now lives in Donegal. His best known play is *Philadelphia, Here I Come!* He has been a full-time writer since 1960 when he gave up teaching.

JAMES JOYCE (1882–1941).
Born and educated in Dublin, Joyce spent most of his life in Paris. His major work, *Ulysses,* has been accepted worldwide as a classic.

HUGH KENNER.
Professor of English literature at John Hopkins University, Baltimore, Kenner is the author of many books on twentieth-century writers, including three on James Joyce and two on Samuel Beckett.

BENEDICT KIELY.
Born and educated in Ulster, Kiely has been a Dublin journalist and a teacher in America. He has written many novels, mostly with Northern Ireland background and characters.

MARY LAVIN.
Born in Massachusetts, Mary Lavin went to live in Ireland at an early age. Her Irish short stories and novels have won wide acceptance both in Ireland and abroad.

HUGH LEONARD.

John Keyes Byrne, who writes under the pseudonym of Hugh Leonard, was born in Dalkey, Dublin. Once an Irish civil servant, Leonard today is one of Ireland's best-known and most commercially successful playwrights. Probably his best work is the play *Da*.

CORMAC MACCONNELL.

Columnist of Dublin's *Irish Press*, MacConnell has many regular avid readers.

BRIAN MACMAHON.

A novelist, short story writer, dramatist and ballad maker, MacMahon comes from County Kerry. For more than 40 years, he has taught in the national parochial school in Listowel, Kerry.

EUGENE J. MCCARTHY.

A recognized poet and essayist, he is the author of ten books and a contributor to leading magazines. A former university professor, he was a U.S. representative and senator from Minnesota from 1949–1970, and became known nationwide through his campaign for the presidency in 1968. Now he devotes most of his time to writing and lecturing and guarding the public interest.

MICHAEL MCLAVERTY.

A novelist and short story writer, McLaverty has been a teacher of mathematics and a headmaster in Ulster, the scene of most of his writings.

JOHN MCNULTY (1896–1956).

American born, McNulty was *The New Yorker's* amusing, highly regarded, first hand observer of Manhattan's Third Avenue Irish pubs and their patrons.

GEORGE MOORE (1852–1933).

A novelist and man of letters, Moore enjoyed a wide reputation both in his native Ireland and in Britain. He was one of the early leaders in the Irish Renaissance around the turn of the century.

HUGH A. MULLIGAN.

American journalist, Mulligan writes "Mulligan's Stew," a popular column distributed by the Associated Press. He was the AP correspondent in Ireland from 1969 to 1977 and is married to a colleen from County Armagh.

FRANK O'CONNOR (1903–1968).
A noted short story writer, and a man of letters, Frank O'Connor is the pseudonym for Michael O'Donovan, born in Cork. Besides his superb Irish literary contributions, O'Connor had resided in the United States and taught in American universities.

JULIA O'FAOLAIN.
A novelist and short story writer, Julia O'Faolain is the daughter of Sean and Eileen O'Faolain. Born and educated in Dublin, she has lived for some years in California where she has worked as a teacher of languages and interpreter and translator.

SEAN O'FAOLAIN.
Born in Cork, and educated there, O'Faolain was among the earlier volunteers in the Irish Republic movement. Later, he was the editor of *The Bell,* the famous Dublin literary magazine. Sean O'Faolain has been long regarded as one of the foremost writers of Irish short stories.

LIAM O'FLAHERTY (1897–1984).
Born in the Aran Islands, off the west coast of Ireland, O'Flaherty was long recognized as a leading Irish novelist and short story writer. His best known work is *The Informer* which, like several other of his novels, became a popular film.

SEAMUS O'KELLY (1875–1918).
A prolific writer, Irish journalist O'Kelly also was a playwright, novelist and author of short stories. He was once known as Ireland's most "neglected genius."

BRIAN O'NOLAN (1911–1966).
A lifetime Irish civil servant and rare character in Dublin, Brian O'Nolan also wrote novels, plays, short stories and an eagerly read column in Dublin's *Irish Times.* Through these, he was widely known by his pseudonyms, such as Flann O'Brien, Myles na gCopaleen, Brother Barrabus, George Knowall, Count O'Blather and James Doe.

HESKETH PEARSON (1894–1964).
A prominent London actor and biographer, Pearson has written popular books on Bernard Shaw, Oscar Wilde, Conan Doyle and Gilbert and Sullivan.

JAMES PLUNKETT.
A novelist, short story writer and playwright, James Plunkett Kelley writes under the pseudonym of James Plunkett. He grew up in Dublin, was active in labor organizations and later as a producer for Irish radio and television.

SOMERVILLE AND ROSS.
This was the famous literary team of Edith Somerville (1858–1949) and Violet Martin (1862–1915) who used the pseudonym Martin Ross. As collaborators, they produced several serious, highly regarded Irish novels. However, their greater reputation was for their series of comic stories entitled *Some Experiences of an Irish R.N.* about the Irish countryside and its people.

HONOR TRACY.
Although an Englishwoman, Honor Tracy is best known for her humorous novels and sketches about Irish contemporary life. She has been a journalist and written excellent books about Japan and Spain.

WILLIAM TREVOR.
A novelist and short story writer, William Trevor is the pseudonym of William Trevor Cox who was born in Cork and educated in Dublin. A member of the Irish Academy of Letters, Trevor has received a number of outstanding literary awards. As an Irish writer, who has lived for periods in Britain, Trevor seems to have most of both Irish and British societies at his fingertips. His English short stories of London swingers, mod clerks and shopgirls are as authentic and convincing as his authoritative tales of Irish priests, farmers and racing characters. Hence, Trevor is widely considered to be one of the best living short story writers.

MERVYN WALL.
Born in Dublin and eduated there and in Germany, Wall is a writer of highly praised short stories as well as several popular

novels and a trio of plays produced by the Abbey Theatre in Dublin. He has served as an Irish civil servant, been Programme Assistant in Radio Eireann, and Secretary of the Irish Arts Council.

LEONARD PATRICK O'CONNOR WIBBERLEY.

An Anglo-Irishman, Wibberley is the author of *The Mouse That Roared, Take Me To Your President, The Trouble With the Irish* and *The Coming of the Green.* Under the name of Patrick O'Connor, he has published a series of juvenile fiction books.